# Ethical Insights

# Ethical Insights
## A Brief Introduction

### Second Edition

## Douglas Birsch

*Shippensburg University of Pennsylvania*

Boston   Burr Ridge, IL   Dubuque, IA   Madison, WI   New York
San Francisco   St. Louis   Bangkok   Bogotá   Caracas   Kuala Lumpur
Lisbon   London   Madrid   Mexico City   Milan   Montreal   New Delhi
Santiago   Seoul   Singapore   Sydney   Taipei   Toronto

# McGraw-Hill Higher Education

A Division of The **McGraw-Hill** Companies

2   3   4   5   6   7   8   9   0   MAL/MAL   0   9   8   7   6   5   4   3   2

**Library of Congress Cataloging-in-Publication Data**

Birsch, Douglas
     Ethical insights : a brief introduction / Douglas Birsch.—2nd ed.
          p.   cm.
     Includes bibliographical references and index.
     ISBN 0-7674-2018-7
     1. Ethics.   I. Title.
BJ1025.B54   2001
171—dc21                                                              2001030579

Sponsoring editor, Kenneth King; production editor, Holly Paulsen; manuscript editor, Kay C. Mikel; design manager and cover designer, Susan Breitbard; text designer, Claire Seng-Niemoeller; manufacturing manager, Randy Hurst. The text was set in 10/12.5 Garth Graphic by TBH Typecast, Inc. and printed on acid-free 50# Finch Opaque by Malloy Lithographing, Inc.

www.mhhe.com

*To my ethics students,*
*past, present, and future,*
*and to my first ethics professor, Dr. James F. Sheridan*

# Preface

*Ethical Insights* is a concise introduction to ethics and ethical theories. Its purpose is to provide students with the conceptual framework to facilitate thoughtful and profitable discussions of ethical problems. It is designed as a supplemental book for applied ethics courses, such as contemporary moral issues, business ethics, computer ethics, engineering ethics, health care ethics, or environmental ethics.

## Organization

*Ethical Insights* contains a general introduction to ethics (Chapter 1), eight short chapters on ethical theories (including one that discusses two theories), and a final chapter exploring a pluralistic approach to ethics. The book is organized around ethical insights, ethical standards, traditional ethical assumptions, and basic ethical themes. (Appendix 1 provides a summary of these elements.) The chapters on ethical theories have a common pattern:

- Identification of the ethical insight related to the theory.
- The theory's ethical standard, which establishes moral guidelines to help solve ethical problems.
- Some of the strengths of the theory.
- Analysis of the theory in terms of traditional ethical assumptions and the four basic ethical themes discussed in Chapter 1.
- Comparison with another theory, usually the one in the preceding chapter.
- Some of the problems that emerge with the theory.
- Appraisal of the theory in terms of the criteria for a successful ethical theory presented in Chapter 1.
- Questions to help the reader review key concepts.

I have chosen not to include some of the subtleties of the ethical theories so that the instructor can spend the bulk of the course discussing ethical problems rather than explaining the intricacies of Kant's ideas or hedonistic utilitarianism. Because this book is designed for use in a variety of applied ethics courses, I have also deliberately omitted case studies. Including such material for each type of course would have excessively lengthened the text.

## About the Second Edition

It is a pleasure to be able to produce a second edition of *Ethical Insights*. I have taken this opportunity to improve on the first edition, and I have made quite a few changes. Some of these changes reflect my ideas, and some were suggested by professors who have used the text. Users of the first edition should be aware that the basic format is the same but that all the chapters contain at least some minor changes. Here are the major changes:

1. A chapter was added on divine command theory.
2. A chapter was added on ethical egoism and ethical subjectivism.
3. The chapters on utilitarianism and virtue ethics are more focused on the relevant philosophers, Bentham and Mill for the former and Aristotle for the latter.
4. The utilitarianism chapter contains a greater concentration on rule utilitarianism.
5. Each chapter includes an expanded section on the strengths of the theory to balance out the section on the problems or weaknesses.
6. The chapter on the ethics of care now contains brief sections on David Hume and on feminist ethics.

## The Ethical Theories

I have chosen to label the approaches to ethics in this book "ethical theories." In Chapter 1, I provide two explanations for the term "ethical theories": (1) Ethical theories attempt to provide clear and reasonable concepts related to moral guidelines. (2) Ethical theories identify and justify moral guidelines to use in solving moral problems and to help us live together successfully. The approaches to ethics discussed in the subsequent chapters can be viewed as "theories" because they attempt to accomplish these objectives.

Each theory begins with an ethical insight. In using the term "insight," I am referring to the sense of the word that relates to perceiving in an intuitive way. In my usage, an insight is an idea that seems to be intuitively correct to someone. As the reader will discover, I think some of these insights or intuitions are misguided. Others seem to hold up better under scrutiny.

The nine moral theories presented in this book are versions of divine command theory, ethical relativism, ethical egoism, ethical subjectivism, Kantian ethics, utilitarianism, moral rights theory, virtue ethics, and the ethics of care. These theories center, respectively, on God's commands, social moral principles, harm and benefit to individuals, feelings and attitudes of individuals, harm and benefit for morally significant beings, consistency and moral equality, moral rights, the virtues, and care.

I have chosen these nine theories because they are the ones I have used most profitably in my classes, perhaps because the insights related to each of them make sense to students. This is crucial for me. I want to provide a conceptual ethical framework for the course using theories that are related to familiar insights. Several of the theories (act utilitarianism, moral rights theory, and virtue ethics) also contain familiar moral vocabularies, such as harm and benefit, rights, and virtues. Divine command theory and the longer versions of ethical egoism and ethical subjectivism are new to the second edition. These additions were prompted by comments from professors using the first edition and by my own experiences with the book.

My choices of divine command theory, ethical relativism, ethical egoism, ethical subjectivism, act utilitarianism, and Kantian ethics are probably not particularly controversial, but the other selections may require some explanation. I have included a chapter on moral rights because I believe we can produce a plausible "ethical theory" centered around moral rights. In my courses, I discuss moral rights theory as well as Kant's ethical theory. Because contemporary moral problems are often discussed in the language of rights, most students are familiar with the key concepts, and they find rights easier to understand and more interesting than the various formulations of the Categorical Imperative. Although I use both theories, many professors prefer Kantian ethics and will probably skip the moral rights chapter.

I chose virtue ethics, or more precisely Aristotle's ethics, because it allows the instructor to develop the idea of ethics in terms of a goal, purpose, or function—in Aristotle's case, a universal human purpose. Aristotle's theory can form the foundation for a discussion of organizational ethics in terms of the goals, purposes, or functions of corporations and organizations, an approach I find especially useful in business ethics. Inclusion of virtue ethics enables both exploration of the concept of virtue in general and discussion of specific virtues. Moreover, like moral rights theory, virtue ethics has a familiar moral vocabulary, such as courage, generosity, and friendliness.

The last and probably most controversial choice is Nel Noddings's version of the ethics of care. I included this theory because it provides a contemporary rejection of many of the traditional ethical ideas, such as universalizability and impartiality. If the instructor is sympathetic to the claim that men and women have different ways of talking about ethics, this theory can also be used to represent a feminine approach to solving moral problems.

## Suggestions for Using This Book

*Ethical Insights* can be used at the beginning of the course to introduce students to ethics and ethical theories and to prepare them for subsequent discussions of ethical problems. A second way to use the book is to integrate the appropriate chapters with the discussion of moral problems or issues. For instance, students could read the chapter on moral rights before discussing the abortion issue.

This book is intended to make the task of teaching ethical theories in applied ethics classes easier. Ethical theories are difficult for many students to understand; unlike ethical problems, they can seem abstract and remote from students' experience. I think this book responds to this concern.

## Acknowledgments

Once again, the person who helped me the most with this book was Ken King, the philosophy editor at Mayfield Publishing Company; there would have been no first or second edition without Ken's assistance and support. Also at Mayfield, I am grateful to Georgia Gero-Chen, editorial assistant; Holly Paulsen, production editor; Susan Breitbard, design manager; and Kay Mikel, manuscript editor. I am also grateful to the reviewers: Keith Green, East Tennessee State University; Joan Whitman Hoff, Lock Haven University of Pennsylvania; BJ Kiehl, Palomar College; Bill Marvin, University of Dayton; Susan Lee Morris, Ferris State University; and Philip A. D. Schneider, Coastal Carolina University. At home, I appreciate the efforts of my wife, Ellen, and my daughter Jocelyn for helping with the index. At Shippensburg University, I received assistance from Dr. Charles Loucks, who edited the entire manuscript.

# Contents

## CHAPTER 5 / Kantian Ethical Theory     68

# Chapter 1

# An Introduction to Ethics and Ethical Theories

Ethics is the investigation into how we ought to live. The part of ethics discussed most often is concerned with how to live successfully with other people. Thus, one basic goal of ethics is to help us live together successfully. Some of the time our relations with other people proceed smoothly; at other times we encounter problems. Many of these problems are ethical problems, which turn up in relation to most human activities. Sustaining friendships, raising children, selling things, or providing others with information can present us with important dilemmas that have serious consequences. Some ethical problems that could confront any college student are described briefly in the following paragraphs. As you read these scenarios, think about what additional information would be helpful for resolving these ethical dilemmas.

You are friends with two people involved in a serious relationship. You find out that one of them is cheating on the other. Should you tell the deceived person? Why, or why not? Suppose the deceived person asks you about the matter. Should you lie or tell the truth?

You need a textbook for a very important class but lack the money to buy it. Should you steal the textbook from the bookstore if you believe there is only a slight chance you would get caught? If you are too scared to steal it from the bookstore, should you steal it from a wealthy friend if you believe he or she would never find out? Why did you give the answers that you did?

You are in your first year of college, and you (or your girlfriend) become pregnant. Would you get an abortion? Would you try to convince your girlfriend to get an abortion? Why, or why not?

You need to get a good grade on the final to pass a class, but you are not confident that you will be successful. Should you cheat on the test if there is almost no chance of getting caught? Why, or why not?

For many years you have been in a serious relationship with another person. Then he or she ends it. You become very depressed and think about killing yourself. Would you try to kill yourself? Why, or why not?

You have been paralyzed from the neck down in a car accident. Your life is filled with pain and humiliation. Would you ask a family member or close friend to kill you? Why, or why not?

You are in a relationship with another person. You love this person, and he or she loves you. Now another person (better looking, richer, smarter, more fun) tells you that he or she loves you. Should you break up with the first person and get involved with this new individual? Why, or why not?

Which of these problems seems most serious to you? Was it hard to arrive at answers to these questions? Do you think everyone would agree with your responses? Would you be able to convince people who disagreed with you that you were right and that they were wrong? Do you think it is a good idea to learn more about problems like these and how to solve them?

If you had trouble answering these questions, this book will help you. Each of the next eight chapters discusses and evaluates one or more ethical theories. Ethical theories identify ethical guidelines. These guidelines are tools we can use to help us solve ethical problems. Each theory claims that its guidelines are the best tools to use in solving all ethical problems. However, just as we use different tools for different jobs—such as a wrench and not a hammer to loosen a bolt—different sets of ethical guidelines may be the optimum tools for particular areas of life (see Chapter 10 for more on this topic).

## Ethics, Theoretical Ethics, and Applied Ethics

Moral philosophers try to understand and solve ethical problems. Thus, another one of the goals of ethics is to solve moral problems. It is not possible to define the term "ethical problems" with enough precision to separate these kinds of problems from all other types of problems. The previous examples of problems have provided a rough "definition by examples," which should help make the concept "ethical problems" reasonably clear. If further explanation is needed, we might say that *ethical problems* are connected to how we ought to live in relation to situations where there is a potential for harm and benefit or respect and disrespect to morally significant beings. Ethical problems come in two forms: (1) specific cases where we must determine the good or right thing to do, say, or believe; and (2) general problems where we attempt to discover the appropriate response to a class or set of actions, statements, or beliefs. If the problems involve significant harm and benefit or respect and disrespect, then a great deal rests on their solution and the task of moral philosophers is an important one.

Philosophers use a variety of conceptual and theoretical resources to investigate ethical problems. This investigation into the conceptual and theoretical resources for solving ethical problems and into the solutions to them is called *ethics*.[1] Ethics is subdivided into *theoretical ethics*, which studies the conceptual and theoretical resources for solving problems, and *applied ethics*, which examines specific problems and offers solutions to them. Ethics discussions have traditionally centered around books and essays written by famous philosophers and other thinkers, but it is open to everyone. If you thought about the brief sketches that raised some common ethical problems, you have already started to participate in ethics.

In the past, theoretical ethics has concentrated on ethical theories. Ethical theories try to answer a variety of questions: How ought we to live? Is it possible to find a rational answer to the question of how we ought to live? What is the difference between good and evil? What makes an action or a belief morally good? Is anything always good or evil? When is a person morally responsible for something? What is virtue in general? What is a particular virtue, and how do these particular virtues relate to virtue in general? What ought we to do or to believe? Why should we act morally? The answers to these theoretical ethical questions help us do applied ethics and solve ethical problems. Finding successful solutions to ethical problems is a serious challenge and of great importance.

## Alternative Sources of Solutions

One way to get help in solving ethical problems is to learn about ethical theories, but there are other sources of help as well. *Religions* provide guidelines about how to live and can help us solve these problems. If I am a Christian, my religion informs me about how I ought to live—for example, to follow the Ten Commandments or the Golden Rule. If I am a Buddhist, I will attempt to follow the Noble Eightfold Path. Each religion has its own guidelines about how to live. Although religions do inform people about how they ought to live, religious answers are arrived at in a different way than ethical ones (see Chapter 2 for more on this topic).

*Laws* also inform us about how we ought to live. Some laws are related to ethical problems, but legal considerations are not the same as moral ones.[2] Laws are rules of conduct established by governments or legislative bodies and usually are connected to specific penalties or punishments. Ethical guidelines do not have to be created by governments, and they have no specific penalties attached to them. If someone asserted that people ought to obey the laws, he or she would be making an ethical claim about how we ought to live. The laws themselves, however, are legislative rules, not ethical claims or guidelines. The laws combine to form a legal code, while the set of moral guidelines constitutes a morality.[3] The distinction between laws and ethical guidelines is reinforced by the possibility that there can be unethical laws. At one time slavery was legal in the United States, but most of us would assert that slavery has always been unethical and that the laws permitting it were immoral ones. The subject of ethics will be clearer if we keep this distinction between laws and ethical guidelines in mind.

Another source of solutions to ethical problems are a particular society's *beliefs, values,* and *attitudes.* To the extent that people can identify the beliefs of their society, they might use those beliefs to help them solve ethical problems. In China the predominant belief or attitude today seems to be that a couple should have only one child. This belief could help a woman who already had one child resolve the problem of whether or not to have an abortion should she become pregnant a second time. She could simply follow the predominant belief, be content with her one child, and have an abortion. This idea of social beliefs being relevant to ethical problems is discussed in Chapter 3.

What might be called *human relationships* can also provide insight into how we ought to live and can help us solve ethical problems. Love, caring, and friendship shape our daily lives. Traditionally, these relationships have not found a central role in ethics because they were thought to be contrary to the search for rational, impartial, universalizable ethical guidelines. In the view of some philosophers, however, love, caring, and friendship are ethically significant. Therefore, ethics is more than the search for rational, impartial, universalizable ethical guidelines. At a later point in this chapter I will discuss rationality, impartiality, and universalizability. In Chapter 9 I will discuss an ethical view centered on caring, and in Chapter 10 I will briefly investigate the importance of special treatment for friends and loved ones.

## Ethical Theories

The approaches to ethics contained in this book are referred to as ethical theories. *Ethical theories* attempt (1) to provide clear and reasonable concepts related to moral guidelines and (2) to identify and justify moral guidelines to use in solving moral problems and helping us live together successfully. This definition of ethical theories relates to the book's account of the basic purpose of ethics. More specifically, ethical theories provide three things: (1) standards or guidelines for determining good and bad or right and wrong, (2) justifications for using these particular standards, and (3) differentiations between what is and what is not morally significant.[4] Most of the proponents of ethical theories are distressed by the profusion of ethical beliefs and competing solutions to ethical problems. Each group believes their particular approach to ethics is the best one—that is, that it provides the legitimate ethical standard to determine good and evil.

Although many ethical theorists emphasize their interest in solving moral problems, Mary Midgley sees that, overall, ethics is about interacting successfully with others:

> Human beings are not limpets or even crocodiles, they are highly social creatures. Except for a few natural hermits, they have to interact fairly constantly if they are to have any sort of a satisfying life. And these interactions are only possible where there is some measure of agreement on basic patterns.[5]

Human beings are indeed social creatures. We live together in societies, and if we are to do so successfully, we must live within certain basic guidelines that reflect a "measure of agreement on basic patterns." Laws provide some of these guidelines and help us to live together successfully, but at least two kinds of situations arise wherein laws are insufficient and we also need ethical guidelines. One situation is illustrated by the slavery example, wherein a law treats one segment of society unfairly or harmfully. An ethical standard allows us to evaluate the questionable law. Another situation arises when society would run more smoothly if people acted in a certain way, but the law is inadequate to produce the desired actions. In general, we believe we can get along better if we do not steal each other's property. Imagine that you find a wallet containing a hundred dollars in a deserted area at night. No one is nearby. You could take the hundred dollars, discard the wallet, and have no reason to fear being caught and punished. However, if you were guided by the moral principle that it is wrong to steal other people's property, you would return the wallet. We get along better if people return wallets and if property is protected. Thus, ethical guidelines help us live together more successfully. The second aspect of ethical theories is that they identify ethical guidelines that can help us live together more successfully.

Ethical theories identify moral or ethical guidelines. *Moral guidelines* are rules, principles, beliefs, and so on that moral agents create and that inform us about how we ought to live. These guidelines usually create a view of ethical activity that contrasts with the unlimited pursuit of self-interest. If people believe it is permissible to do anything that is in their self-interest, they may injure other individuals or society in general to benefit themselves. This will interfere with living together successfully. Ethical theories can help to prevent harm to individuals and to society by identifying a view of "good" that opposes the unlimited pursuit of self-interest. This does not mean that ethical people can never act in their own self-interest, only that there are limitations on the pursuit of self-interest.

In summary, there are two primary aspects to the function or purpose of ethical theories. One aspect is to help us solve ethical problems, and the second one is to help us live together successfully. The two aspects are closely related. Ethical problems usually involve other people. Should I tell the deceived friend the truth? Should I steal the textbook? Should I end the relationship? Our solutions to these ethical problems will affect how successfully we can live with others.

## Evaluating Ethical Theories

The main function of ethical theories is to identify moral guidelines to help us solve ethical problems and live together successfully. Therefore, I will evaluate the ethical theories presented in the text in relation to their success at accomplishing this function. The criteria for this evaluation relate directly to that function:

1. *The ethical theory must be able to identify some ethical guidelines.* Obviously, a theory that cannot identify any guidelines cannot solve any problems or help us live together successfully.

2. *The theory must be able to show that some ethical guidelines are better than others.* A theory that concludes that any ethical guideline is as good as any other would imply that any solution to an ethical problem is as good as any other solution. This would legitimize any actions, even the most harmful or antisocial ones.

3. *The theory must identify ethical guidelines that would prohibit the unlimited pursuit of self-interest.* People cannot live together successfully if they believe it is permissible to do anything that is in their self-interest because they may harm other individuals or society in general to benefit themselves.

4. *The theory must produce effective solutions to ethical problems.* A theory that produced impractical or ineffective solutions or only a limited number of solutions would not be as valuable as a theory without these limitations.

# Some Traditional Assumptions of Ethical Theories

Before discussing specific ethical theories, it is important to understand some basic concepts. Many, but not all, ethical theories have centered on what might be called a set of traditional ethical assumptions. Today some philosophers are calling into question these traditional assumptions, but they remain important to many other thinkers. These traditional ethical assumptions provide a foundation for most ethical theories and they can be briefly stated as follows:

1. Ethics is rational (rationality).
2. Persons are moral equals and ought to be treated impartially (impartiality).
3. A person can universalize some ethical evaluations (universalizability).

Now let's examine each of these assumptions in more detail.

## *Rationality*

Rationality means roughly the ability to think and to act according to reasoned principles. In the context of the traditional ethical assumptions, saying that "ethics is rational" means, in general, that people can use reason to reach theoretical and practical conclusions about ethical matters. More specifically, people can provide reasons to support moral guidelines and solutions to ethical problems; these reasons can be evaluated; and some reasons, guidelines, and solutions are better than others. Thus, persons can arrive at guidelines supported by reason and reasons. They can, then, use these rational guidelines to guide their actions. Finally, the claim that ethics is rational also suggests that well-intentioned people who share an ethical framework (and sometimes even ones who do not) can discuss ethical problems and hope to arrive at mutually acceptable solutions.

Rationality is an important consideration related to ethics. It is a criterion for moral responsibility and is crucial to being a moral agent. *Moral agents* can be defined as beings who can perform morally significant actions and be held morally responsible for them. When we hold people morally responsible or accountable for something, we often feel justified in praising, rewarding, blaming, criticizing, or punishing them. There are three common criteria for moral responsibility. To be held morally responsible for something, an agent (1) needs to have freely or willingly caused something to happen, or allowed it to happen through his or her negligence; (2) must be able to have known or must know the consequences of the thing; and (3) must be rational or able to know the difference between good and evil.

The first criterion means that if my brakes fail and I try to avoid hitting other cars but accidentally run into yours I am not morally responsible for injuring you. You should not criticize me unless you believe I could have done something to avoid the collision. I may be financially responsible for paying compensation, but I am not morally responsible because I did not freely or willingly hit your car. If, however, I have been negligent (for example, if I have been having a serious problem with my brakes but deliberately failed to get them fixed), then I am morally responsible for your injury.

The second criterion implies that I am not morally responsible if I cannot know the consequences of something, but I may be held morally responsible if I deliberately remain ignorant. If it were impossible for me to have known that my brakes would fail, I am not morally responsible for injuring you. If, however, I strongly suspected that there was a problem with my brakes but deliberately chose to remain ignorant about their condition, then I will be held morally responsible for your injuries. I freely or willingly chose to remain ignorant of a potentially dangerous situation, and, therefore, we may say that the second criterion is satisfied.

The third criterion for moral responsibility means that moral agents must have the ability to think and to act according to rational principles. They must be able to understand the difference between moral good and bad. People with mental illnesses or defects and young children who cannot act on rational principles and who do not understand the difference between good and evil cannot be held morally responsible. For example, some people with mental illnesses cannot understand the nature of their actions or rationally evaluate the consequences. They also may be unable to comprehend the difference between good and evil. A psychopath may not be able to understand the difference between killing an ant or a human being. We do not hold the psychopath morally responsible for his or her action, even though the person is causally responsible for doing the killing and will be confined to an institution. The psychopath does not rationally understand what he or she is doing and cannot meet the third criterion.

*Impartiality*

The second of the traditional ethical assumptions is that persons are moral equals and therefore ought to be treated impartially. By this we mean that everyone in a sufficiently similar situation counts the same when we are trying to make ethical judgments or resolve moral problems. Impartiality requires that we ignore "irrelevant factors" or factors that would make us give special treatment to someone and not treat him or her as equal to everyone else. For example, it is usually thought to be irrelevant that a person is my friend. In ethical matters I must be impartial and treat my friend as a moral equal to other persons. The same is true for me. I cannot privilege myself but must consider myself a moral equal to others. Treating persons as moral equals sometimes conflicts with pursuing self-interest. When I act on self-interest, I may proceed as if I had more moral worth than other persons do. In an ethically significant matter, I must recognize that I am only one among equals. I must do what is good or right—not simply what is best for me. Impartiality does not require that we ignore relevant factors. If someone had murdered another person, we would treat that person differently from other persons. People do not remain moral equals in the sense that they are all equally good or bad. The specific sense in which they remain moral equals differs from theory to theory and will be discussed in subsequent chapters.

Moral equality can be illustrated by briefly discussing act utilitarianism, which is one ethical theory (see Chapter 6). *Act utilitarians* claim that ethical actions provide the greatest net benefit or happiness for the persons affected by an action. To be ethical, we must be impartial while acting in accord with this rule. We cannot treat our families, our friends, or ourselves in a special or privileged way. Rather, we must treat everyone as moral equals and take them into consideration in the same way that any other person would be taken into account. For an act utilitarian, every person is the same when calculating the benefit and harm produced by an action. A benefit to your spouse or child is the same as a benefit to a stranger. In some cases, what maximizes benefit for the greatest number of persons might also be in your self-interest, but that would merely be a coincidence. In many other cases, following the act utilitarian rule will conflict with your self-interest. For example, I may want to spend my fifty dollars on more CDs for my collection, but the ethical thing to do might be to donate the sum to an effective charity. Perhaps I already have hundreds of CDs, and giving the money to the charity would save lives. Contributing the money to charity and saving the lives produces more benefit for a larger number of people than buying the CDs. According to utilitarians, in some cases I must sacrifice my self-interest to be ethical.

Act utilitarianism and some other ethical theories claim that people are moral equals. These theories can be called *egalitarian* ethical theories. They can be contrasted with *nonegalitarian* ethical theories, which do not treat all people as moral equals. Four egalitarian theories are discussed in this book: divine command theory, act utilitarianism, Kantian ethics, and the moral rights ethical theory. Five nonegalitarian theories are also examined: ethical egoism, ethical subjectivism, ethical relativism, virtue ethics, and the ethics of care.

The issue of moral equality is connected to one of the most important questions in ethics: What beings should be given moral consideration? Philosophers sometimes use the phrase *morally significant beings,* which can be defined as beings who ought to receive ethical consideration. For example, if good is related to benefit and harm, we must consider the benefit and harm done to all morally significant beings, but we would not need to consider benefit and harm done to beings who are not morally significant. To be more specific, we would consider benefit and harm to human beings because they are morally significant beings, but we would not consider benefit and harm to ants because they are not morally significant. *Full-status morally significant beings* receive the highest degree of moral consideration. There also may be *partial-status morally significant beings* who receive some moral consideration but are not treated the same as those with full status. Some people believe certain animals, such as gorillas, chimpanzees, dogs, and cats, should receive some moral consideration. For example, it may be wrong to kill them even though the value of their lives does not equal that of human lives. Although moral consideration for nonhuman animals may seem extreme to some people, in environmental ethics we encounter theories that would extend moral consideration beyond nonhuman animals to things other than beings, such as trees, rivers, and ecosystems. To answer the question about moral consideration, philosophers need to agree on a criterion or set of criteria that would determine what beings are and are not morally significant. If there are partial-status morally significant beings, then an additional criterion (or criteria) is needed to separate the two categories of morally significant beings.

This question has generated a great deal of controversy, and finding an answer to it is crucial for solving moral problems such as abortion rights and claims of animal exploitation. Whether a fetus or a nonhuman animal is a morally significant being depends on the criterion (or criteria) we choose to determine what beings get moral consideration. The phrase "morally significant beings" must not be confused with the phrase "morally significant actions." Morally significant beings are beings who ought to receive ethical consideration. *Morally significant actions* are actions that concern moral philosophers because moral guidelines are relevant to these actions. Not all actions are worth ethical consideration. For example, the action of tying your right shoe before your left shoe is not morally significant. No moral guideline is relevant to tying your shoe. There is, of course, a connection between morally significant beings and morally significant actions. Most morally significant actions involve harm, benefit, respect, or disrespect to one or more morally significant beings.

## Universalizability

The last of the traditional ethical assumptions is that persons can universalize some moral evaluations; that is, they can extend their ethical evaluations to anyone else in a sufficiently similar situation. Like impartiality, universalizability is connected to the crucial idea of moral equality: I can universalize my legitimate ethical evaluations because I am a moral equal to everyone else. If it is wrong for me to steal in this situation, then it is wrong for anyone to steal in this situation because we are moral equals. No one has special moral status that allows him or her to steal and be ethical. Another reason for the universalizability of certain ethical evaluations is the assertion that some ethical guidelines are universal. Because everyone should endorse the guidelines, they can be applied to everyone's actions. As stated earlier, act utilitarians claim that ethical actions provide the greatest net benefit or happiness for the greatest number of people. This principle is supposed to be universal; it should be endorsed and followed by everyone. Based on this principle, the ethical thing for me to do in the example of the CDs is to give the money to charity. If it is the ethical thing for me to do, I can claim that it is the moral thing for anyone to do in a sufficiently similar situation. If we are all supposed to follow the guideline, then good and bad will be the same for all of us when we are in sufficiently similar situations.

For it to be ethical for someone to act differently in the same moral situation, that person would have to have a different moral standing than the rest of us or be following a different moral guideline. Philosophers who believe in universalizability assert that we are moral equals and that we ought to endorse and follow the same guidelines. To be ethical, everyone in a situation with sufficiently similar morally significant factors ought to do the same thing. Thus, we can universalize some of our moral evaluations, extending them to other people in similar situations.

These three traditional ethical assumptions lie behind most ethical theories and have had a great deal of influence on ethics. Among contemporary philosophers, these assumptions about rationality, impartiality, and universalizability have become controversial and are being called into question. In this book, you will encounter both theories that endorse these traditional ethical assumptions and ones that do not.

## Basic Themes Associated with Ethics

In addition to the traditional assumptions connected to ethical theories, four basic ethical themes associated with moral good and bad can also be identified. These themes can be developed in a variety of ways. Here I will set them up as opposing views and present them in the form of questions.

1. What kind of moral guidelines makes something good or bad: subjective, relative, or objective ones?

2. What makes something good or bad; is it the consequences that are produced or the reasoning that leads up to it?

3. Are good and bad related to following general rules without exceptions or connected to separately evaluating each action, belief, and so on?

4. Are good and bad primarily related to the group, community, or majority of persons or should the focus be on the individual?

The first theme is represented by the question, "What kind of moral guidelines makes something good or bad: subjective, relative, or objective ones?" In this text the term "subjective" will be applied only to moral guidelines that are necessarily a product of the emotions or attitudes of specific individuals. As we shall see in Chapter 4, *ethical subjectivism* refers to any ethical theory that argues that the only legitimate moral guidelines are ones that are necessarily connected to the emotions or attitudes of specific individuals or subjects. Each individual should create and use his or her moral guidelines to determine good and bad. The term "relative" will be applied to guidelines that are the product of an actual society. In Chapter 3 we will discover that *ethical relativists* claim that the only legitimate moral guidelines are those connected to actual societies. Therefore, legitimate moral guidelines are always relative to some actual society. All the members of a society should use their society's moral guidelines to determine good and evil. In contrast to these two concepts, a theory will be said to produce "objective" moral guidelines if the guidelines are the product of considerations of fact and/or reason that do not depend on the perceptions, judgments, or emotions of particular persons or the beliefs of a particular society.[6] For example, considerations of harm and benefit to morally significant beings are *objective* because they do not depend on the perceptions, judgments, or emotions of some particular person or the beliefs of some specific society. Any moral agent has the potential to identify these factual considerations of harm and benefit. The fact that rape and murder harm victims or cause pain and death could be appealed to as factual reasons that they are evil. If a philosopher endorses objective moral guidelines, some actions (such as rape and murder) will always be good or evil for everyone. One of the objectivist theories investigated in this book is the Kantian theory, found in Chapter 5. The conflict between subjective, relative, and objective ethical positions and conclusions is an important consideration in ethics.

Another significant theme in ethics can be introduced by the question, "What makes something good or bad; is it the consequences that are produced or the reasoning that leads up to it?" Although it might seem that the correct answer is a combination of the two, philosophers have often chosen to focus primarily on one or the other aspect. *Ethical consequentialists* believe the goodness of something is a result of the consequences that it produces. *Ethical egoists* focus on the consequences to the individual, whereas *utilitarians* demand the greatest beneficial consequences for the greatest number of people affected. For a utilitarian, sending a check to a charity is not good unless some benefit actually results from it. *Deontologists* deny that good is a result of the consequences. They think this introduces a distressing element of luck into ethics. From the consequentialist perspective, I might try to do something good, but if I am unlucky and no good consequences result from my effort, I have not succeeded in performing a good action. Deontologists focus on the reasoning that leads up to something. They assert that if the right kind of reasoning motivates me to send a check to charity, the action is good regardless of the consequences. Many philosophers focus on actions as the main subject of ethical evaluations. We might assume that they are working with the following model of action:

$$\textit{Reasoning} \rightarrow \textit{Action} \rightarrow \textit{Consequences}$$

Deontologists believe we should look at the reasoning that precedes the action to determine whether it is good or evil. Consequentialists believe we should look at the consequences produced by the action. Action is often the focus of ethical evaluations, but morally significant beliefs, attitudes, commitments, policies, and so on can also provide a focus for evaluation. This dispute between the ethical consequentialists and the deontologists is another important debate in ethics.

A third theme relates to this question, "Are good and bad related to following general rules of behavior without exception or connected to separately evaluating each action, belief, policy, and so on?" People who believe that general rules should guide our behavior feel that these rules should have no exceptions. For example, it is wrong to kill innocent people, it is wrong to steal, it is wrong to break a promise. People who want to evaluate things separately believe we must be open to the possibility that we can appropriately make an exception to even the best moral rule. They want to evaluate each action as independently as possible based on some criterion. The criterion may be similar to a rule, but if it is, then the criterion is the only rule they will always endorse.

The German philosopher Immanuel Kant (1724–1804) believed some rules could never be broken by an ethical person. For example, it is wrong to break your promises. Like Kant, rule utilitarians also believe in following general rules, although unlike Kant, they evaluate the rules by considering the general consequences of following them. If having people always follow a rule produces a greater net benefit than their not doing so, then the rule ought to be followed in all cases. In contrast to Kant and rule utilitarians, act utilitarians claim that we must evaluate each action as independently as possible using the general criterion that what is ethical is what promotes the greatest net benefit for the morally significant beings affected by an action. They have one basic rule or criterion, the utilitarian maxim that we ought to maximize net benefit, but they use this rule to evaluate distinct actions, decisions, beliefs, and so on separately. Breaking your promise may be the ethical thing to do in one case, whereas in another instance it may be unethical. Chapter 5 discusses Kant's ethical theory, and Chapter 6 investigates utilitarianism.

The fourth important theme relates to the question, "Are good and bad primarily related to the group, community, or majority of persons or should the focus be on the individual?" Utilitarians believe the focus of ethics should be the greatest net benefit for the greatest number of morally significant beings. In some cases utilitarians would sacrifice the individual for the greater good of the group because the benefit to the larger number of people outweighs that of the individual. Other philosophers discuss ethics using the language of moral rights (see Chapter 7). Proponents of moral rights focus on the individual. They would never sacrifice the individual for the group, at least not without the individual's consent. Moral rights are often seen as legitimate claims to protection for the essential aspects of the individual, such as life, liberty, and property. The point of providing this protection is to prevent the group from forcing individuals to give up elements that are essential to living successful lives. This debate about the focus of ethical attention is another important conflict in ethics.

Each of the ethical theories discussed in this book takes a position in relation to these four themes about good and bad, and those positions will be discussed in subsequent chapters. The discussion of these themes will help you to recognize the similarities and differences between the different ethical theories and moral guidelines that can help you solve the ethical problems you face in day-to-day living.

## Conclusion

This chapter provided a brief introduction to ethics. Two meanings were provided for the term "ethics." The first was *the investigation into how we ought to live*. The second was *the investigation into the conceptual and theoretical resources for solving ethical problems and into the solutions to them*. These two meanings point to the two aspects of what the text calls the basic goal of ethics: to help persons solve ethical problems and live together successfully. A variety of ethical concepts were identified: ethics, ethical problems, theoretical ethics, applied ethics, ethical theories, moral guidelines, moral responsibility, moral agents, morally significant beings, morally significant actions, traditional ethical assumptions, and ethical themes. Ethics is important because it is vital for us to live together successfully and because we need to be able to reach successful solutions to moral problems.

## QUESTIONS FOR REVIEW

*Here are some questions to help you review the main concepts in this chapter.*

1. What is ethics?
2. What is an ethical problem?
3. What is the difference between theoretical ethics and applied ethics?
4. How do moral guidelines differ from laws?
5. What is an ethical theory? What three things typically are provided by an ethical theory?
6. What four criteria will be used to evaluate ethical theories?
7. What are the three traditional ethical assumptions?
8. What are moral agents? What criteria do we use to determine moral responsibility?
9. What does impartiality "require" of moral agents?
10. What is the difference between egalitarian and nonegalitarian ethical theories?
11. What are morally significant beings?
12. Explain the difference between the terms "morally significant beings" and "moral agents."
13. What are morally significant actions?

14. What are the four basic themes associated with ethics?

15. What position is endorsed by ethical objectivists? How does it differ from the positions of ethical subjectivists and ethical relativists?

16. How do deontologists and consequentialists differ in regard to the question of what makes something good or evil?

17. According to the text, what is the basic goal of ethics?

## NOTES

1. This second definition of "ethics" is centered around solving ethical problems and seems appropriate for a book designed for applied ethics classes. The first sentence of this chapter contains a more general definition. Another more general definition is: "inquiry about ways of life and rules of conduct." *The Encyclopedia of Philosophy,* Vol. 3 (New York: Macmillan, 1967).

2. In this book "ethical" and "moral" are used as synonyms.

3. This text uses the term "morality" to mean a moral code or set of moral principles, rules, ideals, or guidelines usually grounded in a moral theory.

4. In this text the words "good" and "right" are used as synonyms. The same is true for "bad" and "wrong."

5. Mary Midgley, *Can't We Make Moral Judgments?* (New York: St. Martin's Press, 1991), p. 57.

6. Some philosophers would prefer to use the term "absolute" instead of "objective" in this context. I consider this a personal preference and have clearly defined what I mean by "objective" in the text.

# Chapter 2

# Divine Command Theory

Religion provides guidelines about how to live that can help people solve ethical problems and live together successfully. The writings of the Middle Eastern religions of Judaism, Christianity, and Islam describe many of these guidelines for human action, which are written as commandments from God. Some commandments have been general rules such as the Ten Commandments, designed for a whole people or perhaps for everyone. These general commandments provide a set of rules that ought to be followed and that create a view of good and bad actions, attitudes, and beliefs. They inform believers about how to live and can be used to solve many of life's moral problems.

According to the Torah and the Bible, at one point in their history the Israelites were captives in Egypt. Finally, after a series of divine punishments, the Pharaoh allowed them to leave. During their exodus from Egypt, Moses and the Israelites camped near Mount Sinai. God called Moses to the top of the mountain and gave him the Ten Commandments to instruct the Israelites in how they ought to live. Here is a brief version of the Ten Commandments from the book of Exodus:

1. Thou shalt have no other gods before me.
2. Thou shalt not make unto thee any graven image.
3. Thou shalt not take the name of the Lord thy God in vain.
4. Remember the Sabbath day, to keep it holy.
5. Honor thy father and thy mother.
6. Thou shalt not kill.
7. Thou shalt not commit adultery.
8. Thou shalt not steal.
9. Thou shalt not bear false witness against thy neighbor.
10. Thou shalt not covet . . . anything that is thy neighbor's.

These Commandments established a view of good and bad. For example, honoring a person's father and mother was good; not honoring them was bad. Killing, committing adultery, and stealing were bad. To this day, this account of good and bad provides the foundation for morality in everyday life for all who embrace Judaism.

Other commandments have been personal, as when God commanded Moses to go to the top of Mount Sinai to receive the Ten Commandments. These personal commandments provide vital instructions for that individual. Some commandments come directly to prophets from God, as the Ten Commandments did. Angels relay other commandments, such as when an angel instructed Mary to name her baby Jesus. Today, believers usually find God's commandments in holy texts, such as the Bible, the Torah, or the Qur'an, but prophets and other holy people may also be a contemporary source of divine commandments.

## Divine Command Theory

How should a person live his or her life? One way to answer this question is to say that people should follow God's commandments. These religious people start from the insight that *legitimate guidelines for how to live are necessarily related to God.* In calling this idea an "insight," I am referring to the sense of the word that relates to perceiving in an intuitive way. Thus, this idea seems intuitively correct to religious people.

This conception of God and his commandments is sometimes called divine command theory. *Divine command theory* claims that God's commandments establish the requirements for how to live and create an objective view of good and bad conduct. According to this view, good and bad do not depend on human perception, cultures, or conventions— only on God's commandments. These divine commandments make secular ethical guidelines unnecessary. God's commandments create obligations for persons. If God commands people not to steal, then people are obligated to follow that commandment. *The "ethical" standard for this theory is that what God commands people to do is good and what God forbids people to do is bad.* The theory states that whatever God commands is good simply because God commanded it. No other reason is relevant to good and evil. The theory does not endorse speculations about why God commands the things he does.[1] God's reasons are presumably beyond human understanding, possibly because God acts without anything that we would recognize as "reason." God's reasons, if they exist, are irrelevant to identifying what is good and bad. For us, the only reason something is good is that God commands it; the only reason it is bad is that God forbids it.

If God commands a person to do something, then that thing is good, even if ordinary human beings might be inclined to regard it as bad. The book of Genesis relates the story about God's command that Abraham sacrifice his son Isaac. This seems to many of us to be the epitome of evil. What could be worse than killing your own child? The killing is even more horrible when the larger context is known. God had informed Abraham that he would have a son through whom he would become the father of a great nation. Abraham's wife Sarah was thought to be unable to conceive a child, but finally, in her old age, Sarah gave birth to a son, Isaac. This promised son was the child that God commanded Abraham to kill as a sacrifice. Thus, Abraham must not only kill his child, but he must kill the promised child for whom he waited so long and who was supposed to make it possible for him be the father of a great nation.

Most people would regard as evil both this commandment and the action it commanded. It seems cruel and evil to tell a father to kill his child, and the action of killing an innocent child is surely evil. Divine command theory asserts, however, that what people think is irrelevant. Good and bad have nothing to do with individual people's opinions, with society's beliefs, or with whether people are harmed or killed. Good and bad only relate to God's commands.

Divine command theory states that God is the creator of the universe and ultimately the creator of us all. Religious people believe our lives are a gift from God that he can take away at any time. Therefore, when God kills or commands someone to kill, it cannot be evil. It was good of Abraham to set out to kill his son. If God had not later told him to spare the boy, it would have been good for Abraham to kill his son. It is not the place of humans to question or even to try to understand God's commandments. God is omnipotent, omniscience, omnipresent, transcendent, uncreated, and eternal. The ways of such a being are mysterious and are often beyond our comprehension. God, however, is also perfectly good, and people should trust his wisdom, knowledge, and goodness and obey his commandments.

## Justification for the Ethical Standard and Strengths of the Theory

### God's Authority

Why would someone endorse the standard of good and evil put forward by divine command theory? What are the strengths of divine command theory? The main justification relates to a belief in God and God's authority. God is the creator and ruler of the universe. Human beings are part of his creation. God's authority extends over all people because he is the creator of the universe and human beings are part of his creation. If God chooses to make commandments related to human behavior, they should be obeyed because to disobey would be to rebel against our creator. People who believe in God may feel justified in endorsing this "ethical" standard because they accept God's authority. Thus, one strength of the theory is that people who believe in God will be inclined to accept a theory that acknowledges God's authority.

## Clear and Universal Guidelines

The second possible justification for the standard and corresponding strength of the theory is that it seems to make good and evil very clear and universal. We simply need to follow God's commandments, and at first glance, these commandments seem clear and unambiguous: Thou shalt not steal. What could be more clear-cut than that? We do not need to consider the complexities of the particular situation related to a potential theft because the details of the situation are not relevant. We do not need to be confused by all the human opinions about stealing because human opinions about stealing and about good and evil in general are not relevant. We also do not need to be led astray by the many contrasting views of different societies about stealing and good and evil in general because they are not relevant either. Finally, we do not need to worry about the consequences or results of stealing or not stealing, such as whether anyone benefits or is harmed. The only relevant thing is God's commandment. A theory with clear guidelines seems stronger than one with unclear ones.

Divine command theory also makes good and evil universal. If someone asks whether or not he should steal this book, there is a universally correct answer: Thou shalt not steal. Therefore, the answer is "No," in every place and in every time. It is the correct answer here and in every other country in the world. It was correct in the past, is correct now, and will be correct in the future. The correct answer depends only on God's commandments, not on anything about human perception, cultures, or conventions. Thus, unless God's commandment changes, stealing is universally wrong. This idea of universal guidelines also seems like a strength to some people because it reduces the possibility of ethical disagreements.

## Overriding Guidelines for Conduct

The final justification for the ethical standard and related strength of divine command theory is that it provides an overriding set of guidelines that eliminates conflict. To have one set of religious rules and another set of secular ethical rules guiding life would be confusing because the two might conflict. God commands us not to lie, so we should not lie. However, most people's secular ethical view is that it is good to lie in certain situations. For example, you should lie if it will prevent hurting someone's feelings. With divine command theory, we can discard secular ethics and merely follow God's commandments. If God commands us not to lie, then it does not matter what people usually believe about lying. It does not matter if someone's feelings would be hurt. The commandment is that people should not lie, and that is the only rule that needs to be considered. Thus, there is no conflict between religious principles and secular beliefs, and this is another strength of the theory for many people.

## Divine Commands, Human Freedom, and Morally Significant Actions

Jews, Christians, and Muslims believe God has made many commandments. Most of the believers of these religions also assert that God has granted human beings the freedom to choose whether or not to follow his commandments. God does not force people to obey his commandments; the choice is up to them. For example, Abraham had a real choice concerning whether or not to sacrifice his son. He had the option to defy God and refuse or to obey God and kill his son. Both of these options were "live options"—options that were really possible and open to Abraham. For many believers, human freedom makes the divine reward for obeying the commands seem fair. People have the option to obey or disobey. Those who obey are rewarded, and those who disobey are punished. Thus, each group gets what it deserves.

The concept of "morally significant actions" discussed in Chapter 1 refers to the idea that moral guidelines are relevant to some actions and not to others. Stealing someone's property is always morally relevant no matter what ethical theory is providing the moral guidelines. Whether you tie your right or left shoe first is never morally significant. In between are many other actions, some morally significant and some not. Based on divine command theory, an action is morally significant if God commands us to perform it or if God forbids us to do it. If God has made no mention of the action, then it is not morally significant. If we consider any of the major texts of the three Middle Eastern religions, we would discover hundreds or possibly thousands of morally significant actions. The Torah, the Bible, and the Qur'an contain many commandments beyond the Ten Commandments.

## Divine Command Theory and the Traditional Ethical Assumptions

In Chapter 1, I discussed some traditional assumptions that lie behind most ethical theories: rationality, impartiality, and universalizability. Behind divine command theory lie only two of these three assumptions; divine command theory does not assume that ethics is rational.

Declaring that ethics is rational means, in general, that we can use reason to reach theoretical and practical conclusions about ethical matters. More specifically, people can provide reasons to support moral guidelines and solutions to ethical problems; these reasons can be evaluated; and some guidelines and solutions are better than others. These rational guidelines can then inform their actions. In divine command theory, reasons cannot be evaluated. Whatever God commands is good simply because God commanded it. Therefore, the only reason something is good is that God commanded it. No other reason or factor is relevant to good and evil. There can be no evaluation of the reason for the guidelines or the guidelines themselves, only blind obedience. Human reasons are clearly irrelevant, but even if God had some reason for giving the command, it would also be irrelevant to good and bad. Only the commands matter, not any possible reasons for them. Therefore, in the sense used in Chapter 1, good and evil are not rational because the reasons for the guidelines and the guidelines themselves cannot be evaluated. This matter will be discussed further in the section on the problems with the theory.

The second traditional ethical assumption is impartiality—the idea that persons are moral equals and ought to be treated impartially. By this we mean that everyone in a sufficiently similar situation counts the same when we are trying to make ethical judgments or resolve moral problems. We ignore as "irrelevant" factors that would make us give special treatment to someone and not treat him or her as equal to everyone else. For example, it is usually thought to be irrelevant that a person is my friend. In ethical matters, I must be impartial and treat my friend as a moral equal to other persons. Divine command theory assumes that people are initially moral equals. All human beings are considered to be morally significant beings in God's view. All people were created by God and are bound by God's authority. They should all follow God's commands. Therefore, all persons start out equally in their relation to God. People do not end up equally good or bad. Their moral status ultimately depends on the degree to which they follow God's commandments. No matter how often people sin, however, they remain God's creatures and can always beg forgiveness and attempt to be reconciled to God. The different religions have different ideas about how this reconciliation can take place.

The third traditional ethical assumption is universalizability—persons can universalize some moral evaluations. That is, some moral guidelines should be followed by all of us, and some ethical evaluations should be extended to anyone else in a sufficiently similar situation. The assumption of universalizability lies behind divine command theory. The Ten Commandments and many other divine commandments are universal guidelines. They were meant to apply to all human beings. Because they are universal, they allow us to make some universal evaluations. God commands people not to steal: If someone steals something, the evaluation that it is wrong can be made by anyone and applied to anyone who commits that action. The guidelines, or commandments, and the evaluations that follow from God's commands are both universal.

## Divine Command Theory and the Basic Ethical Themes

In addition to the traditional assumptions connected to ethical theories and ethics, some basic ethical themes are related to moral good and evil. The first theme can be represented by the question: *What kind of moral guidelines makes something good or bad: subjective, relative, or objective ones?* Divine command theory asserts that legitimate moral guidelines and good and bad are objective. In Chapter 1, I defined "objective" moral guidelines as the product of objective considerations of fact and/or reason that do not depend on the perceptions, judgments, or emotions of particular persons or the beliefs of some specific society. In divine command theory, good and bad depend on God's commands and prohibitions and not on human perceptions, attitudes, emotions, or social beliefs. If it is a fact that God commanded people not to steal, then it is bad for them to do so. Their personal emotions or attitudes toward stealing are irrelevant. The beliefs and attitudes of their society are also irrelevant. Only the fact that God has made a command is relevant. Therefore, this theory asserts that moral good and bad are objective.

Another significant theme in ethics can be introduced by this question: *What makes something good or bad; is it the consequences that are produced or the reasoning that leads up to it?* Divine command theory relates good and evil to God's commands and prohibitions. If your reason for doing something is that God commanded it, then that action is good. The consequences of following God's command are not relevant to the goodness of your action. Therefore, divine command theory is certainly not a consequential theory. In the case of Abraham, killing his son was good because God commanded it; the consequences of the act were irrelevant to its moral evaluation. Divine command theory is based on the reasoning that precedes the act. If I reason that God has commanded this act, then it is good.

The third theme relates to this question: *Are good and bad related to following general rules without exceptions or connected to separately evaluating actions, beliefs, and so on?* People who believe our behavior should be guided by general rules feel that there are no exceptions to these rules: It is wrong to kill innocent people, it is wrong to steal, it is wrong to break a promise. People who choose to evaluate things separately believe we must always be open to the possibility that we can appropriately make an exception to even the best moral rule. They want to evaluate each action as independently as possible based on some criterion or criteria. The criterion may be similar to a rule, but if it is, then the criterion is the only rule they will always endorse. Divine command theory asserts that "moral" good and bad are connected to following general rules—the commandments—without exceptions. If God commands us not to steal, we do not need to examine every possible case of stealing. We simply should not steal.

The fourth important theme relates to the proper focus of ethical attention and benefit: *Are good and bad primarily related to the group, community, or majority of people or should the focus be on the individual?* Divine command theory emphasizes that individuals must follow the divine commandments. It is not concerned with the good of the group or the majority; it is focused on the individual and his or her response to God's commandments and prohibitions. Therefore, divine command theory asserts that "moral" good and bad are related primarily to the individual.

## Problems with Divine Command Theory

Up to this point I have explained divine command theory, enumerated a few of its strengths, and related it to the traditional ethical assumptions and basic themes. This section discusses problems with the theory, illustrating how an insight that seems appropriate to many people can become problematic as thinkers transform that insight into a theory about good and bad. As the problems are discussed, I will relate them to the criteria for evaluating ethical theories. The final section in the chapter provides an overall evaluation of divine command theory.

### Different Texts and Interpretations of Texts

One problem with divine command theory is our inability to resolve the dispute over the source of divine commandments. Although all monotheistic religions acknowledge that the ultimate source is God, people have different views of God and disparate ideas about how we know God's commandments. Most religions have a sacred text or texts that their believers claim reveal God's commandments. Which of these different texts, however, contains the authentic commandments? Do we look at the Qur'an, the Bible, the Torah, or some other religious text? Sometimes commandments in these different texts conflict, and there is no way to resolve these conflicts. It does not seem possible to resolve this problem because we cannot use reason to examine these texts or to choose the single legitimate one. There is no established set of rational criteria for the single legitimate religious text, and therefore reason cannot arbitrate the conflict.

Most people believe in the religion of their parents or of the community in which they were socialized. Adopting a religion, for them, is primarily a matter of faith, not reason. A person's faith is a faith in a particular view of God and in a particular religious text that reveals God's commandments. Thus, faith is personal and cannot be generalized to arbitrate the claims of different religions nor to select a single legitimate text. This problem cannot be solved in a generally convincing way by either reason or faith, and it remains an ongoing difficulty for divine command theory.

Prophets and other holy people can also be sources of God's commandments. Different religions, however, have different holy people, and these holy people sometimes say things that conflict. Just as we cannot use reason or faith to determine the single correct religious text, so we cannot identify the correct prophet or holy person. This relates to criterion two of the evaluation criteria: The theory must be able to demonstrate that some guidelines are better than others. There is no rational way to show that the commandments endorsed by one religion are better than different commandments asserted by another.

The second aspect of this problem with divine command theory involves the difficulty of interpreting the divine text in order to understand God's commandments. For example, biblical scholars disagree about the correct interpretation of many passages in the Bible. Does God command us never to divorce our spouses, or is divorce permitted? Does "Thou shalt not kill" permit some kinds of killing, and, if so, what kinds? Even this seemingly simple and clear-cut command must be interpreted. Interpretations always depend on the context of the text and on the people doing the interpreting. Meaning is context dependent; there is no way to fix the interpretation by giving the phrase one single, exact, determinate meaning that would apply to every use of the phrase.[2] In addition to the normal difficulty with human interpretation, only God could fix a determinate meaning for a divine text. Nothing contained in the text itself or declared by a prophet could establish God's meaning in a determinate way. Perhaps a common divine revelation, where God appeared to millions of people, might accomplish this. God might appear in Times Square and say, "I meant do not kill except in time of war or in self-defense," but then, of course, he would have to explain "war" and "self-defense." These explanations would lead to the need for further clarification, and the process might go on indefinitely.

Without the divine revelation—and perhaps even with it—the problem is unsolvable. In the roughly two-thousand-year-old controversies between Christian groups related to biblical interpretation, we can see clearly the difficulty of any such resolution. This problem also relates to the second criterion from Chapter 1: The theory must be able to show that some guidelines are better than others. There is no rational way to show that one interpretation of a commandment is better than another plausible interpretation. Without a definite way to decide between alternative interpretations, there is no way to ultimately show that some guidelines are better than others.

## Plato's Problem

The Greek philosopher Plato discusses an important topic related to divine command theory in his dialogue, the *Euthyphro*. Socrates and Euthyphro are discussing piety or holiness. At one point, Euthyphro says that "holiness is what the gods all love, and its opposite is what the gods all hate, unholiness."[3] Socrates then asks the crucial question, "Is what is holy holy because the gods approve it, or do they approve it because it is holy?"[4] This can be related to divine command theory and points to several important considerations. First, let's rewrite Euthyphro's definition: "What is good is what God commands, and its opposite is what God forbids, bad." Next, we can rephrase Socrates' question: "Is what is good good because God commands it, or does he command it because it is good?" Socrates' question points to an important distinction. God's command can make something good, or God can command something because it is good. On the surface, Socrates' question seems rather simple; it merely urges us to choose one of the two options. The difficulty, however, is that whichever option we choose presents serious problems for divine command theory.

Assume that we select the first option: Something is good simply because God commands it. This is the way we have interpreted divine command theory so far: Whatever God commands is good simply because God commanded it. The only reason something is good is that God commanded it. No other reason or factor is relevant to good and evil. Even God's reasons for giving the command, if they exist, are irrelevant to good and bad. Thus, an action is neither good nor bad until God either commands that we do it or forbids our doing it. For example, stealing was not bad until God made the commandment "Thou shalt not steal."

The problem with this position is that it makes good and bad arbitrary. An example can help to demonstrate this. Suppose God had not changed his commandment, and Abraham had killed Isaac. Someone might claim that this human sacrifice was evil. Abraham might reply that it was good because God commanded him to do it, but Abraham would surely be asked, "Why would God command you to kill your own son? What possible reason could God have had?" Abraham might answer that he did not know God's reason but that the act was good, and why God commanded it was a mystery. In addition, Abraham might add that God's reason is irrelevant. No reason of God's prior to the commandment could justify the action of killing Isaac as good because killing Isaac was not good until God commanded it. No factual consideration or reason God might have had prior to making the command is relevant to good and evil because it is the command that makes the action good or evil. Thus, there is no way to answer the question about why God commanded the killing that has any relevance to good and evil. Without any relevant factual consideration or prior reason, God could just as legitimately have commanded Abraham to praise Isaac as to kill him. That makes the killing of Isaac good, but arbitrary.

The problem with divine command theory that surfaces in Plato's *Euthyphro* is that the theory makes good and bad arbitrary. There is no justification for anything being ethical except that God commanded it. Therefore, our ethical discourse will be limited to discussing the content of God's commands with that group of people who share our view of God and a certain divine text. As I argued in a previous section, these discussions about the content of the commands will ultimately be only partly successful because of the interpretation problem. In addition, we will have nothing useful to say to anyone outside our immediate religious group. In fact, many outsiders will probably think we are mad or evil. They may not agree with what we take to be God's commands or perhaps even believe in God. In most modern societies, Abraham would be committed to a mental institution, not regarded as the ultimate model of religious faith.

What about Socrates' other option? Suppose Abraham was asked why God commanded him to kill Isaac. He might respond with an answer related to the other half of Socrates' question, "God commands what he does because it is good." God commanded him to kill Isaac because it was the ethical thing to do. This implies that God had some reason for giving the command; perhaps it led to some greater good. Maybe Isaac was going to grow up to be a mass murderer and God, being omniscient, knew this. Killing innocent people may be bad for some reason that does not depend on God. Thus, slaying Isaac was good because it would prevent the greater evil of the deaths of many innocent people. The difficulty is that this second answer is fatal for divine command theory. It asserts that good and bad conduct are related to some other factor not dependent on God, which makes preventing the deaths of innocent people good. Preventing death and harm to innocent people is good prior to God's commandment about Isaac; therefore, God makes the commandment that he does. This, however, contradicts divine command theory. Based on that theory, preventing the deaths of innocent people is neither good nor bad until God makes a commandment in relation to it. If preventing the deaths of innocent people is good apart from God's command, then there is a standard of good and bad separate from God's commands and divine command theory is misguided.

Socrates' question points to a dilemma. We can embrace divine command theory and a view of good and bad as arbitrary, or we can reject the theory and adopt an independent account of good and bad that does not depend on God's commandments. Most philosophers and theologians have chosen the second option. They have rejected the theory and endorsed some independent, secular account of good and bad. The arbitrariness of divine commands does not satisfy criterion two of the evaluation criteria: The theory must be able to show that some guidelines are better than others. If the commands or guidelines are arbitrary, there is no way to show that they are better than different commandments asserted by another religion or even better than secular moral guidelines associated with an ethical theory.

### God's Goodness

A third problem for divine command theory is that it distorts the usual claim that God is perfectly good. The Middle Eastern religions of Judaism, Christianity, and Islam share a certain conception of God. God is omnipotent, omniscient, omnipresent, transcendent, uncreated, eternal, and perfectly good. If good simply means "commanded by God," then the claim that "God is perfectly good" means "God is perfectly commanded by God," which is an odd claim to make. It is either nonsense or simply circular: God commands God. In either case, it is not what was meant by the believer's claim that God is perfectly good. The rough meaning for "God is perfectly good" is that on some scale of moral goodness God is at the top. God is always good and always does what is good. He is never evil. No being could ever be better than God. This meaning requires an independent standard against which to judge God. We apply the standard to God, and he meets the standard perfectly. Therefore, the usual conception of God shared by the three Middle Eastern religions seems to run counter to divine command theory. This is an internal problem for the theory; it does not relate to any of the criteria for evaluating ethical theories.

# Conclusion

Divine command theory has some strengths, but it also contains some problems that most philosophers and theologians consider to be fatal. To endorse divine command theory, we must acknowledge that good and evil are ultimately arbitrary. We will not be able to use reason to understand ethics and how we ought to live. We must also give up the idea that the claim that "God is perfectly good" is a significant claim. Most of us are not willing to accept these consequences. As we saw in Chapter 1, most philosophers believe ethics is rational. When they say "ethics is rational," they mean, roughly, that we can use reason to reach theoretical and practical conclusions about ethical matters. More specifically, people can provide reasons to support moral guidelines and solutions to ethical problems; these reasons can be evaluated; and some guidelines and solutions are better than others. They also mean that well-intentioned people who share an ethical framework (and sometimes even ones who do not) can discuss ethical problems and hope to arrive at mutually acceptable solutions. Divine command theory makes all of this impossible.

The view that ethics is secular or nonreligious does not deny the existence of God. Actually, it is consistent with religious belief because it enables us to make sense of the claim that God is perfectly good. A person could endorse one of the secular ethical theories in this book and still be a deeply religious person. Immanuel Kant, whose theory is discussed in Chapter 5, was very religious and believed in the Christian conception of God. He also believed his ethical theory was consistent with Christian religious belief.

Rejecting the divine command theory has one final advantage, the general advantage that keeping ethics and religion separate enables us to reach acceptable ethical conclusions with a larger number of people. The basic purpose of ethics is to help us solve moral problems and live together successfully. We encounter people of many different religions in our daily lives. If ethics were based on a particular religion or religious text, there would be many unsolvable problems between people of different religions. Imagine trying to be an ethical businessperson in a foreign country if you had to attempt to get your Hindu business partners to do business based on commandments found in the Bible. The prospects for success would seem to be minimal.

If we want to solve moral problems and live together successfully, we need ethical guidelines that all of us can endorse rather than religious beliefs that divide us even more than we are already divided. Separating religious considerations from ethical ones will make it more likely that we will be able to agree on some ethical guidelines and live together more successfully. In view of the considerations in this chapter, we should reject the ethical "insight" that *guidelines for how to live are necessarily related to God.* Divine command theory is unsuccessful, and we must turn elsewhere for legitimate moral guidelines about how to live. The next chapter investigates whether ethical guidelines can be obtained from society.

## QUESTIONS FOR REVIEW

*Here are some questions to help you review the main concepts in this chapter.*

1. What ethical insight is related to divine command theory?
2. What is the "ethical" standard for divine command theory?
3. Based on divine command theory, explain why the opinions of people are irrelevant to evaluations of conduct.
4. Identify one justification for using the "ethical" standard of divine command theory.
5. How do proponents of divine command theory differentiate between actions that are and are not morally significant?
6. Do proponents of divine command theory accept all the traditional ethical assumptions? Explain why, or why not.
7. What position does divine command theory take on each of the ethical themes?
8. In your opinion, what is the greatest strength of divine command theory? Support your answer.
9. In your view, what is the most serious problem with divine command theory?
10. Is divine command theory a successful ethical theory based on the criteria presented in Chapter 1? Support your answer.

## NOTES

1. This chapter uses "he" and "his" to refer to God. This is merely a convention; it does not imply that God is male.

2. This is a controversial matter, and a complete explanation is beyond the scope of this book. In short, meaning is dependent upon context. To have a single, exact, determinate meaning, we would need a single, exact, determinate context, yet a phrase can and must be meaningful in multiple contexts. Thus, it is not the case that there is only a single context that can be the setting for a meaningful phrase. Without a single, exact, determinate context, there can be

no single, exact, determinate meaning. This is correct for words and phrases used in ordinary language, but it may not be correct for science and mathematics where convention may be able to provide a single determinate context.

3. Plato, *The Collected Dialogues of Plato,* edited by Edith Hamilton and Huntington Cairns (New York: Bollingen Foundation, 1961), p. 178.

4. Ibid.

# Chapter 3

# *Ethical Relativism*

When we study people around the world, we observe what appear to be different ethical guidelines and disparate solutions to ethical problems. In Ireland the prevailing view is that abortion is wrong, whereas in China women who already have one child are encouraged to have abortions. Some observers conclude that these differences are primarily related to the fact that people live in different societies. Each society seems to have some moral guidelines, and these guidelines often differ from society to society. Despite these differences, each society seems to have adequate guidelines to satisfy its ethical needs. This chapter explores whether this observation is correct. Are these social moral guidelines really adequate to allow us to solve moral problems and live together successfully?

The initial claims are that societies already have moral guidelines and that there are differences between the guidelines of different societies. Connected to these claims is an approach to ethics that discusses the status of a society's moral guidelines and their adequacy. *Ethical relativism* asserts that the only legitimate moral guidelines are those of actual societies or groups and that moral good and bad are connected to these actual ethical guidelines. Therefore, any moral guidelines created by ethical theories (such as those of utilitarianism) would be misguided and irrelevant. Because legitimate ethical guidelines are always associated with an actual society or group, and because these actual societies and groups do not endorse exactly the same moral guidelines, there is no legitimate universal set of moral guidelines. To many people, the idea that legitimate moral guidelines are always relative to an actual society seems intuitively correct. Ethical relativism is an approach to ethics connected to the ethical insight that *legitimate moral guidelines are necessarily related to an actual society.* Philosophers offer many different accounts of ethical relativism, but the discussion in this chapter builds directly on the ideas presented in this paragraph. In this chapter, I will also show how problems develop with ethical relativism when we try to move beyond these initial ideas to a better understanding of the view.

## One Version of Ethical Relativism

Ethical relativism relates moral good and bad to the ethical guidelines of actual societies or groups. It often starts from the observation that ethical beliefs and practices are not identical in all societies. This observation is consistent with cultural relativism. *Cultural relativism* is the view that different societies or cultures do things differently. For example, people wear different kinds of clothes, are governed by different kinds of political systems, and believe in different religions. Some societies also have different sets of ethical guidelines. If individuals from these different societies were to discuss their ethical principles and practices, they would probably disagree about what practices were right and wrong. These ethical disagreements would arise even though the individuals agreed on the description of the practices (e.g., they agreed on what constituted an abortion).[1] The progression from cultural relativism to ethical relativism occurs when the observation about ethical differences is followed by the claim that the only legitimate moral guidelines are those of actual societies. These actual moral guidelines create good and evil. If society's guidelines approve of something, it is ethical, and if these guidelines disapprove of something, it is unethical. *The ethical standard for ethical relativism is that a society's actual moral guidelines determine good and bad.*

If ethical relativism is to be effective, proponents of the theory must be able to identify the actual moral guidelines of a society. These guidelines create moral obligations for the members of the society. They determine what people ought to and ought not to do. If a woman's society has a moral guideline that asserts that abortion is evil, then she ought not to get an abortion. Her personal feelings about or attitudes toward abortion are irrelevant. Only the social moral guidelines of her society are legitimate for her.

Ethical relativists maintain that there is no universal or objective ethical standard that holds for all societies at all times.[2] This idea is an essential claim of ethical relativism. Legitimate notions of good and bad often vary from society to society and may change within a society over time. Therefore, ethical guidelines are relative to some society or group in a particular historical setting. Different ethical positions may be appropriate for different peoples. No single legitimate set of ethical guidelines is endorsed by every society; therefore, no legitimate universal or objective ethical guidelines can be identified.

## Ethical Relativism and Tolerance

Based on these ideas, many people believe ethical relativists ought to endorse tolerance for the different ethical guidelines and practices of other societies. They conclude that it is wrong for people in one society to condemn the moral guidelines or ethically significant practices of another. Without a legitimate set of universal ethical guidelines, condemnation by members of one society of the practices of another is unjustified. The ethical guidelines of one society would have no legitimate application to any other society.

This idea can be illustrated with an example about some ethically significant practice that is simultaneously endorsed by one society and condemned by another. For instance, modern-day Cuba presumably still condemns capitalism as exploitative and evil. In contrast, the ethical guidelines of the United States endorse capitalism. Here it seems that both of these societies would agree on a description of capitalism. The ethical relativist would suggest that the different moral guidelines produced different moral evaluations of capitalism. Capitalism is ethically right for citizens of the United States and ethically wrong for Cubans. Neither group is objectively right or wrong; therefore, each group should tolerate rather than condemn the other.

I believe it is a mistake to include in ethical relativism the idea of tolerance for the different ethical guidelines and ethically significant practices of other societies. This position supporting cross-cultural tolerance is a serious problem for ethical relativism, and the theory will operate without it. Bernard Williams, a contemporary British philosopher, explains that the assertion that we should not condemn the different beliefs and practices of other societies is a nonrelative or objective claim, and the ethical relativist has no grounding for such a claim.

> The central confusion of relativism is to try to conjure out of the fact that societies have differing attitudes and values an a priori nonrelative principle to determine the attitude of one society toward another; this is impossible.[3]

It is impossible because, according to ethical relativism, people have no basis for making ethical claims that are not related to the actual moral guidelines of their society. The most that ethical relativists are justified in claiming is that in our society we approve of tolerance or noninterference with other cultures and hence we should be tolerant. This, however, is not the position endorsed by the proponents of cross-cultural tolerance. They assert that everyone ought to tolerate the ethical differences of other societies regardless of their own moral guidelines. Williams's point is that there is no justification for this claim about what everyone should do. In the United States, our moral guidelines seem to approve of interference with other cultures and societies. We intervene regularly in the interest of promoting peace and preventing violations of human rights. Ethical relativists have no grounds for condemning our interference if such intervention is in accord with the moral guidelines of our society.

This idea, that we should leave cross-cultural tolerance out of ethical relativism, can be illustrated with an example. Assume that moral rights are part of the ethical guidelines endorsed by U.S. society. Rose is an ethical relativist and therefore believes that the legitimate moral guidelines are those endorsed by her society. She is especially insistent about the right to life. When she sees people in other countries being killed merely because of their political views or because they belong to certain ethnic groups, she claims the killing is evil and ought to be stopped. Rose's view of good and bad is based on the moral guidelines of her society—the only legitimate ethical standard available to her—and in her view other societies are acting unethically when they execute people for political reasons. Rose is not tolerant of these executions; she condemns them (and perhaps wants to eliminate them). She would not tolerate a society like Nazi Germany but rather would condemn it and want to see it destroyed.

To avoid Williams's problem, ethical relativism should endorse the idea that people will use the moral guidelines of their own society to evaluate everything. The key to ethical relativism is that good and bad are established by the actual moral guidelines of a society, and those actual guidelines may not include cross-cultural tolerance. Only if a society's actual moral guidelines include the principle of tolerance should citizens of that society tolerate the different ethical guidelines and practices of other societies. Although this version of ethical relativism avoids the serious problem with cross-cultural tolerance, it will have other problems. Before discussing them, however, I want to provide some support for the theory and discuss how it relates to the ethical assumptions and themes.

## Justification for the Ethical Standard and Strengths of the Theory

An earlier section identified the moral standard of ethical relativism, that a society's actual moral guidelines determine good and bad. The second thing an ethical theory is supposed to provide is a justification for the ethical standard. Why would someone endorse the ethical standard put forward by ethical relativism? What strengths does the theory have that would lead someone to endorse it? In this section, four possible justifications or arguments will be discussed; the first will be rejected and the other three left standing for the your consideration.

## Cultural Relativism

The first possible justification is based on cultural relativism and is actually a group of related arguments. A simple version of it goes like this. We observe that ethical guidelines vary from society to society (or are relative to a society). Therefore, ethical guidelines ought to vary from society to society. If ethical guidelines ought to vary from society to society, then no single set of guidelines is correct for all societies. If ethical guidelines ought to vary from society to society and there is no single legitimate set of them, then each society ought to consider its existing set of ethical guidelines to be legitimate. This argument is, of course, incorrect. First, even if ethical guidelines ought to vary, it does not follow that the existing guidelines are the appropriate ones. This would only legitimate their being different, not that the actual ones were somehow the best ones to have. More important, however, is the idea that just because things are a certain way does not allow us to conclude that they ought to be that way. The fact that many children are starving in the world today does not necessitate the conclusion that those children ought to be starving. If you think they ought to be starving, you need a separate argument to support that conclusion. From the observation that ethical guidelines vary from society to society, there can be no justified conclusion about what the legitimate ethical guidelines ought to be. Perhaps ethical guidelines ought to vary from society to society, and perhaps no one set of guidelines is correct for all societies. However, it is also possible that there is one correct set of ethical guidelines and that the people in many societies are simply wrong. Cultural relativism does not provide adequate support for ethical relativism.

## Moral Guidelines as a Social Institution

A second and more interesting reason for endorsing ethical relativism is related to morality. In this book, the term *morality* is used to refer to a specific set of moral guidelines. People might endorse ethical relativism because they view morality as a social institution. Societies create various institutions to help them function successfully. One such institution is morality. For example, relativists would claim that the United States has a morality, or a specific set of moral guidelines. Morality is necessary because the laws, by themselves, are not adequate to produce the kind of conduct that enables society to operate successfully. (This idea was discussed in Chapter 1.) People need to respect other people's lives, liberty, property, and privacy to produce a successfully functioning society. Without morality, people will only respect these things when they believe they might get caught and punished. Therefore, morality helps society function more successfully. If morality is a social institution, then the appropriate morality would be the actual moral guidelines of society. Presumably the society has the moral guidelines it does because these guidelines have proven to be effective in helping society function successfully. Because they have proven to be effective, they constitute the best morality. This reasoning acts as the justification for using the ethical standard of actual social moral guidelines as the basis for good and bad. Adopting this justification for ethical relativism supports the idea that each society has a legitimate set of moral guidelines and that good and evil are related to them. Therefore, one strength of the theory is that it is consistent with the way many people think about morality. People are more inclined to accept a theory that is consistent with an existing belief than one that is at odds with it.

## Cultural Relativism Once Again

Another justification for using the moral standard of ethical relativism and a related strength of the view is that it seems to fit with our observations about the world. Even though we cannot use cultural relativism to validate ethical relativism, at least ethical relativism does not contradict cultural relativism. The two positions are consistent. We observe that many societies seem to have different moral guidelines. This is consistent with cultural relativism, the idea that different societies do things differently. Cultural relativism is, of course, correct. Different societies eat different foods, have different political systems, and so on. Some societies also have different moral guidelines. Thus, ethical relativism is consistent with the facts of cultural diversity. This consistency with cultural relativism is another possible justification for using the ethical standard and a related strength of the theory.

## Ethnocentrism and Nationalism

A rough definition for *ethnocentrism* is the belief in the superiority of one's own ethnic group and its ways of doing things. A similarly imprecise definition for *nationalism* is the belief in the superiority of one's own nation and its ways of doing things. Social scientists often condemn both of these ways of thinking, but many people find them satisfying. It is agreeable to think that one's own group and nation are better than others. People can feel proud of their group and country and be happy to be associated with them. Certainly many Americans have no hesitation in declaring that the United States is the best country in the world. A third strength of this version of ethical relativism, at least for some people, is that it is consistent with ethnocentrism and nationalism. Ethical relativism asserts that the moral guidelines of a person's society are the appropriate ones for the person to endorse. In a sense, these guidelines are superior to all others. People can be confident in and proud of their moral judgments because they are based on guidelines that are superior to all others. Presumably this also could be a reason for using this ethical standard and a strength of the theory.

## Determining Morally Significant Actions

An ethical theory must distinguish between what are and are not morally significant actions. This is not an issue that ethical relativists frequently discuss; however, if a society's moral guidelines relate to an action, moral relativists believe it is morally significant. For instance, most societies have a guideline about keeping and breaking promises; therefore, keeping promises is morally significant in these societies. If a society does not have a guideline about something, then the action is not morally significant. For example, U.S. society has no opinion about whether you should dye your hair to change its color, therefore this action has no moral significance.

## Ethical Relativism and the
## Traditional Ethical Assumptions

It is difficult to decide whether or not ethical relativism accepts the traditional ethical assumptions. We might be inclined to say that ethical relativists would agree that ethics is rational. People can provide reasons related to actual social moral guidelines to support their ethical evaluations and their solutions to moral problems. However, ethical relativism and divine command theory have a similar limitation. The reasons a society has particular guidelines are irrelevant, just as the reasons God commands what he does are irrelevant. Thus, there are no ultimate reasons, based on reason, for the moral guidelines and judgments. The moral guidelines are arbitrary because the only reason for following them is that they are the actual guidelines of the society. People in different societies with different guidelines would have no way to discuss and debate the merits of their different ethical guidelines. Even ethical relativists within the same society could not legitimately debate the merits of their society's moral guidelines; they can only accept them. Therefore, in the sense of "rational" used in Chapter 1, ethical relativists cannot claim that ethics is rational.

Whether or not ethical relativism accepts moral equality is also an interesting question. In one sense it does; all members of a particular society are moral equals in that the moral guidelines of their society bind all of them. Also, all people are moral equals in that I judge all of them by the same set of moral guidelines, those of my society. In a wider sense, however, all human beings are not moral equals. Members of other societies are not treated impartially or in the same way as members of a person's own society. The actions of members of other societies are not judged by the moral guidelines of their own societies but by the moral guidelines of the society of the person doing the judging. For example, I judge myself and the members of my society by the moral guidelines of the United States, which are our guidelines, but I also judge members of other societies by the moral guidelines of the United States, which are foreign to them. Therefore, ethical relativists judge some people by ethical guidelines that those people accept and other people by ethical guidelines that are foreign to them and that they would probably not accept. On the whole, this version of ethical relativism does not consider people to be moral equals because it does not judge all people by their own society's ethical guidelines.

The issue of universalizability is also a contentious one. The version of ethical relativism I elaborated could accept the idea that people are capable of universalizing legitimate moral evaluations. If we simply apply the ethical guidelines of our own society to everyone, then we are universalizing our moral evaluations. The version of ethical relativism that includes cross-cultural tolerance would not universalize moral evaluations. Legitimate ethical evaluations made by members of other societies should be based on their own ethical guidelines. These guidelines might be the same as ours or different from ours. In either case, we cannot legitimately universalize our moral guidelines and evaluations. They are only appropriate for persons in our society. Any legitimate ethical conclusion should be grounded in the specific ethical guidelines of a particular society; it could not come about by universalizing our guidelines.

## Ethical Relativism and the Basic Ethical Themes

Ethical relativism takes a position on each of the ethical themes discussed in Chapter 1. The first theme was represented by this question: *What kind of moral guidelines makes something good or bad: subjective, relative, or objective ones?* Ethical relativists answer this question by claiming that the only legitimate ethical guidelines are relative ones. Legitimate ethical guidelines are those endorsed by an actual society. For an ethical relativist, personal moral guidelines and an individual's attitudes and emotions are irrelevant to ethical evaluation. Legitimate moral guidelines cannot be objective because they are not based on considerations of fact or reason that do not depend on the perceptions, emotions, or judgments of particular persons or the beliefs of a specific society. Ethical relativism is characterized by assertions that legitimate ethical guidelines are relative.

The second ethical theme was highlighted by this question: *What makes something good or bad; is it the consequences that are produced or the reasoning that leads up to it?* Ethical relativists seem to believe the reasoning that leads up to something is what makes it ethical. If an action is in accord with one or more of society's moral guidelines, then that action is ethical regardless of the consequences. If it violates one or more of society's moral guidelines, then it is unethical regardless of the consequences. The society's ethical guidelines create moral good and bad and are the only relevant ethical consideration.

A third ethical theme relates to this question: *Are good and bad related to following general rules without exceptions or connected to separately evaluating each action, belief, and so on?* The position of ethical relativism in relation to this theme is debatable, but I believe ethical relativists would be compelled to claim that we should faithfully follow the moral rules of our society. If society believes stealing other people's property is evil, then stealing is always evil, no matter what the benefit to the individual. Allowing exceptions to the basic moral rules of society would violate the idea that society needs morality to function smoothly. Of course, if the belief is that sometimes it is ethical to steal and other times it is not, then people would still be following a general rule even if they steal on some occasions and not on others.

The fourth important ethical theme relates to the proper focus of ethical attention: *Should the group, community, or majority of persons be the focus of ethics or should the focus be on the individual?* Ethical relativists focus on the group or society as the source of legitimate ethical guidelines. Individuals who disagree with the moral guidelines of their society and hold different ones will not be acting ethically if they act in accord with their personal moral principles and in opposition to the societal ethical principles. It is the actual ethical guidelines of the society or the group that are identified as the legitimate moral guidelines by ethical relativism.

## Contrasting Ethical Relativism with Divine Command Theory

Ethical relativism and divine command theory have many differences and only a few similarities (see Appendix 1). Ethical relativism relates moral guidelines to actual societies, whereas divine command theory connects moral guidelines to God. The ethical standard of ethical relativism is that a society's actual moral guidelines determine good and evil, whereas the ethical standard for divine command theory is that what God commands people to do is good and what God forbids people to do is bad. In regard to the traditional ethical assumptions, both ethical relativism and divine command theory assume that ethics is not rational and that some ethical evaluations can be universalized. They disagree on the assumption related to moral equality and impartiality. Proponents of ethical relativism do not treat people impartially, whereas advocates of divine command theory would claim that all people originally stand in the same relation to God. In relation to the themes about moral good and bad, both theories base good and bad on the reasoning that precedes an action and focus on general rules of conduct. Ethical relativism, of course, asserts that good and bad are relative to societies, whereas divine command theory argues that good and bad are objective. According to ethical relativism, good and bad relate to the group or society, whereas proponents of divine command theory state that good and bad are connected to the individual.

## Problems with Ethical Relativism

Until now I have presented and briefly elaborated on the ethical insight central to ethical relativism: that legitimate ethical guidelines are necessarily related to an actual society. In this section, you will see that problems develop with the theory as we try to fill out the basic ideas of ethical relativism and develop a better understanding of the theory. As I discuss the problems, I will relate them to the criteria for evaluating ethical theories presented in Chapter 1. In the final section of the chapter, I will present an overall evaluation.

### *Actual Ethical Guidelines*

The first step to a better understanding of ethical relativism is to try to locate the actual ethical guidelines of a society. This will help us to better understand what the ethical relativist means by the ethical guidelines of a society. Assume that I am an ethical relativist and a citizen of the United States; I must know the ethical guidelines of my country so that I can follow them. I am, of course, assuming that the society as a whole has a set of ethical guidelines.

Where do I find the actual ethical guidelines of my society? Laws are written down and can be discovered in law libraries, but ethical guidelines are not recorded in ethics libraries. There is no determinate set of ethical guidelines written down for the guidance of U.S. citizens. If there is an unwritten set, I am not aware of them. Therefore, I will have to look for them. There would seem to be four promising alternatives.

One way to find the actual ethical guidelines of a society is to examine the beliefs of the majority of the members of the society. To discover what guidelines are actually endorsed—for example, if I wanted to know whether my society approves of abortion—I might take a survey. In doing this, I would be assuming that other people are more knowledgeable than I am—even though I am a concerned citizen (and a teacher of ethics). I am hoping that they know the ethical guidelines of our society and will respond to my survey. They have to respond to the survey based on the ethical guidelines of our society and not on their personal preferences or feelings. If they did the latter, the results would reflect an ethical subjectivist approach (which will be discussed in Chapter 4). The ethical guidelines of a society are not simply the subjective guidelines of the majority of the citizens. This would result in the foundation of the social ethical guidelines (the citizens' subjective beliefs) being plagued with all the problems of ethical subjectivism, which are a very serious set of problems. Ethical guidelines are legitimate because society endorses them. However, if we do not already know what society endorses or what the ethical guidelines are, a survey of citizens' opinions will not be a successful way of discovering them. I do not believe citizens know what society approves and disapproves in all cases—especially with respect to issues like abortion where emotions run deep—therefore, this approach would be unsatisfactory. If we are unclear about the social ethical guidelines, we could not discover them by surveying citizens.

Another idea would be to look at the guidelines of the government or ruling group. Perhaps the government establishes the ethical guidelines for the society. In the United States the President and members of Congress try to reflect the opinions of their constituents, so this method would work no better in the United States than the first method, which I have argued is unsuccessful. In a dictatorship, we could discover the ethical guidelines if they were grounded in the feelings of the dictator and he or she imposed them on the whole society. We would need to know, for example, whether the dictator had a good feeling about abortion. The problem with this variation is that the ethical guidelines are founded on the dictator's feelings, and once again the foundation of the social moral guidelines would have the serious problems that affect ethical subjectivism. Therefore, this second approach to discovering the actual ethical guidelines is unsuccessful also.

A third possibility would be to examine the laws and then work backward. The assumption would be that ethical guidelines inspire laws. By looking at the laws, one might attempt to discover the society's moral guidelines. U.S. law allows abortion, so abortion must have been ethical when the law was made. This view implies that although we are unclear about the ethical guidelines of today, people in the past must have been better informed. They were clear enough about the ethical guidelines to make laws based on them. The problem is that the ethical guidelines are supposed to be based on the current moral guidelines of the society, but this "legal view" makes the dominant guidelines those of a past version of the society because the authority to establish ethical guidelines lies with the earlier version of society that created the laws. This seems illegitimate for ethical relativism. These moral guidelines are for an earlier version of society, and we would not know if they are still the ethical guidelines of the current society. Some laws are no longer endorsed by the majority of people. For example, the majority of people in the United States disapproved of Prohibition before ratification of the constitutional amendment that allowed people to once again produce and sell alcoholic beverages. A problem with this "legal view" is that existing laws may not all actually reflect the ethical guidelines held by the majority of people in the society.

A fourth possibility would be to look at the society's moral tradition. Presumably this moral tradition would be articulated in the society's fundamental documents. By consulting political documents, works of literature, art, and so on, we could discover whether the moral tradition of the United States approved of abortion. As ethical relativists, however, why should we be bound by moral tradition? The legitimate moral guidelines are those endorsed by society today, not those endorsed in the past. Like the "legal view," moral tradition makes the dominant guidelines those of a previous society and seems to deny the current society the authority to create its own moral guidelines. In addition, this seems incorrect because we would not know if these traditional guidelines are still the ethical guidelines of the current society.

All of these are possibilities for discovering the actual ethical beliefs of a society. One could also conceivably assert that the correct morality would be the intersection of all of them. In any case, the difficulty is obvious and twofold: (1) all of the ways of identifying the actual ethical guidelines are seriously problematic, and (2) we have no way to choose among them. In general, the problem for ethical relativism is that the theory does not seem to be able to identify the actual moral guidelines of a society. Therefore, ethical relativism cannot satisfy any of the criteria for evaluating ethical theories. The first criterion states that the ethical theory must be able to identify some ethical guidelines. If we cannot determine the actual moral guidelines of our society, then the idea proposed by ethical relativism about how to identify the ethical guidelines is incorrect. Ethical relativism will not be able to identify the necessary moral guidelines, nor can it satisfy any of the other criteria. It is not successful as an ethical theory.

## Multiple Sets of Ethical Guidelines

A better understanding of ethical relativism also requires us to determine whether the ethical guidelines of other groups, besides society as a whole, should count as legitimate moral guidelines. If the ethical guidelines endorsed by ethnic groups, local communities, special interest groups, and so on count, ethical relativism will have to deal with multiple sets of legitimate moral guidelines that may conflict. For the sake of this discussion, we shall assume that these groups have ethical guidelines that are written down. (If they do not, the first problem would apply to them as well as to society as a whole.) Imagine that Rose is a citizen of the United States, but she is also a member of other groups with their own particular ethical beliefs. She is a woman, a Latino, part of a family, and a resident of a local community. She also works for a large corporation. If all of these groups have ethical guidelines, would each set constitute legitimate guidelines? If they are all legitimate ethical guidelines, how should she resolve conflicts among them? Suppose the majority of women in the United States are "pro-choice," the majority of Latinos "pro-life," the majority of her family "pro-life," the majority of people in her local community "pro-choice," and the position of her corporation is "pro-choice." As an ethical relativist, Rose cannot determine which position to take on abortion. This situation would seem to imply that ethical relativism has additional problems with at least the second and fourth criteria for evaluating ethical theories. Ethical relativism would not be able to demonstrate that one set of moral guidelines is better than another (criterion two). Further, if Rose is faced with the problem of whether or not to get an abortion, ethical relativism would be unable to help her resolve the dilemma (criterion four).

Some form of ethical relativism (usually the kind involving cross-cultural tolerance) seems more plausible if we concentrate on tribes that are isolated in remote regions or on islands. It is relatively easy to regard a tribe on an isolated island as a distinct group or community. In the pluralistic contemporary world, however, it is much harder to find such distinctive societies. We tend to belong to a number of groups (an ethnic group, a socioeconomic class, a country, a company, a local community, a family, and so on). Given the existence of multiple groups with legitimate ethical guidelines, ethical relativism will not be a successful ethical theory because it will neither identify unambiguous ethical guidelines nor show why some moral guidelines are better than others.

This problem with multiple groups could be solved if we interpret the ethical relativist as saying that only the moral guidelines of the society as a whole count as legitimate ethical guidelines. This solution, however, makes resolving the first problem even more crucial, and we could not solve it.

## Moral Change and Dissent

An ethical theory must be able to identify some moral guidelines, but ethical relativism makes the production and identification of new ethical guidelines mysterious. Legitimate ethical guidelines are those that are endorsed by the society, and we know that sometimes these change (e.g., slavery is now unethical in the United States). The mystery is that guidelines change even though there is no apparent reason for change. Moral good and bad depend on the current ethical guidelines of a society, not on objective reasons the society has the guidelines it does, such as that people are being benefited or harmed. (If people grounded moral guidelines on objective reasons, they would be endorsing another ethical theory, perhaps rule utilitarianism.) If, however, the reasons why people create the guidelines they do are not important, then there is no motivation for change in the moral guidelines. Without any motivation for change, it is a mystery why a society would do so.

Another aspect of the mysterious nature of the production and identification of new ethical guidelines surfaces when we think about what ethical relativists must say about the relation between the moral guidelines of a society and the people who disagree with those guidelines. For them, there can be no legitimate ethical dissent within a society. If "good" equates to whatever is approved of by the moral guidelines of the society, then members of the society who dissent from the dominant ethical guidelines would always be wrong. In pre–Civil War Alabama, a member of the white community who believed slavery was evil would be wrong. According to an ethical relativist, good and evil for whites was determined by the white community at large or by the prevailing view in Southern society, not by dissenters. The slaves might agree with the dissenter, but because the dissenter is not a member of the slave community, the ethical position of that community cannot legitimate his or her dissent. The problem here is that dissent is always wrong, but dissent is a major factor in changing a society's ethical beliefs. Once again the production of new ethical guidelines seems mysterious.

As well as being mysterious, the production of new moral guidelines is arbitrary. If the only legitimate moral guidelines are those endorsed by an actual society, then any new moral guideline is unjustified. There could be no compelling ethical reason for the change. If there is no ethical justification or reason for a particular new guideline, then any added guideline is as good as any alternative addition. A society can add any moral guideline it wants to because as soon as it adds it the guideline will be legitimate. This makes the addition of new moral guidelines arbitrary.

## Conclusion

Although grounded in an initially reasonable ethical insight, ethical relativism is not a successful ethical theory based on the criteria established in Chapter 1. Individual members of a society hold many personal moral beliefs, but we cannot identify the actual ethical guidelines of the society as a whole. We would also not know how to arbitrate between the differing moral guidelines of the different groups to which a person belonged. Therefore, ethical relativism does not meet any of the criteria for a successful ethical theory. We need to reject the "ethical insight" that legitimate moral guidelines are necessarily related to an actual society. Although we cannot, with any certainty, find the moral guidelines of a society, there would seem to be no such problem identifying those of specific individuals. Certainly we could, with some work, identify an individual's personal moral guidelines. In the next chapter we will look at two theories based on specific individuals. These theories will not have the problems that plague ethical relativism, although they may have problems of their own.

QUESTIONS FOR REVIEW

*Here are some questions to help you review the main concepts in this chapter.*

1. What ethical insight is related to ethical relativism?
2. What is cultural relativism? What is ethical relativism? Explain the difference between the two.
3. What ethical standard do ethical relativists use to determine good and bad?
4. Why do some philosophers claim that ethical relativism leads to tolerance of other societies' different moral guidelines and judgments? Why does the author reject that position?
5. In your opinion, what is the best justification for the moral standard and the related strength of ethical relativism?
6. How do ethical relativists differentiate between what is and what is not a morally significant action?
7. Would ethical relativists accept any or all of the traditional ethical assumptions? Support your answer.
8. What position does ethical relativism take on each of the four ethical themes?
9. Discuss one similarity and one difference between ethical relativism and divine command theory.

10. In your opinion, which problem with ethical relativism is the most serious? Explain why.

11. Is ethical relativism a successful ethical theory? Support your answer.

## NOTES

1. This assumes that people from different societies could agree on the descriptions of the practices (e.g., what counts as a lie, a bribe, a theft, or self-defense). A more radical version of ethical relativism claims that people from different societies could not even agree on the descriptions of the practices.

2. There could be a legitimate universal moral code if by coincidence all societies developed the same set of moral guidelines. This, of course, has not happened so far.

3. Bernard Williams, *Morality: An Introduction to Ethics* (New York: Harper & Row, 1972), p. 23.

# Chapter 4

# Ethical Egoism and Ethical Subjectivism

The previous chapter showed the difficulty in identifying the actual ethical guidelines of a society. Without clear moral guidelines provided by society, it would appear that we should be unable to make ethical evaluations or judgments, yet people make them all the time. If someone breaks into my house and steals my stereo equipment, I am furious and quick to tell anyone who will listen that the person who did it is a jerk who should be caught and punished. I got a lot of pleasure out of listening to my stereo, and now I cannot do that. The loss of my stereo has harmed me, and I am angry about it. Obviously, I think the theft was morally bad or wrong. Individuals seem to have no trouble making ethical evaluations and, therefore, perhaps legitimate moral guidelines are related to something about particular individuals instead of something about societies. For many people, this idea that legitimate moral judgments necessarily connect to something about particular individuals seems intuitively correct. They would endorse the ethical insight that *legitimate moral guidelines necessarily have something to do with particular individuals.*

To develop this insight, we must discover what it is about particular individuals that relates to good and bad. In the above example, I claimed that the loss of my stereo harmed me. I got a lot of pleasure out of listening to it, and now I cannot do that. My loss of pleasure harms me. We might connect harm to the individual with something being morally bad. If harm to the individual is bad, then benefit to the individual should be good. Therefore, the initial claim related to a theory associated with individuals is that whatever harms individuals is bad or wrong and whatever benefits them is right or good.

## Ethical Egoism

The idea that moral good and bad relate to harm and benefit to an individual is an essential component of an ethical theory called ethical egoism. *Ethical egoism* claims that to act ethically moral agents should act in their own self-interest and maximize benefit for themselves. *The ethical standard of ethical egoism is that what is good for an individual is what produces a net benefit for that individual, and what is bad is what produces a net harm for that individual.* Individuals have only one fundamental moral duty: to maximize net benefit and minimize net harm to themselves. They have no basic moral obligation to other people. Ethical egoism leads to the conclusion that there is no difference between "good for me" and "good." Whatever is beneficial for me is morally good, no matter what the effects on others may be. Other people's harm and benefit simply should not count in our moral considerations. If it is beneficial for me to assault you and steal your money because I need it, I know that I can do it without being caught, and I will not be bothered by bad feelings about it afterward, then it is morally good to do it. The fact that you are injured and lose your money is irrelevant.

This version of ethical egoism is making a claim about how everyone should act: Everyone should act based on their self-interest. You will act to maximize benefit to you, and I will act to maximize benefit to myself. This ethical position does not mean that a person can never act in a way that would benefit someone else. If helping someone else is the best way to maximize benefit to me, then I ought to help that person. If I depend on another person for a ride to work each day, it would be consistent with ethical egoism for me to lend that person a hundred dollars to get the car fixed. Although I am temporarily out the hundred dollars, I gain the significant benefit of being able to go to work and make money. In this case, I should help the person because that is the best way to maximize benefit to myself. Therefore, an ethical egoist may have secondary moral obligations to other people that are related to the basic moral obligation to maximize benefit to himself or herself. I ought to loan the other person money for repairs because I am obligated to maximize benefit to myself. An egoist does not have to be a selfish person. If the best way to maximize benefit to myself is to be generous to others, then I should do that. Perhaps my generosity will be repaid by that person being generous to me, and I will achieve a net advantage. Egoists may be concerned about world poverty, the environment, and other global problems. Their basic reason for being concerned with these problems, however, is that they believe their concern will produce benefits for them.

Ethical egoism does not claim that I should always do what is pleasant. I should be rational about what is best for me. Sometimes I may have to do something unpleasant or painful to achieve a greater benefit in the future. I may regard exercising for an hour every day as unpleasant, but as an ethical egoist, I should do it because it would produce significant benefits for me. As this example implies, egoists do not have to concern themselves solely with short-term consequences. An egoist needs to think about whether a short-term harm, like the pain of getting a cavity filled, will produce a greater amount of long-term benefit, such as a healthy tooth.

Ethical egoism is a consequentialist ethical theory because it determines good and bad based on the consequences to the individual. If the consequences of an action are only benefits, then the action is good. If the consequences are only harms, then it is bad. If the consequences include both benefits and harms, then the egoist must determine whether there is a net benefit or harm. Thus, egoism involves calculations of potential or actual benefit and harm. The object of these calculations is to determine the actions that produce the greatest amount of net benefit for the individual.

## Justification for the Ethical Standard and Strengths of the Theory

An ethical theory should provide an ethical standard to determine good and bad and offer some justification for that standard. The ethical standard was presented in an earlier section, and now the justification will be considered.

### *The Natural Inclination to Be Self-Interested*

The best justification for using the ethical standard and a corresponding strength of the theory is that the standard and theory seem to fit people's natural inclination to be self-interested. By self-interested, we usually mean that people want to promote their own well-being or maximize benefits to themselves. They tend to look out for their own well-being first, and then consider the well-being of other persons later. Ethical egoism endorses this self-interested attitude and asserts that self-interested actions are the only ethical ones. Thus, one justification for using this standard is that it is consistent with people's inclinations. A theory that is consistent with human nature has an advantage over a theory that is at odds with human nature because people will be more inclined to accept it. This consistency with people's natural inclinations is a strength of the theory.

## Respect for the Individual

Another justification for the standard and a corresponding strength of the theory is that it respects the individual. As philosophers like Friedrich Nietzsche and popular thinkers like Ayn Rand have argued, we must endorse the integrity of the individual and not obligate the individual to serve others. To obligate Rose to help John is to devalue Rose's life because it means she must live at least a small part of her life for John's benefit. The egoist would claim that she should live for her own benefit, not for someone else's. Also, theories that obligate people to help others do not necessarily limit that help to a small amount. People might find themselves obligated to spend all their time helping others. Thus, in one sense their lives are of no value, only the lives of these other people matter. The egoist position is that every individual has an equal right to pursue his or her benefit and that people should not be devalued and obligated to serve others. For some people, this respect for the individual is a reason to use this standard and a strength of the theory.

## Content and Efficiency

A third strength of the theory is that it gives good and bad a clear content: benefit and harm to the individual. This content also seems to promote simplicity and ethical efficiency. That is, we can identify and compare potential harm and benefit to one person with relative efficiency. Certainly ethical egoism is simpler and more efficient than a theory that tries to identify and compare the benefits and harms to everyone affected by an action. The egoist will only have to determine the harms and benefits to one person, whereas the utilitarian will have to identify all the people who are affected by an action and then discover all of the harms and benefits to each of these people. It is much easier for the egoist to make an ethical judgment than for the utilitarian to do so. Thus, another strength of egoism is that it is more efficient than some other theories.

# Morally Significant Actions

A theory should also delineate morally significant actions from ones that are not morally significant. For an ethical egoist, morally significant actions are ones that either benefit or harm the particular individual. When someone steals my stereo, it is morally significant because I have been harmed. Wearing a blue-striped white shirt rather than a plain white one with my blue suit is not morally significant because the choice of shirts does not benefit or harm me.

## Ethical Egoism and the Traditional Ethical Assumptions

Ethical egoism accepts only one of the traditional assumptions associated with ethical theories: It assumes that ethics is rational. Ethical egoism assumes that we can use reason to reach theoretical and practical conclusions about ethical matters, including why we should be ethical egoists. More specifically, people can provide reasons based on harm and benefit to the individual to support egoistic solutions to ethical problems, these reasons can be evaluated, and some solutions will be better than others. Ethical egoism does not endorse moral equality and impartiality. The individual is the only one whose harm and benefit matter; thus, he or she is morally superior to everyone else. The individual certainly does not have to treat people impartially. Friends and family should be given special treatment because that will presumably result in more benefit to the individual. Finally, ethical egoism does not assume that any ethical evaluations can be universalized. Because people are different, what maximizes net benefit for an individual in a particular situation may not maximize net benefit for another person in the same situation. In any case, the individual is only concerned with his or her own moral evaluations, not with extending those evaluations to other people.

## Ethical Egoism and the Basic Ethical Themes

In addition to the traditional assumptions connected to ethical theories, the basic ethical themes about moral good and bad can also be related to ethical egoism in an effort to obtain a better understanding of the theory. The first theme can be represented by this question: *What kind of moral guidelines makes something good or bad: subjective, relative, or objective ones?* This is an interesting issue. The ethical egoist's guidelines are clearly not relative because they do not depend on society. It would seem that the ethical egoist's moral guidelines should be subjective because they are related to something about particular individuals. Chapter 1, however, defined "subjective moral guidelines" as ones that are necessarily a product of the emotions or attitudes of specific individuals. Ethical egoism does not relate good and bad to emotions or attitudes but instead to supposedly objective considerations of harm and benefit to the individual. If it is a fact that telling the truth in this situation will harm me, then it is bad for me to do it. Thus, although this may seem odd, ethical egoism claims that good and bad are objective because they are based on factual considerations of harm and benefit.

Another significant theme in ethics is this: *What makes something good or bad; is it the consequences that are produced or the reasoning that leads up to it?* As stated earlier, ethical egoism is a consequentialist theory. Good and bad are based on consequences to particular individuals.

The third theme relates to this question: *Are good and bad related to following general rules without exceptions or connected to separately evaluating actions, beliefs, and so on?* People who believe we should guide our behavior by general rules feel that these rules should have no exceptions. People who want to evaluate things separately believe we must always be open to the possibility that we can appropriately make an exception to even the best moral rule. They want to evaluate each action as independently as possible based on some criterion or criteria. The criterion may be similar to a rule, but if it is, then the criterion is the only rule that they will always endorse. Ethical egoism could endorse either of these approaches depending on which one maximized overall benefit. Clearly, egoists have one moral rule with no exceptions: The individual ought to maximize net benefit to himself or herself. An individual egoist could take either approach, however, depending on which one would do the best job of maximizing overall benefit for that individual.

The fourth important theme relates to the proper focus of ethical attention and benefit: *Are good and bad primarily related to the group, community, or majority of people or should the focus be on the individual?* Ethical egoism is focused on the individual. The group, community, or majority of people are irrelevant except to the extent that they affect the individual.

## Contrasting Ethical Egoism with Ethical Relativism

Ethical egoism and ethical relativism are very different theories, but they do have some similarities (see Appendix 1). Egoism originates with the insight that moral guidelines are necessarily connected to something about specific individuals, whereas ethical relativism asserts that guidelines relate to actual societies. The ethical standards differ in a corresponding way. The ethical standard for egoism relates good and bad to benefit and harm to the individual, whereas ethical relativism connects good and bad to the actual moral guidelines of a society. In relation to the traditional ethical assumptions, the theories have only one common position: Egoism and ethical relativism both assume that people are not moral equals. The two theories differ with regard to the other ethical assumptions. Ethical egoism assumes that ethics is rational, whereas ethical relativism makes the production of moral guidelines mysterious and arbitrary. Egoism does not assume that ethical evaluations can be universalized, but ethical relativism claims that a person should use the moral guidelines of his or her society to judge everything. In regard to the themes related to good and bad, the two theories differ on everything. Egoism claims that good and bad are objective because they are based on factual considerations, whereas ethical relativism asserts that good and bad are relative to society. Egoism determines good and bad by focusing on consequences, whereas ethical relativism endorses following general rules without exceptions. Egoism focuses on either following rules or evaluating actions separately depending on which course would maximize net benefit to the individual. Ethical relativism is committed to following general rules without exceptions. Finally, egoism relates good and bad to the individual, whereas ethical relativism connects them to the society or group. In summary, the two theories have many important differences, and only one similarity.

## Problems with Ethical Egoism

There are a number of problems with ethical egoism, three of which are discussed in this section. The concluding section on ethical egoism relates these problems to the criteria from Chapter 1.

### Determining the Consequences and Doing the Calculations

The first problem with ethical egoism is one that is found in all consequentialist theories; it involves the difficulty in identifying all the consequences or harms and benefits that follow from an action. Whether an action is good or bad depends on the beneficial and harmful consequences. Therefore, the egoist must identify all the consequences of an action. The effects of actions are often widespread, however, and it is difficult to identify all of them. Also, when someone tries to determine whether or not a proposed action is ethical, the individual must predict future consequences. Predicting the future is notoriously difficult, and an incorrect prediction will produce a faulty moral judgment. Thus, one problem with ethical egoism is that it will be hard to make accurate moral judgments in cases where the consequences are difficult to identify or predict.

Another problem with ethical egoism is related to doing the calculations. Ethical egoism involves weighing or comparing the harms and benefits of an action to determine whether there is a net harm or benefit. It also involves comparing the harms and benefits of alternative courses of action to determine which is best. It is difficult to do this, however, when the harms and benefits are very different kinds of things. Perhaps I could make ten thousand dollars by taking advantage of a friend in a business deal. It will cost me a friend, but I will make a lot of money. As an egoist, I should do whatever benefits me the most, but which action produces more benefit? Is the person's friendship or the ten thousand dollars more beneficial to me? It is hard to weigh these two because they are such different kinds of things. If ethical egoists cannot successfully weigh the competing sets of consequences, they will not be able to solve moral problems.

## Inconsistency

A second and more serious problem is that, in a sense, ethical egoism is inconsistent. The inconsistency involves the two basic principles of ethical egoism. The first principle is that what is good for an individual is what produces the greatest net benefit for that individual. The second is that everyone ought to act based on his or her self-interest. You will act to maximize benefit to you, and I will act to maximize benefit to me. These two principles are difficult to reconcile. If what is good for me is what produces the greatest net benefit for me, then it is not good for me for everyone to act based on his or her self-interest. I will gain more benefit from your actions if you act in my best interest rather than in your best interest. As an ethical egoist, I would reject the second principle of ethical egoism—that everyone should act based on their self-interest—and claim that everyone ought to act so as to maximize net benefit to me. This is, of course, not a very plausible scenario. It would be against people's natural inclinations to disregard their benefit and simply act for my benefit. Thus, ethical egoism is either inconsistent or it goes against people's natural inclination to be self-interested instead of being in accord with it.

## Living Together Successfully

The final problem with ethical egoism is related to one of the basic purposes of ethics as identified by this book. One purpose of ethics is to help us solve moral problems and live successfully with each other. Ethical egoism would not help us accomplish this purpose. Ethical egoism asserts that what is good is what maximizes net benefit for the individual. Other people's harm and benefit, in itself, simply does not count. Therefore, egoism would legitimize even the most harmful and antisocial acts as long as they benefited the individual. Harming others and committing antisocial acts is not an effective way to live successfully with other people. Ethical egoism cannot assist us to successfully resolve conflicts of interest between people because it gives the individual a superior moral status to everyone else. Other people are merely the means to achieve the individual's benefit. It is doubtful that a person could live successfully with other people if he or she thought of them merely as a means to achieving his or her own self-interest.

## Evaluation of Ethical Egoism

The previous section discussed several problems with ethical egoism. At this point, however, we should consider whether or not ethical egoism would be a successful ethical theory based on the criteria in Chapter 1. First, can ethical egoism identify some ethical guidelines? The theory does identify a basic ethical guideline: People should act based on their self-interest and maximize net benefit to themselves. We can use this guideline to evaluate particular cases; for example, that in this situation I should lie if it will produce more benefit than harm for me. Second, the theory can also show that some ethical guidelines are better than others. "I should lie whenever it benefits me" is a better guideline than "I should always tell the truth no matter what the consequences may be" because the first one will maximize net benefit to me. Skipping to the fourth criterion, ethical egoism can help us solve some moral problems, but the difficulty in identifying all the consequences and doing the calculations will limit its effectiveness to some degree. The theory does not, however, satisfy the third criterion. Nothing in the guidelines identified by the theory prohibits the unlimited pursuit of self-interest. Indeed, individuals ought to pursue self-interest in any and all ways that really maximize benefit to them. It would permit acts that are harmful to others or to society in general if these acts really benefit the individual ethical egoist. Therefore, ethical egoism is not a successful ethical theory based on the criteria from Chapter 1. It does not identify ethical guidelines that would control the unlimited pursuit of self-interest and help us to live together successfully.

Most philosophers reject ethical egoism because it can be used to validate brutal and harmful behavior. If the egoist would receive a net benefit from killing you and stealing your money, then it is ethical for him or her to do it. This does not seem to be an adequate approach to ethics because it clearly would not help us live together more successfully.

## Ethical Subjectivism

The second half of this chapter investigates another ethical theory focused on the individual. Consider once again the example at the beginning of the chapter. Someone breaks into my house and steals my stereo equipment. Upon discovery of the theft, I am furious and quick to tell anyone who will listen that the person who did it is a jerk who should be caught and punished. Ethical egoism focuses on the harm to me, but we might also consider my attitude or emotional reaction. I am angry that my stereo has been stolen. Perhaps good and bad are related to our attitudes and emotions. *Ethical subjectivism* can be used to identify any theory that claims that the emotions or attitudes of individuals are the source of ethical guidelines. If a particular individual has a positive attitude or emotional response to something, it is ethical. If he or she has a negative attitude or emotional response to it, it is unethical. The specific version of ethical subjectivism that will be considered in this chapter is called emotivism.

## Emotivism

The philosopher Charles Stevenson produced a version of ethical subjectivism called *emotivism.* Stevenson argued that good and evil (or, to be more precise, moral judgments or expressions) are related to the attitudes of specific individuals.[1] Stevenson's theory is not really an ethical theory in the sense of the term used in this text. His theory is about the nature of moral judgments, not about producing and justifying an ethical standard. We can, however, build a simple ethical theory about how to live using Stevenson's ideas.

Stevenson's theory is based on the idea that there are different kinds of language with different functions or uses. Some language is used to describe possible facts. For example, the sentence "The book's cover is green" states a possible fact—that the book's cover is green. The proposition expressed by the sentence is true if, and only if, the book's cover really is green. Thus, the statement is true if it corresponds accurately to an actual fact. Descriptive language states or describes possible facts and can be true or false.

Moral language does not describe possible facts. It has two functions, the first of which is to express positive and negative attitudes. Stevenson uses the word "attitude" to indicate psychological dispositions of being for or against something. These expressions of attitudes have an emotional aspect and an *emotive* meaning. The phrase "Lying is evil" expresses the person's disapproval of stealing. It is like saying, "Lying, boo!" "Giving to charity is good" expresses approval and is the same as "Giving to charity, yea!" Examples of moral language are similar, but not identical, to exclamations, such as "Hurrah" or "Damn." Because moral expressions are like exclamations, they cannot be true or false. "Hurrah" cannot be true or false, and neither can "Lying is evil." Stevenson's idea is that ethical judgments express a particular individual's attitudes of being for or against things.

It is important to understand that according to Stevenson moral language does not report attitudes—it expresses them. In contrast to Stevenson's view, someone else might claim that the expression "Lying is evil" reported my negative feeling about lying. This would mean that my expression is another kind of descriptive language. Instead of reporting things about the world, such as the color of book covers, it reports people's attitudes about actions. Thus, moral language could be true or false depending on whether or not it was an accurate report of the person's attitude. Suppose that Rose has a negative attitude about lying, but says "Lying is ethical." Her statement is false because it is an incorrect report of her attitude. Thus, based on this "reporting view," moral language reports people's attitudes about actions and can be true or false. This "reporting view" account of moral language is not Stevenson's view.

Perhaps Stevenson declined to endorse the "reporting view" of moral language because he realized that it misrepresented the nature of ethical argument and disagreement. If you say "abortion is wrong" and I insist that it is ethical, we are disagreeing about the moral status of abortion. Using the "reporting view," however, there would be no disagreement. You are reporting your attitude and I am reporting mine. Both of our claims are true, and there is no disagreement between us even though the claims themselves seem to contradict each other. This view misrepresents ethical disagreement. When we make our different claims, we are making different claims about abortion, not merely about our attitudes. We are disagreeing about the moral status of abortion. I think you are wrong and I am right; I do not think that both claims could be true. Therefore, this "reporting view" seems seriously flawed because it greatly distorts the nature of ethical disagreement.

Stevenson's view avoids this problem. When you say "Abortion is wrong," you are expressing your negative attitude about abortion. When I claim it is ethical, I am expressing my positive attitude. Thus, we have a real disagreement over the status of abortion. For you it is the kind of thing that produces negative feelings, whereas for me it is the kind of thing that creates positive feelings. Thus, our moral disagreement is not only about our different attitudes but also about the nature of abortion. This produces a less distorted view of ethical discourse and disagreement.

According to Stevenson, the second aspect of moral language is that it possesses a prescriptive function. That is, moral language prescribes certain actions or is used to influence people to act in certain ways. In relation to this aspect of moral language, when I say "Stealing is evil," I am trying to keep you from stealing. When I say "Giving to charity is good," I am encouraging you to give to charity. This second aspect of moral language suggests that examples of moral language are similar to commands as well as to exclamations. When I say "Stealing is evil," it is similar, although not identical, to commanding you: "Do not steal." I am commanding you to do or not do a certain kind of action. Based on Stevenson's ideas, moral language attempts to influence people not by appealing to considerations of facts or reason but instead by encouraging them to develop a similar attitude. It is an emotional appeal, not a rational one. Moral language has a prescriptive function because it is used to encourage certain attitudes and kinds of actions in other people.

This second aspect of moral language increases the disagreement between the people in the earlier example. When you say "Abortion is wrong," you are trying to influence women not to have abortions. When I say it is ethical, I am attempting to influence women to have abortions. Thus, once again we are disagreeing about the moral status of abortion. You urge people not to have abortions, and I assert that it is an acceptable kind of action. Stevenson's view seems to create a less distorted view of moral disagreement than the "reporting view."

Stevenson claims that moral language is different from descriptive or fact-stating language. Moral language does not state possible facts. It has both emotive and prescriptive aspects because it expresses an attitude and tries to influence others. Stevenson's position concerns the nature of moral language, but in the next section I will attempt to use it as the basis for a simple ethical theory.

## Emotivism as an Ethical Theory

Based on Stevenson's ideas, we can create a very simple theory about how one ought to live. Although Stevenson might have been unwilling to endorse it, this theory is similar to a view put forward by some ethics students. Based on this "emotive ethical theory," moral obligation could be related to attitudes or emotional responses. If someone has a positive attitude or emotional response to something, it is good. If a person has a negative attitude or emotional response to it, it is bad. Thus, the ethical standard would be that *what is good for an individual is what produces a positive attitude or emotional response in that individual, and what is bad is what produces a negative attitude or emotional response.* Presumably my outrage or anger at having my stereo stolen would count as the appropriate kind of attitude or emotional response and would make the action of stealing my stereo a bad one. Therefore, good and bad would necessarily depend on particular individuals.

The emotive ethical theory might assert that attitudes and emotional responses to actions are involuntary. A person does not collect the facts about the action, evaluate them, and then decide how to feel. This would make good and bad ultimately dependent on facts about particular persons, as in ethical egoism. The attitudes or emotional responses are simply involuntary responses to actions. The individual is confronted with an action and experiences a certain response. In any case, how the attitudes and emotional responses arise is morally irrelevant; only the attitudes about or emotional responses to actions would matter.

In the emotive ethical theory, all persons would use their attitudes or emotional responses as the basis for moral judgments. This theory asserts that ethics is not related to facts or reasoning but to attitudes or emotional responses. Any other view of ethical judgments, such as ethical relativism or ethical egoism, is based on the wrong considerations.

## Justification for the Ethical Standard and Strengths of the Theory

The previous section presented the ethical standard of the emotive ethical theory. This section offers some justifications for using this ethical standard and some corresponding strengths of the ethical theory.

### Moral Disagreement

The best justification for the ethical standard of the emotive ethical theory is that it explains why we have such a large amount of disagreement over ethical matters. When we disagree over factual matters, such as the distance to the moon, we can collect data and reason about them. With accurate observations and measurements, we can often resolve these factual disagreements. Ethical issues, such as the debate over abortion, seem more difficult. People can agree about the facts but still disagree on the issue. For some reason, solving ethical problems is more than a matter of collecting facts and reasoning about them. The emotive ethical theory explains why this is the case. Ethical matters are related to attitudes and emotions; therefore, collecting data and reasoning are useless. It is very difficult to resolve emotional differences. People simply feel whatever they feel. Also, emotions are notoriously inconsistent, varying from person to person for no apparent reason and changing for a particular individual over time. I may feel one way about something today and another way about the same thing tomorrow. Thus, one justification for using this standard is that it explains the large amount of disagreement over ethical issues. The ability to explain this matter is seen by some people as a strength of the theory.

### The Difference between Science and Ethics

A second way to justify using this standard and a related strength of the theory is similar, although not identical, to the first one. The emotive ethical theory provides a plausible explanation for the difference between science and ethics. Science operates in a certain way involving hypothesis, experimentation, and theories. It rests primarily on observation. Ethics seems quite different. Moral philosophers rarely do experiments, nor do they make many observations of the physical world around them. Why are these two areas of human endeavor so different? The emotive ethical theory provides an answer to this question. Ethics is unlike science because science deals with observables, whereas ethics deals with attitudes and emotional responses, which cannot always be observed. This ability to explain the difference between science and ethics is one reason to use this standard and a strength of the theory.

### Moral Certainty and Confidence

The final justification for using the standard and a corresponding strength of the emotive ethical theory is that it produces moral certainty and confidence. Presumably, individuals know their own attitudes and can identify their emotional responses with certainty. Therefore, individuals can be certain about and confident in their moral judgments because these judgments depend only on their attitudes or emotional responses. Also, no one else knows these attitudes and emotional responses as well as the individual, so the person can be confident that he or she cannot be effectively challenged. Thus, a justification for using this standard and a corresponding strength of the theory is that it provides moral certainty and confidence.

## Morally Significant Actions

An ethical theory should also delineate morally significant actions from ones that are not morally significant. For a proponent of the emotive ethical theory, a morally significant action is one that elicits an attitude or emotional response. The theft of my stereo was morally significant because I was angry about it. Other actions, such as filling my car's tank with gasoline, would not be morally significant because I would not have any attitude or emotional response toward them at all.

## Emotive Ethical Theory and the Traditional Ethical Assumptions

Emotive ethical theory would not accept any of the traditional assumptions associated with ethical theories. First, it does not assume that ethics is rational. Ethical guidelines and judgments relate to involuntary attitudes or emotional responses, not to considerations based on reason. Emotivists would not assume that we could use reason to reach theoretical and practical conclusions about ethical matters. Only the attitudes or emotional responses matter, and they are not necessarily rational. Emotive ethical theory also does not endorse impartiality and moral equality. Each individual's attitudes and emotional responses determine good and bad for him or her; the attitudes of others or the effects of our actions on them are irrelevant. Thus, the individual is morally superior to everyone else and does not have to treat people impartially. Finally, emotive ethical theory does not assume that any ethical evaluations can be universalized. Good and bad relate to a particular individual's attitudes or emotional responses. Other people may have very different dispositions and responses and make very different moral judgments. Thus, we cannot assert that another person should make the same judgment in a similar situation. Although moral language has a prescriptive element, there is no intention to or possibility of influencing every existing person with a particular expression.

## Emotive Ethical Theory and the Basic Ethical Themes

In an effort to better comprehend the emotive ethical theory, let's examine how the basic ethical themes about moral good and bad can be related to it. The first theme can be represented by this question: *What kind of moral guidelines makes something good or bad: subjective, relative, or objective ones?* As was stated in an earlier section, emotivism is one kind of ethical subjectivism. The moral guidelines of the emotive ethical theory are subjective because they are based on the particular attitudes or emotional responses of specific individuals. Emotivist guidelines are not relative because they do not depend on society. They are also not objective, in the way that term was used in Chapter 1, because they are not a product of objective considerations of fact and/or reason that do not depend on the perceptions, emotions, or judgments of particular persons.

Another significant theme in ethics is this: *What makes something good or bad; is it the consequences that are produced or the reasoning that leads up to it?* This contrast is not really appropriate for the emotive ethical theory because good and bad are clearly not based on reasoning. In one sense, labeling an act as good or bad might be said to be based on consequences. If an action produces a positive attitude or emotional response, it is good. Some might say that the emotional response is a consequence of the action, but this seems to distort the meaning of "consequences" as discussed in Chapter 1. The best answer would seem to be neither; good and bad are based on attitudes, not on consequences or reasoning.

The third theme relates to this question: *Are good and bad related to following general rules without exceptions or connected to separately evaluat-*

*ing actions, beliefs, and so on?* People who believe we should guide our behavior by general rules feel that these rules should have no exceptions. People who want to evaluate things separately believe we must always be open to the possibility that we can appropriately make an exception to even the best moral rule. They want to evaluate each action as independently as possible based on some criterion or criteria. The criterion may be similar to a rule, but if it is, then the criterion is the only rule that they will always endorse. The emotive ethical theory does not propose that we follow general rules. Each action is evaluated based on the attitude or emotional response connected to it. Thus, actions are evaluated individually.

The fourth important theme relates to the proper focus of ethical attention and benefit: *Are good and bad primarily related to the group, community, or majority of people or should the focus be on the individual?* The emotive ethical theory is focused on the individual. The group, community, or majority of people are morally irrelevant. Only the attitudes and emotional responses of the individual matter. Even if the attitudes were somehow a product of society, this would be morally irrelevant because it is the attitudes themselves that matter, not why the individual has those attitudes.

## Contrasting the Emotive Ethical Theory with Ethical Egoism

Both the emotive ethical theory and ethical egoism relate moral guidelines to something about specific individuals, but they are very different theories (see Appendix 1). The ethical standard for egoism relates good and bad to benefit and harm to the individual, whereas the emotive ethical theory joins good and bad to individuals' attitudes and emotional responses. In regard to the traditional ethical assumptions, the two theories agree that people are not moral equals and that moral judgments cannot be universalized. The theories disagree, however, on whether ethics is rational. The emotive ethical theory assumes it is not, and ethical egoism claims the reverse. Related to the themes concerning good and bad, the theories have some similarities and some differences. First, emotive ethical theory asserts that good and bad are subjective, whereas ethical egoism claims that they are objective. Second, both theories claim that good and bad are related to specific individuals, not to the group, majority of people, or society. Third, ethical egoism relates good and bad to consequences, not to reasoning before the action, whereas the emotive ethical theory connects good and bad to attitudes rather than to either consequences or reasoning. Finally, ethical egoism focuses on either following rules or evaluating actions separately, depending on which would maximize net benefit to the individual. The emotive ethical theory relates good and bad to specific actions. Although the two theories relate to the same ethical insight, they have important differences.

## Problems with the Emotive Ethical Theory

This section discusses three of the many problems with emotivism. The final section of the chapter provides an overall evaluation and reviews why most philosophers reject the theory.

### Moral Language

One problem with emotive ethical theory is that it is based on Stevenson's view of moral language, which many philosophers believe is misguided. Stevenson argues that moral language always has an emotive and a prescriptive element: It expresses an attitude and prescribes a certain kind of conduct. I cannot adequately analyze and evaluate Stevenson's view of language here, but one criticism of it can be summarized. Stevenson claims that every example of moral language has emotive and prescriptive aspects, yet many examples refute this. In a discussion of different kinds of theft, Rose might say, "Although I don't feel sorry for the companies, it is clear that stealing from large stores is still unethical." There is no emotional aspect to this expression at all. Rose is not bothered by retail theft from large stores; she is just acknowledging that it is still unethical. In a similar manner, someone could use a moral expression without prescribing anything. For example, John might say, "Although I would never tell a woman she had to give birth to a child, I personally believe abortion is wrong." John is not prescribing that anyone refrain from getting an abortion. He is simply stating his personal position, which, for some reason, he is unwilling to extend to any pregnant woman. There is no prescriptive element to his expression. If Stevenson had stated that moral expressions sometimes have emotive and prescriptive elements, there would be no problem. When he claims that they always do, he is mistaken. If Stevenson's view of moral language is misguided, then the ethical theory based on it is suspect.

### Ethics as Mysterious and Arbitrary

Another serious problem with emotive ethical theory is that it makes ethical guidelines and ethical judgments mysterious and arbitrary. If I ask why you think euthanasia is unethical, as an emotivist, you will answer, "Because I have a bad attitude toward disconnecting from life support someone in the last stages of dying from a disease." If I ask why you hold this negative attitude, you would have to reply that why does not matter. Nothing except the actual attitude is morally relevant. Therefore, we are left with these mysterious attitudes and with no explanation for why we have the ones we do. Consequently, we have no real explanation for why we have the ethical guidelines that we do. In addition to these matters being mysterious, any attitude or ethical guideline would be as good as any other one. Thus, the attitudes and moral guidelines are arbitrary. A theory that makes moral guidelines and moral judgments mysterious and arbitrary is not a very valuable theory for many people.

### Preventing the Unlimited Pursuit of Self-Interest

The final problem is that emotive ethical theory implies that any conduct can be ethical. If a person has a positive attitude or emotional response when contemplating rape, then rape is ethical for that person. There is no way to objectively declare rape to be evil because only individual attitudes and emotional responses are morally significant. Any action, no matter how brutal or cruel, could be ethical. The third criterion for a successful moral theory stated that an ethical theory must identify moral guidelines that would prohibit the unlimited pursuit of self-interest. Clearly, the emotive ethical theory cannot satisfy this criterion. It would legitimate even the most harmful or antisocial conduct if the person had a positive emotional response or a positive attitude toward that behavior. Allowing people to act in harmful and antisocial ways is not appropriate if we want to solve moral problems and live together successfully. This tendency of the theory to legitimatize any conduct is a serious problem for many philosophers.

## Evaluation of the Emotive Ethical Theory

The emotive ethical theory has both strengths and weaknesses. Most philosophers reject this theory, and if it is examined in the context of the criteria from Chapter 1, it would be discarded. First, can emotive ethical theory identify some ethical guidelines? If we believe moral language has a prescriptive function, and if we are not too rigid or exclusive about what counts as "ethical guidelines," the answer is that emotive ethical theory can identify some moral guidelines. Moral expressions or judgments are attempts to influence particular people either to do or not to do various things, and these attempts could be viewed as ethical guidelines. According to emotive ethical theory, individuals produce the ethical guidelines, and the theory informs us about how to identify them.

Second, can emotive ethical theory show that some ethical guidelines are better than others? If the attitudes and emotional responses of particular individuals determine the ethical guidelines, then any moral guideline would be legitimate if it were related to a judgment that actually expressed an attitude. The moral guideline related to the specific attitude is better than others for the particular individual—but not for people in general. If we want an ethical theory to show that some moral guidelines are better than others for all of us, emotive ethical theory cannot help us.

Third, can emotive ethical theory help us live together successfully? Emotive ethical theory cannot satisfy this criterion. It would legitimate even the most harmful or antisocial conduct if the person had a good attitude toward that behavior. A theory that does not prohibit brutal and cruel actions cannot help us to live together successfully.

Finally, can emotive ethical theory help us solve ethical problems? If solving ethical problems simply means that we can arrive at personal solutions, then emotive ethical theory can help solve moral problems. My attitudes and emotional responses can guide me in solving ethical problems. If I have a positive attitude toward stealing a book and no negative attitude toward the possible legal consequences of doing so, then I should do it. If solving ethical problems includes being able to support my solutions with reasons that other people would understand and might even endorse, then emotive ethical theory cannot help us solve moral problems in a satisfactory way. My only reason for saying that stealing the book was good is that I had a good attitude toward doing it. Why I have the attitude is morally irrelevant. Thus, in a personal sense emotive ethical theory satisfies the fourth criterion, but in an interpersonal sense it does not.

Based on the serious problems with at least two of the four criteria, emotive ethical theory would not be a successful ethical theory. It would not show that some moral guidelines were better than others, and it would not help us solve moral problems and live together successfully.

## Conclusion

In this chapter, I have discussed two approaches to ethics that relate legitimate moral guidelines to something about particular individuals. Neither of these theories is successful in the context of meeting the criteria outlined in Chapter 1. My conclusion is that we should also reject the "ethical insight" that legitimate moral guidelines necessarily have something to do with particular individuals. In Chapters 2 and 3, we considered God and society as the sources of legitimate moral guidelines. In this chapter, we investigated whether legitimate moral guidelines had their source in specific individuals. All of these approaches to ethics have proved unsuccessful. In Chapter 5, we will turn to a theory that relates legitimate moral guidelines to reason and that exemplifies the three traditional ethical assumptions of rationality, impartiality, and universalizability. Perhaps an approach to ethics more in line with traditional ethical assumptions will be more successful.

## QUESTIONS FOR REVIEW

*Here are some questions to help you review the main concepts in this chapter.*

1. Explain how ethical egoism and ethical subjectivism relate to the same moral insight.

2. Explain the difference in the ethical standards of ethical egoism and the emotive ethical theory.

3. Why does ethical egoism initially seem to be consistent with people's natural inclinations? Explain the problem that calls this consistency into question.

4. In your view, what is the greatest strength of ethical egoism? What is the greatest strength of the emotive ethical theory?

5. In your opinion, what is the most serious problem with ethical egoism? What is the most serious problem with emotivism?

6. How does Stevenson think "moral language" differs from "descriptive language"? What problem does the author suggest exists with Stevenson's view of moral language?

7. If you had to choose between ethical egoism and the emotive ethical theory, which one would you choose? Why is this the better theory?

8. Compare and contrast ethical egoism and the emotive ethical theory on the traditional moral assumptions.

9. Compare and contrast ethical egoism and the emotive ethical theory on the themes connected to good and bad.

10. In terms of the criteria from Chapter 1, is ethical egoism a successful ethical theory? Explain why, or why not.

11. In terms of the criteria from Chapter 1, is the emotive ethical theory a successful ethical theory? Explain why, or why not.

## NOTE

1. Charles L. Stevenson, *Ethics and Language* (New Haven: Yale University Press, 1944).

# Chapter 5

# Kantian Ethical Theory

Most people who drive automobiles occasionally exceed the posted speed limits, but assume you have an acquaintance who never does this. You ask the person why he or she never speeds, and the answer is, "I'm afraid I'll be caught by the police and have to pay a fine." This would be a consequentialist approach to speeding. This individual does not speed because of the fear of bad consequences. There is, however, another answer a person might give: "I do not speed because I respect the law. Sometimes I want to speed because I'm in a hurry, but because I respect the law I never do it." This is a very different answer; it is not concerned with either consequences or personal wants. The person's action is guided simply by respect for the law. It may seem odd that someone would respect the speeding laws, but assume that this person respects the law in general and therefore obeys all the laws, even the posted speed limits.

This example concerns the laws established by a government—the kind of law that I argued needs to be separated from ethics (see Chapter 1). We know this kind of law exists, but the German philosopher Immanuel Kant (1724–1804) argues that another kind of law also exists, *moral law.* It is not the law of any one country or society; moral law applies to all persons. Many people would intuitively agree with Kant. Their ethical insight is that *there are moral laws that apply to all persons.* This chapter discusses an ethical theory related to this insight and to the idea of acting from respect for the moral law.

In Chapter 1, I suggested that philosophers often work with this model of action:

*Reasoning* → *Action* → *Consequences*

Consequentialist ethical theories, such as ethical egoism claim that good and evil are related to the consequences that result from an action. In contrast, *deontological ethical theories* focus on the reasoning that precedes the action. The word "deontology" relates to the Greek word "deon," which translates roughly as "duty." Immanuel Kant is the most influential of the deontological philosophers. He believed persons had a duty to obey the moral law. Kant's ethical theory is extremely complicated.[1] I will not provide an exact explication of his ideas but instead discuss a simplified "Kantian ethics" centered around acting from respect for the moral law.

## Rules and Actions

The relation between rules and actions is essential to Kantian ethics. The key idea is that, for any action, we can identify a personal rule that guides the action. Suppose I send some money to a charity because I believe everyone ought to help those who are less fortunate. My reasoning might be described in this way. I performed the action (giving money to this charity) because I thought I should act from my personal rule: Everyone ought to help those who are less fortunate. The initial Kantian idea is that every action is guided by a personal rule. Consequently, Kantian theory states that if persons want to be ethical the personal rules that guide their actions must be able to be willed to be moral laws. It is not enough that by coincidence personal rules of action are consistent with these moral laws; persons must be acting because they could will their personal rules to be moral laws. Subsequent sections will explain this position.

## Developing the Kantian Ethical Insight

Consider once again the person who always obeys the speed limit laws. The person acknowledges that the laws exist and respects them; therefore, he or she obeys them. In theory the laws apply to everyone. That is, everyone is supposed to be equal with regard to the law. If I am caught going fifteen miles an hour over the speed limit, I should be treated the same way you would be treated if you were caught doing the same thing. The law exists, and everyone is equal in regard to it. The Kantian position on ethics is similar to this, except, of course, it refers to the moral law. *The Kantian ethical insight is that there are moral laws and that these laws apply to all persons.* If the moral law applies equally to everyone, all persons are moral equals in regard to the law. If the Kantian insight was filled out, it would state that (1) there are moral laws connected to reason, and (2) that all persons are equal in regard to the moral law and should be treated consistently in sufficiently similar situations. The moral law and the moral equality of persons or rational beings are crucial to Kantian ethics. The idea of moral equality among persons means that moral laws equally bind all persons and that all persons count the same when we are applying moral laws. Assume that the rule "It is wrong to steal other people's property" can be willed to be a moral law. If persons are moral equals, they are all bound by the rule, and the rule protects all property. No one has a privileged ethical position that allows him or her to ignore the rule. Therefore, moral laws place obligations on everyone; that is, they are universal.

The ideas of moral equality and ethical consistency for persons are closely connected. Suppose that the rule "It is wrong to steal other people's property" is legitimate. If I believe two persons are moral equals and that they are in sufficiently similar situations, then I ought to act from the moral rule in a consistent way—I should refrain from stealing either person's property. If I do not act this way, I am being inconsistent in two ways. The first inconsistency concerns the rule; I am not consistently acting from the rule. The rule orders me not to steal, but in one case I act from it, and in a sufficiently similar case I disregard it. The second inconsistency relates to my attitude toward persons. I have said that persons are moral equals, but I treat them as if they were not moral equals, stealing from one and not from the other. Kantian ethics claims that persons ought to be consistent, both in acting from moral laws and in the treatment of persons. Moral equality and ethical consistency are key ideas in Kantian ethics.

## Rational Beings, Persons, and Moral Laws

According to Kantian ethics, moral laws are connected to reason, and they bind all free, rational beings. In this context, to be a "rational being" means, at least, to be capable of acting in accord with rational rules or principles. In more detail, a rational being must be able to deliberate, follow rules, make decisions, and support those decisions with reasons. Rational beings must also be able to understand the idea of the moral law and decide how to act based on reasoning about personal rules of action and moral laws. Finally, rational beings must be able to act from respect for the moral law. If a being cannot meet these criteria, he or she will not qualify as a rational being or a person under Kantian ethics.

Moral laws are perceived by persons as universal commands. Because moral laws command persons universally or absolutely, they must be followed without exceptions. They are not conditional rules. Conditional rules tell us what actions persons should take to attain some desired goal and have an "if–then" form: If you want to lose weight, then you ought to exercise and watch what you eat. The rule is conditional because it will only guide you to act if you want to lose weight. Therefore, conditional rules do not obligate everyone—only those people who desire to reach the goal. In contrast, legitimate moral rules or laws place an obligation on everyone regardless of their desires; they are universal.

If moral laws are a product of reason, then it is rational for a person to act from these moral laws. If a person violates the moral laws, he or she has acted inconsistently or irrationally. Persons are capable of being rational and ought to act rationally, presumably out of respect for their rationality. Therefore, ultimately, acting from respect for the moral law is based on acting from respect for rationality. Some might ask, "Why should rational beings act from respect for their rationality?" It is clearly possible and sometimes in our self-interest to act irrationally and inconsistently. As Kant himself acknowledged, persons are imperfectly rational beings. A Kantian would presumably say that we have given up a large part of our freedom and rationality if we do not act from respect for the moral law. We should endorse our nature as free, rational beings —not reject it by acting irrationally.

## The Ethical Standard of Kantian Ethics

Kantians use a basic moral law, principle, or ethical standard called the *Categorical Imperative* to determine the legitimate rules or more specific moral laws that ought to guide action. The Categorical Imperative is similar to an essential principle in many religions. In Christianity this principle is called the Golden Rule. One version of the Golden Rule is, "Do unto others as you would have them do unto you." The first formulation of the Categorical Imperative or ethical standard might be phrased: *Act only from those personal rules that you can at the same time will to be moral laws.* The difference between the Golden Rule and the first formulation of the Kantian Categorical Imperative is subtle, yet important, because the Kantian formula is less likely to lead to a subjective interpretation. I might interpret the Golden Rule as telling me to treat persons the way that I would like to be treated. This interpretation runs the risk of having someone understand it as the instruction to use his or her personal likes and dislikes as the ethical standard for how to treat everyone else. This would extend the person's subjective standard to everyone and would have the problems related to ethical subjectivism. In my opinion, this is not what was meant by the Golden Rule, and it is certainly not what Kant meant. Persons are to act from those personal rules that they could will to be ethical laws because they are rational, moral equals. The first formulation is related to the idea that the moral law is universal. If individuals follow the Categorical Imperative and act on personal rules that they could will to be moral laws, they will have acted ethically.

Kantian ethical theory identifies another version of the Kantian ethical standard that also relates to moral equality and consistency. The second formulation of the Categorical Imperative might be stated like this: *Act in regard to all persons in ways that treat them as ends in themselves and never simply as means to accomplish the ends of others.* Persons are free, rational beings who have various purposes and goals that they wish to accomplish. The second formulation of the Categorical Imperative or ethical standard acknowledges these characteristics when it refers to persons as ends in themselves. Kantian ethics demands that persons evaluate their personal rules and act only on those that they could will to be universal laws. Persons must also acknowledge that other persons should do the same thing because they are moral equals. They must never forget that persons are free and can reason and act, and they should never treat others merely as tools to accomplish their goals, the way they would use a hammer to fix something. For example, I cannot simply order you to help me repair my roof and expect you to do it regardless of whatever plans you may have. This disregards your status as a free, rational being who can make decisions and has goals and instead treats you merely as a means for me to get my roof fixed. I need to ask you to help me fix my roof. This leaves the decision up to you and acknowledges your status as a free being who can make decisions and has his or her own goals. I am still using you as a means to get my roof repaired, but not merely as a means. Rational beings can use persons to accomplish their ends, but they should never use them merely as means to accomplish those ends. Persons are moral equals and, therefore, must act only from personal rules that treat persons as ends in themselves, and never from rules that treat persons merely as means to accomplish their ends. If they do this, they will have acted ethically.

## Legitimate Moral Laws

How are persons to know the rules that they should will to be moral laws? To answer this question, Kantian ethics appeals to consistency, universalizability, and moral equality. First, individuals must determine the personal rule on which they propose to act. Second, they should only act from rules that are internally consistent. Third, they should only follow rules that are universal. Fourth, they should only act from rules that treat persons as moral equals. Finally, people should never act from rules that treat persons merely as means to accomplish the ends of others.

Consider this proposed rule: "I may promise to do something and then break that promise if it is in my self-interest to do so." Assume that I may break the promise for any self-interested reason, no matter how trivial. Therefore, based on willing this rule to be a moral law, everyone would make promises and then in many cases break them. This rule does not meet the consistency criterion because it is internally inconsistent. When I promise to do something, perhaps help you fix your roof, I am saying that I *will* do it. However, this rule is also stating that I *will not* do it if something trivial, but in my self-interest, arises. It is saying that I *will* help you fix your roof and that I *will not* help you. These two aspects of the rule are inconsistent and would make my promise to help you fix your roof meaningless. If this rule were extended to guide all promises, it would make promises in general meaningless. We would never know if the person were going to do the thing he or she had promised to do. Thus, this rule would not meet the first criterion because it is internally inconsistent.

Rational beings should also reject potential rules that are not universal and that do not treat persons as moral equals. Because we are moral equals, legitimate moral laws apply to all of us. A rule may be rejected if it is not universal, that is, if it does not apply to everyone. Suppose someone proposes the rule that "Only women should help those less fortunate than themselves." This rule should be rejected because it is not universal; it does not apply to all persons. The rule implies that women have a special ethical standing, but this is incorrect if all persons are moral equals. All legitimate moral laws treat persons as moral equals and hence apply to everyone. To be ethical, persons must follow only rules that they could will to be moral laws.

Moral agents should also reject potential rules that treat persons merely as means to accomplish the ends of others. Consider the proposed rule, "Whenever my lawn needs mowing, John should mow it for me." This rule disregards John's status as a free, rational being with ends and purposes of his own and considers him merely as a means for me to get my lawn mowed. It is irrational and unethical to treat John as merely a means when he is really a free, rational being. Thus, this potential rule could not be legitimately willed to be a moral law.

Kantians believe that many rules could be willed to be moral laws. One is that "Persons ought to keep their promises." First, keeping all of our promises is internally consistent because the rule, by its formulation, does not interfere with our doing that to which we have obligated ourselves. There might be a promise that is foolishly made—one which it turns out the person does not have the ability to keep—but the inability to keep this promise is a problem with the particular promise and not a necessary problem with the moral rule. Second, this moral rule is universal because it applies to everyone and all promises. Third, this moral rule also treats persons as moral equals because persons will be keeping their promises to everyone, rather than keeping them to some persons and not to others. Finally, it does not treat persons merely as means; by keeping my promise to someone, I respect the person's ends that may be related to the promise. Therefore, persons can will the rule to be a moral law.

Another example would be the rule that "It is unethical to enslave persons." This rule could be willed to be a moral law because it is internally consistent and would treat persons as moral equals and ends in themselves. Slaves meet the criteria as persons, but they are not treated as persons (as free, rational beings and moral equals). They are treated merely as means to satisfy the ends of their owners. If we claimed that slavery was ethical, we would be claiming that some persons (rational beings) ought not to be treated as persons (rational beings). This would be inconsistent and would violate the idea that rational beings must treat persons as moral equals. Conversely, the rule that slavery is unethical supports the idea that persons must always be treated as rational beings and moral equals, and as ends in themselves.

There is no other method to determine the rules that should guide action. Kantians cannot claim that the moral laws would be the rules that produce the best consequences. This is the position taken by rule utilitarianism (see Chapter 6). According to rule utilitarians, we should follow rules that maximize net happiness or human benefit for the greatest number of persons affected. In contrast, Kantians claim that the legitimacy of moral laws is not connected to consequences. Therefore, the Kantian ethical standard does not specify the kinds of consequences that must be produced. The rules that persons should will to be moral laws ought to be rules that fit the criteria of internal consistency, universalizability, and moral equality.

Kantian ethics would not provide a complete list of all the rules that could be willed to be moral laws. As rational beings, persons ought to evaluate their personal rules of action. It would be inconsistent and unethical to reject being a rational being and not to evaluate those personal rules. Of course, Kantians believe persons will all arrive at the same conclusions about which rules could be willed to be moral laws if they use reason correctly. The emphasis, however, is on the moral standard and the procedure used to identify the legitimate rules to guide action, not on identifying a specific set of moral laws.

When a person contemplates a morally significant action, he or she must be able to identify or arrive at a description of the action. From the description, the personal rule that would guide the action can be identified. For example, suppose that my contemplated action is helping you fix your roof, which is related to my promise to help you fix your roof. The rule that would guide my action if I help you is, "Persons ought to keep their promises." As discussed earlier, this rule could be willed to be a moral law; therefore, it is ethical for me to keep my promise and help you fix your roof. We would have to be able to know what counted and did not count as making a promise, the relevant personal rule, and whether that rule could be willed to be a moral law. In some cases, there may be more than one relevant rule. If both rules could be willed to be moral laws, the action is ethical. However, if one rule could be willed to be a moral law and the other could not, there would be a conflict. Conflicts between rules will be discussed further in the section on the problems with Kantian ethics.

## Justification for the Ethical Standard and Strengths of the Theory

An earlier section identified the two Kantian ethical standards or versions of the Categorical Imperative: (1) *Act only from those personal rules that you can at the same time will to be moral laws* and (2) *Act in regard to all persons in ways that treat them as ends in themselves and never simply as means to accomplish the ends of others.* In this section, we turn to justifications for the standards and corresponding strengths of Kantian ethics. These justifications and strengths relate to the three traditional ethical assumptions.

### Ethics Is Rational

The first justification for using the standard and corresponding strength of the Kantian ethical theory is that it makes ethics rational. The theory enables us to provide reasons to support our moral rules, and we can show why some reasons and rules are better than others. Kantians can discuss ethical issues, and if they are well intentioned, they ought to be able to arrive at mutual conclusions. For most people, a theory that makes ethics rational is stronger than a theory that makes it irrational because it enables us to better understand how to live and why we should live that way. It also enables us to reach agreements with other people over moral problems; therefore, we should be able to live together more successfully.

### The Moral Equality of Persons

The second justification for the ethical standard and related strength of the theory is that it asserts that persons are moral equals. This is a positive feature for many people because it prevents prejudiced attitudes like racism and sexism. Sexism, for example, claims that women are inferior to men. Although sexists may claim that women are physically and intellectually inferior, it is the implied claim that women are morally inferior that is most objectionable. If women are morally inferior, then they are not worth as much as men. Their interests can be legitimately sacrificed to serve the interests of men, or women can be forced to live their lives merely to benefit men. The Kantian ethical theory argues that all persons are rational beings and moral equals. No man can legitimately use a woman merely as the means to achieve his ends or those of another person. Thus, the Kantian ethical theory provides the reasoning to refute sexism, racism, and other prejudiced attitudes. This is a justification for using the ethical standard and a strength of the theory for many people.

*Universal Moral Guidelines*

The third justification for using the ethical standard and corresponding strength of the theory is that it allows for the universalizability of moral guidelines and judgments. The moral guidelines or laws generated by the use to the Categorical Imperative ought to be the same for all rational beings. The example of the moral law "It is unethical to enslave persons" was discussed earlier. This is a legitimate moral law and ought to be lawful for all rational beings. These universal moral guidelines enable us to produce universalizable moral judgments. For example, "Enslaving illegal immigrants to work in New York City garment sweat shops is evil." This judgment is correct no matter what part of New York City and whatever time period. For many people, a theory that gives one the justification to declare that certain actions are universally good or bad is a stronger theory than one that does not do this. It is stronger because the capacity to make universal moral judgments provides a justification for taking firm and confident positions on various moral issues.

These strengths of the Kantian ethical theory make it seem to many like an improvement over the earlier theories. In a later section of the chapter, some problems with the theory will be discussed.

## Determining Morally Significant Actions

The legitimate ethical standard identified by Kantians provides a means of separating morally significant actions from those that are not morally significant. With respect to actions, any action performed from respect for the moral law is morally significant. It is also morally significant if we fail to act from respect for the moral law; for example, acting on self-interest in a situation relevant to a legitimate moral law would also be morally significant. If someone asks me a question, I ought to provide a truthful answer or refuse to answer. I should not lie even if it is in my self-interest to do so. It is morally significant if I tell a lie. In general, in Kantian ethics anything related to acting from respect for the moral law is morally significant.

## Kantian Ethics and the Traditional Ethical Assumptions

As has been shown in the previous section, Kantian ethical theory accepts the traditional ethical assumptions. It would claim that ethics is rational. We can use reason to reach theoretical and practical conclusions about ethics. We can also provide reasons to support moral laws and solutions to ethical problems, evaluate those reasons and solutions, and conclude that some of them are better than others. More specifically, we can evaluate personal rules and see if we could will them to be moral laws. Kantians would also agree that there are mutually acceptable solutions to moral problems, assuming we agree on the description of the proposed action and on the evaluation of the proposed rule.

Kantian ethics also accepts the view that all persons are moral equals and should be treated impartially. All persons are rational beings equally bound by the moral law, and, therefore, they are all moral equals. If "Breaking a promise is unethical" is a moral law, then all persons ought to keep their promises to everyone. No one has a special moral status that allows him or her to break promises and still be ethical. Thus, all persons must be treated impartially if a moral agent wants to act ethically.

Finally, Kantian ethics endorses the idea of universalizing moral guidelines and judgments. If one person can legitimately will the rule "Breaking a promise is unethical" to be a moral law, then any rational being can do so, and it would be unethical to break promises. The moral law applies equally to all of us. Assuming that we can will some rules to be moral laws, we can universalize our ethical evaluations connected to those laws.

## Kantian Ethics and the Basic Ethical Themes

Kantian ethics has a position on each of the four basic ethical themes. The first theme was represented by this question: *What kind of moral guidelines makes something good or bad: subjective, relative, or objective ones?* Kantians believe good and bad are objective because they depend on or are the product of considerations of reason that do not depend on the perceptions, judgments, or emotions of particular persons or the beliefs of a particular society. If a personal moral rule can be willed to be a moral law based on the Categorical Imperative, then that law is objective. Its justification is this use of reason, not considerations related to societies. It also is not connected to the emotions or attitudes of specific individuals. The moral law is based on reason and has nothing to do with emotion. Thus, in the sense of "objective" as discussed in Chapter 1, any Kantian moral guideline is an objective one.

Another significant theme in ethics is indicated by this question: *What makes something good or bad; is it the consequences that are produced or the reasoning that leads up to it?* Kantian ethics asserts that the rightness or wrongness of something depends on the reasoning that guided it. The ethical evaluation of an action depends on whether or not the action was done because the personal rule that guided it could be willed to be a moral law.

The third theme is related to this question: *Are good and bad related to following general rules without exceptions or connected to separately evaluating each action, belief, and so on?* Kantians believe ethics involves following rules that could be willed to be moral laws. They allow no exceptions to acting from these rules; making an exception would mean that the moral agent had been inconsistent in acting from the moral law or that he or she had not treated persons as moral equals.

The fourth theme is connected to the proper focus of ethical attention: *Should the group, community, or majority of persons be the focus of ethics or should the focus be on the individual?* Kantians believe the focus of ethics should be the individual person, or rational being. Each person must evaluate his or her personal rules of action and act from those that he or she could will to be moral laws. If individuals use reason correctly, however, everyone will arrive at the same set of legitimate rules of action.

## Contrasting Kantian Ethics with Ethical Egoism

Kantian ethical theory and ethical egoism are very different theories (see Appendix 1) with very different ethical standards. Kantian ethical theory endorses the two forms of the Categorical Imperative: (1) act only from those personal rules that you can at the same time will to be moral laws, and (2) act in regard to all persons in ways that treat them as ends in themselves and never simply as means to accomplish the ends of others. Ethical egoism claims that what is good is what produces a net benefit for a particular individual and that what is bad is what produces a net harm for the individual. A similarity between the two theories relates to the first traditional ethical assumption: Both theories assume that ethics is rational. Kantian ethics differs in that it accepts impartiality, moral equality, and universalizability, whereas ethical egoism accepts none of these. In regard to the ethical themes, there is agreement on two themes, and disagreement on two others. The theories basically agree on the first theme. Kantians assert that good and bad are objective because they depend on general considerations of reason and not on society or the emotions and attitudes of specific individuals. Ethical egoism also claims that good and bad are objective because they relate to factual considerations related to harm and benefit to the individual. The two theories disagree on the second ethical theme. Egoism determines good and bad by looking at the consequences to the individual, whereas Kantian ethical theory looks at the reasoning that precedes an action. There is also disagreement on the third theme, with Kantians connecting good and bad to following general rules without exceptions and ethical egoists evaluating actions on a case-by-case basis. Finally, the theories agree that the focus of ethics should be on the individual, although Kantians focus on the individual willing moral laws and egoists concentrate on considerations of individual benefit. Thus, there are some similarities between the two theories, but a greater number of important differences as well.

## Problems with Kantian Ethics

Kantian ethical theory, historically, has been very important, but it does have some problems. In the next section, three of the more clear-cut of these problems will be discussed. The conclusion of the chapter will evaluate the theory in terms of the criteria from Chapter 1.

### Descriptions for Actions

One problem with Kantian ethical theory relates to the procedure for creating moral laws. Persons must be able to identify an action ("making a promise" or "killing an innocent person") and then decide on the rule that guides the action ("persons ought to keep their promises" or "it is unethical to kill innocent people"). This identification is essential; without it there will be no personal rule. Without the personal rule, there will be no way to determine ethical action because an action can only be ethical if it follows from a personal rule that could be willed to be a moral law. Kant seems to have assumed that there is only one correct description for an action and that each action only connects to one rule. Examples suggest otherwise. Suppose I contemplate taking some food from a grocery store to feed my starving children. What is the correct description of the action? Is it a case of stealing, of saving the lives of innocent people, or of caring for my children? There are certainly incorrect ways to describe this action (for example, taking a walk in the park), but which of the plausible descriptions is the one to use in determining the appropriate rule and ultimately whether the action is ethical? If we cannot identify a single description for the action, we are faced with multiple personal rules. Is this the relevant rule? Whenever my children are starving and I can get no money for food, I ought to take the food from large stores. Is it this rule? It is unethical to steal the property of others. Is it this rule? Persons ought to try to save the lives of innocent people. Finally, is it this rule? We ought to care for our children. It seems that all of these rules (and perhaps others) apply to this case. The problem is that we do not know the proper description or rule. If we cannot identify the single relevant personal rule, we will not be able to decide how to act ethically because we will not know what rule to examine to see if it can be willed to be a moral law. If we cannot do this, we will not obtain help in solving the relevant moral problem. Although this is a serious criticism, the theory would still work in areas where there is no question about the correct description of the action. This criticism shows that the theory will have only limited success as an ethical theory.

## Conflicting Moral Laws

One way to solve the problem of not being able to identify a single description and rule is to declare that several descriptions and rules are relevant to any action. This, however, creates a new dilemma, the problem of conflicting moral laws. Suppose a person could will both of these rules to be moral laws: (1) It is unethical to steal, and (2) Persons ought to try to save the lives of innocent persons. In a case where children are starving and the only way to get food is by theft, which rule should we follow? Kantian theory does not provide the means to allow us to rank moral laws; hence, we will not know what is the ethical thing to do. In fact, even if there could be a legitimate ranking of moral laws, this would not be sufficient. There might be cases where we would have a conflict between a very serious violation of a less important moral law and a minor violation of a more important law.[2] Once again, the theory provides no way to resolve this problem. If persons do not know which rule to follow, they will not have help in solving moral problems. To the extent that conflicting rules arise, Kantian ethics will not be a successful ethical theory.

## Exceptions to Moral Laws

The third main difficulty with Kantian ethics is connected to the idea that Kantians allow no exceptions to moral laws. Using Kantian ethics, there can be no exceptions to legitimate moral laws because we must be consistent and treat persons as moral equals. Kant thought, for example, that persons should never lie, even if a lie might prevent someone from being hurt or even killed. This might seem ridiculous, but we must remember that Kantians are not concerned with consequences. They endorse respect for the moral law, not maximum benefit. When we disregard consequences, what could possibly motivate us to break our moral rule and lie? This aspect of the theory seems rigid and inflexible. If there can be no compromises, Kantian theory will not help us to solve many real moral problems.

In connection to this problem, there is a potential solution that Kantians could offer. They could claim that although moral laws need to be followed without exceptions there is no reason moral laws cannot have exceptions built into them. An example of such a rule might be: It is unethical to steal the property of others except when stealing is the only way to save the lives of innocent people. The only difficulty with this solution is that the exception built into the rule would have to be motivated by considerations related either to consistency or moral equality, and not to consequences. We might argue that we could incorporate this exception about saving the lives of innocent people by stealing into the previous law out of respect for the moral equality of those people whose lives are in danger. Unfortunately, while respecting the moral equality of the people whose lives are in danger, we are not respecting the moral equality of the people from whom we are stealing. A main problem with these exceptions to the rules is that they bring us back to the problem of conflicting moral laws. Why is it more important, based on Kantian ethics, to respect moral equality related to life than moral equality connected to property? Without some policy concerning the relative moral value of ethical laws, this strategy is doomed to fail. Once again, we see a criticism that leads to the conclusion that Kantian ethical theory will be only partially successful in helping us solve ethical problems.

These three problems with Kantian ethics have led many moral philosophers to reject it. Others, however, insist that Kant's work is the most important in the history of ethics and that the theory is the best one we have.


## Conclusion

The Kantian approach to ethics has been very influential. Many persons intuitively believe in the moral law and find acting from respect for that law compelling. Also, most people believe moral equality is an important element in ethics, and no ethical theory takes a stronger position on moral equality than Kantian ethics. Using the formulations of the Categorical Imperative, Kantian ethical theory identifies ethical guidelines, argues that these guidelines are better than those produced by other theories, and distinguishes guidelines that would prevent the unlimited pursuit of self-interest. Thus, it satisfies the first three criteria for a successful ethical theory.

The problems with Kantian ethics relate to the fourth criterion, that the theory must produce effective solutions to ethical problems. One problem with Kantian theory is related to the correct descriptions for actions. This is a serious problem although it is hard to determine how serious it is. To what extent do people disagree on what constitutes lying, theft, breaking promises, and so on? If the degree of disagreement is great, then Kantian ethics will not be very effective at all. The second problem—the inability to resolve conflicting moral laws—is probably the most serious and may be an adequate reason to reject the theory. Many serious moral issues—abortion, gun control, drug testing—involve such conflicts. These are the issues with which we need the most help, and Kantian theory is not equipped to provide that assistance. The third problem with allowing no exceptions to moral laws is a serious one for people who believe effective solutions can never be merely a matter of following rules. They require a more flexible theory that will consider exceptions to basic moral rules. Therefore, although Kantian ethical theory satisfies the first three criteria for a successful ethical theory, it has problems producing effective solutions to moral problems. Based on the criteria from Chapter 1, Kantian ethical theory is only partially successful as an ethical theory.

What are we to conclude about the partially successful Kantian ethical theory and the ethical insight related to it? Should we reject it as we rejected divine command theory, ethical relativism, ethical egoism, and emotivism? Kantian ethical theory seems stronger than these others and should not be rejected unless we can find a better theory. In the eighteenth and nineteenth centuries, a group of moral philosophers, called utilitarians, did believe they had an ethical theory superior to Kant's. In the next chapter, we will look at this utilitarian theory. It takes a completely different approach to ethics and avoids the problems that plague the Kantian view. Utilitarianism examines the actual consequences of actions to determine whether they are good or evil. Perhaps you will agree with the utilitarians that their ethical theory is superior to Kant's.


QUESTIONS FOR REVIEW

*Here are some questions to help you review the main concepts in this chapter.*

1. What is the basic ethical insight connected to Kantian ethical theory?

2. How do moral laws and conditional rules function differently?

3. What are the two formulations of the Kantian ethical standard or Categorical Imperative? Do you think they are really saying the same thing, or do they have an important difference? Support your answer.

4. In general, how are persons to know what personal rules they should will to be moral laws?

5. Identify one potential rule that Kantians would reject, and explain why they would do so.

6. Identify one specific rule that Kantians would will to be a moral law, and explain why they would do so.

7. In your opinion, what is the most significant strength of Kantian ethical theory? Support your answer.

8. How do Kantians differentiate between what is and what is not morally significant?

9. What position do Kantians take on aspects of the traditional ethical assumptions?

10. What view does Kantian ethical theory take on each of the four ethical themes?

11. Identify one similarity and two differences between Kantian ethical theory and ethical egoism.

12. What do you think is the most significant problem with Kantian ethical theory? Support your answer.

13. Is Kantian ethical theory a successful ethical theory based on the criteria from Chapter 1? Support your answer.

## NOTES

1. A primary source for Kant's ideas on ethics is Immanuel Kant, *Groundwork of the Metaphysics of Morals,* translated by H. J. Paton (New York: Harper & Row, 1964).

2. This second aspect of the problem with conflicting moral laws, that even with a ranking there would still be a serious difficulty, was mentioned by one of the reviewers of the first edition of this text.

# Chapter 6

# Act and Rule Utilitarianism

In most cases, human beings seem to have no trouble making moral evaluations or judgments. Every day people do things we easily classify as morally good or bad. When I read in the newspaper that a woman has been violently raped and murdered, I do not have to consult the moral law to conclude that the act is evil. The woman has been harmed and killed, and that is sufficient for me. The ease with which we make most moral judgments seems to conflict with the abstract, complicated, and problematic nature of Kantian ethics. The approach to ethics considered in this chapter, utilitarianism, can perhaps better explain the ease with which most moral judgments are made. Utilitarianism may also be more effective at providing guidance on the difficult moral issues where Kantian ethics suffers from the problems of accurate descriptions for actions and conflicting moral laws.

Utilitarianism can explain how people reach their everyday moral conclusions because it is an ethical theory that focuses on harm and benefit or happiness and unhappiness to morally significant beings. The theory is related to the ethical insight that *an action is morally bad if it harms someone, whereas it is morally good if it helps or benefits someone.* Many people think about good and bad in this way. When you consider whether or not to do something that will affect others, do you think about whether anyone will be harmed or helped by your action? If you do, then utilitarianism may appeal to you.

When we focus on the harm and benefit or happiness and unhappiness produced by our actions, we are looking at the results or consequences of those actions. Ethical theories that claim that good and evil are related to consequences or results are called *consequentialist theories.* Utilitarianism is a consequentialist ethical theory that provides a means to evaluate actions.

## Act Utilitarianism and Ethical Egoism

Ethical egoism, another consequentialist ethical theory, was discussed in Chapter 4. Both ethical egoism and utilitarianism are consequentialist theories and both could relate to the previous insight, but it is important to clearly differentiate between them. The crucial differences concern the objective the theory assigns to the moral agent and their respective views of good and bad. Ethical egoism states that moral agents should act in their own self-interest and maximize net benefit for themselves. What is good is what produces a net benefit for a particular individual; what is bad is what produces a net harm to the individual. In contrast, utilitarianism claims that moral agents should maximize net benefit for the greatest number of morally significant beings affected by a certain action. As a utilitarian, I cannot merely act in my own self-interest; I must consider everyone who will be benefited or harmed. What is good is what promotes more benefit than harm for the morally significant beings affected; what is bad is what promotes more harm than benefit for the morally significant beings affected. The utilitarian position, and the difference between it and ethical egoism, will become even clearer in the remainder of this chapter.

## Utilitarianism

Utilitarianism was popularized by two British thinkers, Jeremy Bentham (1748–1832) and John Stuart Mill (1806–1873).[1] They centered their ideas on a common principle: *What is good is what tends to produce a net utility for the persons affected.* The word "utilitarianism" comes from the idea of "utility," which roughly means usefulness. Bentham defines it more precisely:

> By utility is meant the property in any object, whereby it tends to produce benefit, advantage, pleasure, good, or happiness (all this in the present case comes to the same thing) or (what comes again to the same thing) to prevent the happening of mischief, pain, evil, or unhappiness to the party whose interest is considered.[2]

In place of "utility," Bentham primarily uses the term "pleasure," whereas Mill mostly employs the term "happiness," but the two formulations are similar in that both Bentham and Mill thought that pleasure was the essential component of happiness. Both philosophers would have accepted the idea that good was what promoted more pleasure or happiness than pain or unhappiness for the persons affected.

This chapter will discuss both versions of utilitarianism. Bentham's view illustrates a theory called act utilitarianism. Mill's view adapts Bentham's ideas in two primary ways. Although Mill joins Bentham in being concerned with the quantity of pleasure, Mill adds the idea of the quality of pleasure to his utilitarian view. The other main difference is that Mill is more concerned than Bentham with moral rules. Recently some moral philosophers have argued that Mill was a rule utilitarian, whereas Bentham was an act utilitarian. Although there is agreement on the claim about Bentham, the assertion about Mill remains controversial. The subtleties of interpreting the ideas of these famous philosophers is beyond the scope of this book. Thus, this chapter will be limited to a discussion of some of Mill's statements about moral rules, and I will use these statements as a stepping stone to a description of the rule utilitarian position.

## Jeremy Bentham and Act Utilitarianism

Jeremy Bentham begins *An Introduction to the Principles of Morals and Legislation* by declaring that people are governed by two masters, pleasure and pain. In general, human beings are subject to pleasure and pain and desire pleasure while avoiding pain. In addition to observing this fact, Bentham goes on to assert that pleasure and pain or happiness and unhappiness are the only concepts that can give meaning to moral good and bad. His ethical standard could be phrased as follows: *Actions are good and bad according to the tendency they have to augment or diminish the pleasure or happiness of the parties whose interests are in question.* The only actions that one ought to perform are those that are in accord with this principle. According to Bentham, connecting "ought" to pleasure or happiness is the only way that "ought" can gain a legitimate moral meaning. Bentham did not claim that he could definitively prove that pleasure and happiness were the source of moral goodness and obligation; he merely insisted that this standard was better than any alternative one.

Bentham claimed that it could not be conclusively proven that happiness was the source of moral goodness. One explanation, however, for Bentham's identification of happiness as the source of goodness is as follows. We might assert that happiness is the ultimate end of all our activities and that we should use whatever is the ultimate end of all our activities as our standard of ethical evaluation. Some of our goals have *instrumental value;* that is, they are a means to achieve other goals. I may want to do well on a test so I can earn a good grade in a course. The good grade on the test is a *means* to achieve the *end* of the good grade in the course. The good grade in the course is a means to a further end— graduating from college with a superior grade point average. Graduating from college with a superior grade point average may be a means to the end of getting a well-paying job, and getting a well-paying job may be the means to obtain money. The money allows me to buy a house, a car, and other possessions. It allows me to take vacations and so on. Why do I want these possessions and vacations? They are the means to happiness—but why do I want to be happy? I believe I am better off when I am happy than when I am unhappy. The whole chain ultimately ends with happiness and the idea that happiness is best for us. Philosophers would say that whatever lies at the end of the chain possesses *intrinsic value*. Bentham's idea could be interpreted as claiming that happiness has intrinsic value and that we should use whatever has intrinsic value to ethically evaluate our actions and beliefs.

Bentham uses the term "happiness" at times and "pleasure" at others. In his definition of "utility," he also mentions "benefit." There are advantages and disadvantages to all of these terms. Utilitarianism needs a concept that will accomplish three main things. First, it must provide a content for "good" and "bad" that will be open to observation and calculation. Second, the concept must provide a common denominator for different moral matters. There will be no Kantian problem with conflicting moral laws because all competing moral claims will be able to be translated into the common denominator of happiness, pleasure, or benefit. Finally, the theory requires a concept that includes everything of intrinsic value. "Pleasure" seems to be the most narrow and definite term, and this has the advantage of making it seem the easiest to observe and calculate. The fact that it is narrow, however, suggests that it leaves out a lot of what is really valuable. "Happiness" appears broader, so it probably leaves out less of intrinsic value but will be harder to observe and calculate. "Benefit" may be the widest term and would seem to contain everything of ultimate value, yet it may be the hardest to observe and calculate.[3] In this chapter, "happiness" will be used most often, but "pleasure" and "benefit" will be used at times. Remember that all of these terms refer to the same basic concept: whatever is of ultimate or intrinsic value for persons.

Bentham focuses on individual actions. An action is good if it produces more happiness or pleasure than unhappiness or pain for everyone affected by it. He is primarily interested in the quantitative aspects of pleasure and pain. It does not matter if the action involves reading poetry, playing chess, eating chocolate ice cream, or watching game shows on television. All that matters is the amount of pleasure and pain produced by the action. The moral agent should sum up the value of all the pleasures to all the people involved and then add all the pains to everyone affected. If there is a greater amount of pleasure, then the act is good; if the pain is greater, it is bad. Thus, the essential elements for Bentham are the focus on specific actions and the contrasting quantities of pleasure and pain to those affected.

The assumption made by Bentham is that all people calculate pleasure and pain or happiness and unhappiness. Some do it consciously, others unconsciously. Some calculate carefully, others carelessly. Obviously, Bentham felt that conscious and careful calculation were superior. He also rejected ethical egoism wherein people calculate only the effects on themselves. He argued that an action was only ethical if there was more pleasure than pain after everyone affected had been considered.

Whose pleasure and pain must be taken into account when we are trying to act ethically? In Chapter 1, the term "morally significant beings" was used to identify those beings who ought to be given ethical consideration. Bentham observed that traditionally only human beings, and at one time only adult male human beings, were regarded to be full-status morally significant beings. In contrast to this view, he thought that any being who could experience pain and pleasure must be considered. This would presumably include, at least, all mammals because they have nervous systems like ours and experience pain and pleasure. Peter Singer, a contemporary act utilitarian, claims that the capacity to have interests is the crucial criterion, although he adds that "The capacity for suffering and enjoying things is a prerequisite for having interests at all, a condition that must be satisfied before we can speak of interests in any meaningful way."[4] Singer adds that sentience is enough to make a being worthy of equal consideration of interests, so his position may not be very different from Bentham's.[5] Singer would also presumably include all mammals as morally significant beings, although he argues that a stronger case can be made for some of them such as chimpanzees, gorillas, and orangutans.

## Act Utilitarian Calculations

Bentham assumed that happiness or what benefits people is a good thing and that unhappiness or what harms people is bad. On that basis, he claimed that people ought to maximize pleasure, happiness, and benefit and minimize pain, unhappiness, and harm for as many morally significant beings as possible. To discover actions that produce a net pleasure, happiness, or benefit, this ethical theory utilizes calculations of benefits against harms, benefits against alternative benefits, and harms against alternative harms.

Here is a simplified example of act utilitarian ethical evaluation, although it will make more sense if the term "benefit" is substituted for "pleasure" or "happiness" and "harm" replaces "pain" or "unhappiness." Benefit and harm are superior because they are more general words and can cover a wider variety of things.

Suppose that a management team decides not to upgrade the safety of a new model of automobile by adding a certain part that would provide greater protection for the fuel tank. If they do not add the part, they believe they will save money. Because they want to make as much money as possible, they decide not to add the part. As time goes by, people are killed in low-speed accidents who would not have been killed if the part had been added.

Years later we might look back on that decision and its consequences to determine if the decision was ethical. First, we would identify the significant consequences and divide them into harms and benefits. The significant benefits were that the company saved about eighteen million dollars during the six years that the car remained unaltered. The company also was able to save the one million dollars it would have cost to alter the assembly lines so that the part could have been added. A final benefit is that each car was finished two minutes faster than if the part had been included, which meant that over the years more cars were built. Assume that this produced another two million dollars in profits. The significant harms were that, during the six years, thirty people were killed in low-speed crashes who would have survived if the part had been added. Another sixty people were seriously injured or burned. The relatives and friends of the victims suffered because of the deaths and injuries. Fifty vehicles were destroyed by fire. The company spent fifty million dollars to settle lawsuits connected to the deaths and injuries. The company's reputation was temporarily damaged, and it lost five million dollars in profits because of the lower sales associated with their poor reputation.

After identifying the consequences, we would try to decide whether the benefits outweigh the harms or vice versa. In this case, it is easy to see that the harms outweigh the benefits: The company lost more money than it saved, people were killed and injured, their friends and families suffered, vehicles were destroyed, and the company's reputation was damaged. There is nothing on the benefit side to outweigh these consequences. Therefore, a utilitarian would conclude that it was unethical for the managers to decide not to upgrade the safety of the fuel system.

This sample of a utilitarian analysis is incomplete and simplistic, but a more complete treatment would reach the same conclusion. According to Bentham, a complete utilitarian analysis would have to look beyond the obvious harms and benefits. Bentham discusses seven aspects of a utilitarian evaluation: intensity, duration, certainty, propinquity, fecundity, purity, and extent. This procedure is sometimes called the "utilitarian calculus" or "hedonistic calculus."

First, the agent must consider the intensity or significance of the harms and benefits, which I did to some extent in the example. The deaths were a very significant occurrence, and it would require a lot of benefit to outweigh them. Mill suggests that the more significant aspect when we weigh the significance of competing benefits or harms is the one that a competent agent would prefer. Contrary to Mill, one might also argue that the significance is inherent in the benefits and harms. This controversy did not arise in the automobile example because it was clear that the harms outweighed the benefits.

Second, the duration of each harm and benefit must be considered. A minor pain that lasts for years is more of a harm than a serious pain that is over in a couple of seconds. In my example, the deaths had the consequences of greatest duration because these people were deprived of lives that might have lasted many years. None of the other factors were that far-reaching.

A third factor mentioned by Bentham is certainty: the certainty that the consequences we anticipate will follow from the action actually do so. In the automobile example, I was looking back on this action with something approaching total knowledge. Certainty was not an important factor because I was certain about all the occurrences. I did not have to predict the consequences; I knew what they were.

A fourth consideration is what Bentham called propinquity. How remote is the harm or benefit? How soon will we experience the consequences? Bentham thought that an immediate harm was worse than one that would not happen for a long time. Once again, because I was looking back at the management decision, this aspect is not vital.

A fifth factor is the fecundity of the consequences; that is, how likely is it that the action will produce future benefits? An action that will promote future benefits is better than one that will not do so. Because the decision about the automobiles took place in the past and no further consequences would result from it, there are no future benefits.

A sixth factor is the purity of the consequences. How likely is it that the action will produce future harm? In my example, future harm was not relevant because I had already identified all the harms that had occurred over time.

The last factor is the extent or number of people affected by the harms and benefits. In the management case, I tried to identify the extent of the consequences by considering all the people who were affected.

Although act utilitarianism grows out of a relatively simple insight about benefit and harm, it becomes complicated when we try to identify all of the consequences connected to an action and all of the morally significant beings affected by it. Utilitarian calculations are often difficult to carry out. In some cases, they can be performed completely. In other cases, such as the automobile example, we can produce a reasonable conclusion with which most people would agree. In still other cases, we will probably not be able to determine the consequences and affected persons with sufficient accuracy.

# Justification for the Ethical Standard and Strengths of the Theory

Bentham's version of utilitarianism has a number of strengths. This section discusses those strengths and related justifications for using his ethical standard. A later section investigates problems with act utilitarianism.

## A Clear Content for Ethics

Bentham thought that act utilitarianism would make ethics more scientific. It would provide a clear content—pain and pleasure—for good and bad. This content would enable the determination of good and bad in a straightforward way using the utilitarian calculus. This clear content also provides a common denominator for different moral matters. There will be no Kantian problem with conflicting moral laws because all competing moral claims will be able to be translated into the common denominator of happiness, pleasure, or benefit. This clear content is one of the justifications for using this ethical standard and a related strength of the act utilitarian theory. Act utilitarianism's clear content makes it seem simpler to understand, to use, and at least in one way less problematic than Kantian ethical theory.

## Responding to the Situation of the Agent

A second justification for the standard and a related strength of the theory is that the ethical theory responds to the particular situation faced by the moral agent. Ethics is not a matter of following abstract and general rules without exceptions, but instead investigates the actual situation in which the moral agent finds himself or herself. Many people seem more comfortable with an ethical theory that allows them to evaluate each action separately. They do not want to be compelled to follow general moral rules without exceptions. Thus, this is a strength of the theory and a reason for using Bentham's ethical standard.

## Consistency with the Basic Objective of Human Beings

A third justification for the standard and related strength of the theory is that the theory appears to be consistent with the basic objective of human beings. As a general observation, it does seem accurate that persons seek pleasure, happiness, and whatever benefits them. People differ in many ways, but they have this in common: They all want to be happy. It is reasonable to connect moral good and bad to what is sought by everyone. The controversial step is the one from the individual's happiness being the source of moral good to the greatest happiness of the greatest number of people being the source of moral good. If people want to live together successfully, however, they should take this step.

There are some significant strengths to Bentham's act utilitarian position but also some problems connected to it that will be discussed in a later section. Some contemporary philosophers have endorsed the act utilitarian position, but as will be discussed later, it competes for adherents with another version of utilitarianism called rule utilitarianism.

## Determining Morally Significant Actions

The third thing we have been looking for in an ethical theory is a means of separating morally significant actions from those that are not morally significant. Whatever produces significant pleasure or pain, happiness or unhappiness, or benefit or harm for a morally significant being and is brought about by a moral agent is morally significant. Matters that have no significant pleasure or pain, happiness or unhappiness, or benefit or harm are not morally significant. In an effort to better understand act utilitarianism, the next two sections relate it to the traditional ethical assumptions and the themes related to good and bad.

## Act Utilitarianism and the Traditional Ethical Assumptions

Act utilitarianism accepts the traditional ethical assumptions. First, ethics is rational; we can use reason to reach theoretical and practical conclusions about ethics. We can provide reasons related to pleasure and pain, happiness and unhappiness, and benefit and harm to support our ethical evaluations and our solutions to moral problems, and these reasons and solutions can be evaluated. Some reasons and solutions will be better than others. Moral agents can use their rational considerations about pleasure and pain, happiness and unhappiness, and benefit and harm to guide their actions. Finally, act utilitarians believe people who share an ethical framework can discuss moral problems and arrive at mutually acceptable solutions.

Second, act utilitarians endorse the view that all persons (full-status morally significant beings) are moral equals and should be treated impartially. They treat persons impartially because identical benefits count the same no matter who is the beneficiary: a benefit to a stranger counts as much as a benefit to a family member, or even to you. Act utilitarians must maximize benefit for the greatest number of morally significant beings. When they are doing this, all people are moral equals.

This means that there may be times when to be ethical you must act contrary to your own self-interest. Think about the CD example from Chapter 1. I wanted to buy a few new CDs for my collection, but I already have a couple hundred of them. Instead of buying the CDs, I could donate the money to a legitimate charity that would use it to cure some people from potentially fatal diseases. I may want to buy the CDs, but the ethical thing to do is to donate the money to the charity. The benefit of saving the lives will outweigh the pleasure I get from listening to the CDs. I must remember that even though the sick people are strangers they are my moral equals. Therefore, if I want to be moral, I should help them.

Finally, act utilitarianism accepts the idea of universalizing ethical judgments. As in the CD example, if it is ethical for me to donate the money to a legitimate charity, then it is the ethical thing for anyone to do in a sufficiently similar situation. A "sufficiently similar situation" is sufficiently similar with respect to net harm and benefit. Assuming that we can identify sufficiently similar situations, we can universalize our ethical judgments.

## Act Utilitarianism and the Basic Ethical Themes

Act utilitarianism has a position on each of the four basic ethical themes discussed in Chapter 1. The first theme is represented by this question: *What kind of moral guidelines makes something good or bad: subjective, relative, or objective ones?* Act utilitarians believe the source of legitimate moral guidelines is objective considerations of fact; that is, facts about pleasure and pain, happiness and unhappiness, or benefit and harm. Thus, act utilitarians endorse objective guidelines. Individual actions or groups of related actions that cause more net harm than benefit are objectively evil. For example, the murder of millions of Jews and other people by the Nazis during the thirties and forties was objectively evil because the harm of murdering these innocent people far outweighed any benefits for the Nazis.

Another significant theme in ethics is indicated by this question: *What makes something good or evil; is it the consequences that are produced or the reasoning that led up to it?* Utilitarians are ethical consequentialists who believe the goodness or badness of something is a result of the consequences that are brought about by it. The reasoning is secondary for a utilitarian; our reasons are good if we intend to bring about beneficial consequences. However, an action that was meant to benefit someone might turn out to be bad if it actually causes harm.

The third theme relates to this question: *Should we faithfully follow general rules of behavior, or should we separately evaluate each action and belief?* In theory, act utilitarians evaluate each action separately, but they point out that there are classes of actions wherein the harm or benefit might always outweigh any other factor. For example, rape would always seem to cause more harm than benefit. We do not have to recalculate every case of rape. Sometimes the verdict of human experience is so clear that we know the answer without actually doing the calculation. In relation to such classes of actions, utilitarians could save time by making use of ethical rules. Of course, act utilitarians should always be open to the possibility of an exception to the rule if in a particular case disregarding the rule maximized net benefit. There might be cases where it is ethical to kill, steal, lie, cheat, or break promises (for example, if keeping a promise to someone would cause that person great harm). The ultimate focus for act utilitarians is on specific actions, but they can use rules as timesaving devices.

The fourth theme is connected to the proper focus of ethical attention: *Should the group, community, or majority of persons be the focus of ethics or should the focus be on the individual?* Utilitarians believe the focus of ethics should be the greatest good for the greatest number of people. In some cases, utilitarians would sacrifice the individual for the greater good of the group because the good of the larger number of persons outweighs the good of the individual. We believe automobiles are an ethical product for a business to produce even though thousands of individuals are killed in automobile accidents each year. The enormous benefit of automobiles outweighs the deaths of these people. Act utilitarianism focuses on the group, not the individual, and promotes the greatest good or benefit for the greatest number of people.

## Contrasting Act Utilitarianism with Kantian Ethical Theory

Act utilitarianism has some similarities to and some differences from Kantian ethical theory (see Appendix 1). The basic ethical guideline identified by act utilitarianism is the utilitarian principle that actions are good and bad according to the tendency they have to augment or diminish the happiness of the parties whose interests are in question. Kantian theory uses the two forms of the Categorical Imperative and concentrates on acting from respect for the moral law. Act utilitarianism and Kantian ethical theory both accept all of the traditional ethical assumptions: rationality, impartiality, and universalizability. The two theories also agree on the first ethical theme. They both claim that legitimate moral guidelines are based on objective considerations. Act utilitarianism, however, bases moral guidelines on objective considerations of fact (pleasure, pain, happiness, and so forth), whereas Kantian ethical theory bases moral guidelines on objective considerations of reason. The theories diverge on the other ethical themes. Act utilitarianism focuses on consequences, whereas Kantian ethical theory concentrates on the reasoning that precedes the action. Act utilitarianism relates good and bad to specific actions, whereas Kantian ethical theory connects good and bad to following general rules without exceptions. Finally, act utilitarianism relates good and bad to the group, whereas Kantian ethical theory centers on the individual. Act utilitarianism does not have the problems Kantian ethical theory does, but as will be discussed in the next section, it has its own set of problems.

## Problems with Act Utilitarianism

Act utilitarianism does a reasonable job of satisfying the first three criteria for a successful ethical theory. It identifies the utilitarian principle as the basic ethical guideline and asserts that this guideline is better than others. This ethical guideline would prohibit the unlimited pursuit of self-interest. Although act utilitarianism satisfies the first three criteria for a successful ethical theory, it has difficulty with criterion four: the theory must produce effective solutions to ethical problems. I will discuss several of the problems connected to act utilitarianism and relate them to criterion four. The focus will then shift to John Stuart Mill's version of utilitarianism.

### Doing the Calculations

The first problem with act utilitarianism is the difficulty connected to doing the utilitarian calculations. If we cannot successfully complete the calculations, the theory cannot help us to effectively solve ethical problems. This problem with the calculations has three main aspects.

First, it is difficult to identify all the consequences of an action. An accurate utilitarian analysis must go beyond the immediate consequences and find all the results. This is a difficult undertaking. Short-range consequences can be difficult to identify, and long-range consequences are even harder to identify, especially when you are trying to predict them before the action has occurred. In the automobile example described earlier, we were looking back over time and therefore could identify the results with some accuracy. If we had to try to judge in advance whether the act was ethical, it would be much harder because we would have to predict future consequences. With accurate and extensive information, we can make reasonable predictions about the future, but such predictions are never guaranteed to be correct. In addition, how can we be sure we have extended our search for consequences far enough into the future? Assume that there is a great public outcry after the deaths and injuries related to not improving the safety of the automobile. The public begins to put pressure on legislators to improve automobile safety, and legislators apply pressure on the National Highway and Traffic Safety Administration (NHTSA). After a year of study, the NHTSA issues a regulation to prevent this kind of safety problem in the future. Is this a consequence of the decision of the managers not to improve the safety of their automobiles? If so, does it change our ethical evaluation of that case? This question would be difficult to answer in a satisfactory way. An ethical theory should help us to solve moral problems, but sometimes difficulties with doing the calculations will interfere with act utilitarianism accomplishing this objective.

The second aspect of the problem is that it is difficult to weigh pleasures and pains, happiness and unhappiness, or harms and benefits when they are very different kinds of things. Imagine that a NHTSA mandated safety feature for automobiles will save twenty lives a year but cost U.S. car buyers one hundred million dollars. How do we weigh twenty lives against one hundred million dollars? We place a high value on human life, but is it worth five million dollars to save a life? Perhaps we really cannot even make a reasonable judgment about this matter unless we know what would be done with the one hundred million dollars. If people will spend it to improve their lives, will they improve them sufficiently to balance the loss of twenty lives? Utilitarians depend on calculations, but the elements that must be weighed are sometimes impossible to compare. Once again, this factor will make it hard to solve some ethical problems.

The final aspect of the problem is less serious than the others and would not even occur if the act utilitarian primarily relied on the time-saving rules mentioned earlier. Without these rules, act utilitarians would have to spend a lot of their time identifying and weighing pleasures, pains, harms, and benefits. The utilitarian calculations might take up an enormous amount of our time, making solving ethical problems very time-consuming. This difficulty, coupled with the previous two aspects of the problem, suggests that act utilitarian theory will only be partially successful at meeting criterion four. In relatively simple and clear-cut cases, we will be able to do the calculations, but in other cases, we will encounter trouble.

### Results Contrary to Moral Intuitions

Another serious problem, also relating to criterion four, is that act utilitarianism produces a variety of results that are contrary to many people's moral intuitions. People normally think that stealing, cheating, breaking promises, and killing innocent people are all wrong. Act utilitarianism, however, would justify these actions in certain situations where performing them would produce more benefit than harm. This seems misguided to many people because they think these actions should always be unethical. An even more serious problem for many thinkers is that act utilitarianism focuses on the majority or group and is willing to sacrifice a minority if it would bring about the greatest good of the greatest number of people. This seems intuitively wrong to many people. Why should it be ethical to allow some people to be harmed or killed to benefit a greater number of other people? This practice would be particularly disturbing should you be a member of the minority that is being sacrificed. It might balance out if sometimes you were part of the majority and were benefited and at other times were part of the minority and were harmed. However, it is also possible that you might always end up in the minority; thus, you would always suffer harm to benefit the majority. It seems intuitively wrong that some minority should always be sacrificed for the good of the majority. To cite a complicated and controversial example, many people think the U.S. government was wrong to kill and seriously injure about two hundred thousand civilians at Hiroshima and Nagasaki to hasten the end of World War II and make an Allied invasion of Japan unnecessary. Most people would agree that it is ethical to kill combatants in a war (and it may even be fair or just to kill noncombatants, such as munitions factory workers, who are directly supporting the war effort), but it is unethical to kill noncombatants or civilians (who are not directly supporting the war effort). Many Japanese civilians in these cities, especially children and elderly people, had no role in supporting the war effort, and it was wrong to kill them. The critics of the U.S. action would argue that the bombs should have been dropped elsewhere or not at all. Thus, some thinkers believe utilitarianism is a poor moral theory, charging that it does not really treat persons as moral equals because it is willing to sacrifice some of them for the benefit of others. Because of these various results inconsistent with people's moral intuitions, some philosophers claim that act utilitarianism is not really helping us to solve ethical problems in an effective manner.

## Moral Luck

The final problem undercuts the ability of act utilitarianism to help us solve ethical problems. If good and evil depend on the consequences of an action, then the ability to perform good actions is not totally in the control of the moral agent. An element of luck enters the moral realm.[6] Imagine that I send a check to a charity but that the check is permanently lost in the mail. No beneficial consequences resulted from my action, and therefore the action was not good. In a sense, my bad luck prevented me from performing a good action. When I realize that the check has never been cashed, I can cancel it and send another one—but that is a different check and a different action. Many philosophers believe the ability to perform good actions should be completely in the control of the moral agent; they reject consequentialist theories for this reason. This problem relates to the fourth criterion for evaluating ethical theories. When I mailed my check, I thought I had solved my ethical problem. I had given money to charity and had done the ethical thing. It turns out that I had not really solved the problem in the way that I thought; I had not done anything ethical. Because consequences can never be guaranteed beforehand, utilitarian theory does not always help us to effectively solve ethical problems.

These problems with act utilitarianism have led many moral philosophers to reject this theory. However, many of them are not satisfied with Kantian ethics either. Some of these thinkers have turned to rule utilitarianism as a way to get the best of both act utilitarianism and Kantian ethics. Before rule utilitarianism is discussed, however, it is important to understand John Stuart Mill's version of utilitarianism and his ideas on the quality of pleasures and moral rules.

## Mill's Utilitarianism

John Stuart Mill starts off his moral theory in a way that is very similar to Bentham by claiming that an ultimate ethical principle could act as the foundation for moral guidelines. According to Mill:

> The creed which accepts as the foundation of morals "utility" or the "greatest happiness principle" holds that actions are right in proportion as they tend to promote happiness; wrong as they tend to produce the reverse of happiness. By happiness is intended pleasure and the absence of pain; by unhappiness, pain and the privation of pleasure.[7]

Thus, Mill's formulation of the utilitarian ethical standard is that *actions are good in proportion to which they tend to promote happiness and bad as they tend to produce unhappiness.* He has arrived at this position in the same basic way that it was speculated Bentham did. Mill argues that all action is undertaken for the sake of some end. Although there may be many intermediate ends for our actions, ultimately all action is designed to produce happiness or avoid unhappiness. Happiness is the only ultimate end and should be the foundation of moral goodness. For Mill, the source of moral goodness is not connected to what people ought to desire but simply to what they do desire. His justification comes from looking at what people do, and he claims that no other justification would be more convincing.

Mill claims that actions are right in proportion as they tend to promote happiness. Part of what he means is that the more happiness or the more unhappiness prevention associated with an action, the better it is. This idea of quantity of desirable ends was the only important one for Bentham. Mill, however, is equally concerned with the quality of the pleasure. He uses "pleasure" because he associates pleasure and the absence of pain with happiness. He says,

> If I am asked what I mean by difference of quality in pleasures, or what makes one pleasure more valuable than another, merely as a pleasure, except its being greater in amount, there is but one possible answer. Of two pleasures, if there be one to which all or almost all who have experience of both give a decided preference, irrespective of any feeling of moral obligation to prefer it, that is the more desirable pleasure. If one of the two is, by those who are competently acquainted with both, placed so far above the other that they prefer it, even though knowing it to be attended with a greater amount of discontent, and would not resign it for any quantity of the other pleasure which their nature is capable of, we are justified in ascribing to the preferred enjoyment a superiority in quality so far outweighing quantity as to render it, in comparison, of small account.[8]

Mill thinks we can use human preferences to distinguish the quality of pleasures.[9] Those that are preferred are higher in quality than those that are not, and presumably the quality increases with the intensity of the preference. He also seems to claim that the quality of a pleasure is more important than its quantity. Thus, actions are good in proportion as they tend to promote pleasures of greater quantity and especially greater quality. If quantity and quality were to come in conflict, we should presumably choose quality.

Mill used this notion of quality to refute critics of Bentham's utilitarianism who had called it a philosophy suitable for pigs. Bentham's idea was that whatever produced pleasure was good. Thus, if eating chocolate or watching situation comedies on television gave more pleasure than reading Shakespeare or listening to Mozart, then it is better for you to eat chocolate or watch television. Mill thought this was mistaken. Those who had the experience of both under the right conditions would prefer the higher pleasure. He concludes, "Now it is an unquestionable fact that those who are equally acquainted with and equally capable of appreciating and enjoying both do give a marked preference to the manner of existence that employs their higher faculties."[10] Mill understands that there will be objections to this. What about people who prefer lower pleasures? Mill responds that we all have a capacity to enjoy higher things but that this capacity is easily destroyed by hostile influences, or by lack of time and opportunity. Simply because some people prefer lower pleasures does not prove that higher and lower pleasures have equal value.

Like Bentham, Mill argues that his position is not a form of egoism. The utilitarian standard seeks to promote the greatest net happiness for the greatest number of people, or as he remarks about the utilitarian ethical standard, "for that standard is not the agent's own happiness, but the greatest happiness altogether."[11] The ethical goal, therefore, is a life rich in pleasure or happiness both in point of quantity and quality for the greatest number of people. This view requires the agent to count his or her happiness no more than any other person's. Mill comments, "As between his own happiness and that of others, utilitarianism requires him to be as strictly impartial as a disinterested and benevolent spectator."[12] An ethical person should strive to maximize the happiness of the greatest number of persons, not simply his or her personal happiness.

In summary, Mill's view is that actions are good in proportion to the extent to which they tend to produce more happiness than unhappiness for the persons affected. Actions are bad in proportion to which they tend to produce more unhappiness than happiness for the persons affected. We should evaluate our conduct using considerations of the quality and the quantity of happiness/pleasure and unhappiness/pain produced. The test of quality and the way to measure it will be the preferences of those who have experienced the actions in question and are best able to make an informed comparison.

## Mill and Moral Rules

Moral rules play a much larger role in Mill's moral theory than in Bentham's. One of the contexts in which he discusses rules is in his response to the objection that utilitarianism will be too time-consuming because it will force us to evaluate every individual action. Mill points out that the history of the human species has provided us with a great deal of information about actions. People have learned about the tendencies of actions to produce happiness and unhappiness, and morality is based on this knowledge. Thus, human experience has produced moral rules that correspond to the tendencies of actions to promote happiness or unhappiness. For example, persons have realized that killing innocent people produces more unhappiness than happiness and that keeping promises is more beneficial than breaking them. Thus, we conclude that "killing innocent people is wrong" and "keeping promises is good." Mill refers to these as secondary principles or secondary moral rules. The primary moral rule is, of course, the utilitarian ethical standard. He adds, "Whatever we adopt as the fundamental principle of morality, we require subordinate principles to apply it by."[13] In his opinion, it is impossible to do without these secondary principles. He comments, "There is no case of moral obligation in which some secondary principle is not involved."[14] In light of these comments, Mill's view of moral life seems different from Bentham's. Bentham is more focused on evaluating individual actions, whereas Mill endorses following these secondary principles.

Mill realizes that secondary principles can conflict. For example, we usually agree that lying is wrong and that hurting people's feelings is wrong also. There may be times, however, when telling someone the truth might hurt the person's feelings. How do we resolve these conflicts? Mill answers that we can resolve them using the utilitarian ethical standard: "If utility is the ultimate source of moral obligations, utility may be invoked to decide between them when their demands are incompatible."[15] In fact, in the same paragraph Mill adds that it is only in cases of conflict between secondary principles that the primary moral rule needs to be invoked. Therefore, Mill believes he has avoided the Kantian problem with conflicting moral rules.

The vital issue is whether people are morally justified in making exceptions to these secondary principles. Kant's position was that no exceptions could be made to moral laws. Mill clearly appears to favor exceptions to moral rules when he states, "It is not the fault of any creed, but of the complicated nature of human affairs, that rules of conduct cannot be so framed as to require no exceptions, and that hardly any kind of action can safely be laid down as either always obligatory or always condemnable."[16] Thus, Mill seems to believe exceptions to these secondary principles are justified in some cases. A particular lie or breaking a promise might be morally justified if it maximized happiness in a significant way. Thus, exceptions to the secondary moral principles would be allowed if the exceptions are in accord with the basic utilitarian standard or principle. Of course, no exceptions to the basic utilitarian principle would be allowed. Although Mill's theory is more focused on rules than Bentham's, Mill seems willing to allow legitimate exceptions to those rules.

## Mill's Idea of Justice

Mill's discussion of justice in the last chapter of *Utilitarianism* contains a number of important additional considerations about moral rules. Here Mill introduces the idea of rights, which will be vital in Chapter 7 for the discussion of moral rights theory. Mill states:

Justice is the name for certain classes of moral rules which concern the essentials of human well-being more nearly, and are therefore of more absolute obligation, than any other rules for the guidance of life; and the notion which we have found to be of the essence of the idea of justice—that of a right residing in an individual—implies and testifies to this more binding obligation.[17]

Thus, one kind or class of moral rules is designated by the term "justice." These moral rules take the form of rights. Rights reside in persons and can be violated by the actions of others. Mill explains rights as follows, "When we call anything a person's right, we mean that he has a valid claim on society to protect him in possession of it, either by force of law or by that of education and opinion. If he has what we consider a sufficient claim, on whatever account, to have something guaranteed to him by society, we say that he has a right to it."[18] To have a right is to have something that society ought to defend.

Mill tries to differentiate the moral rules related to justice from moral rules or secondary principles in general. Both kinds of rules relate to duty, but philosophers speak of two kinds of duties. *Duties of imperfect obligation* are those in which, although the actions are obligatory, the particular occasions on which we perform them are left up to us. These are general moral rules, not examples of justice as Mill is using the term. For example, Mill thinks charity is obligatory but that we are not obligated to be charitable to any particular person at any particular time. The charitable actions we perform and when we perform them are up to us. *Duties of perfect obligation* are duties related to the rights of others and are examples of justice. If a person has a certain right, then I have a duty to respect that right. This is not a duty that allows me to choose the person, time, and place to fulfill it. I must always respect the rights of this particular person. This strong position on respecting the rights of others makes Mill look less like an act utilitarian. He is not clear, however, about whether there can be legitimate exceptions to respecting the rights of others.

Mill believes moral rights or the rules of justice are common to all human beings or moral agents; they are universal. Why should a society acknowledge and defend these supposed universal rights? Mill answers that it should do so because they promote general utility. People should realize that our security and happiness are linked to the security and happiness of other members of our society. Only a system of rights can maximize overall happiness.

At this point, it is clear that Mill thought that moral rules played a crucial role in ethics. Some philosophers believe Mill should be designated a "rule utilitarian." In a subsequent section, the rule utilitarian moral theory will be discussed. Mill, of course, did not use the phrase "rule utilitarianism" and for the purpose of this text, it is not important whether he should or should not be included under this heading. The important point is that rule utilitarianism provides an interesting alternative to act utilitarianism and Kantian ethics. Before looking at this theory, however, two problems with Mill's view ought to be mentioned.

## Two Problems with Mill's Version of Utilitarianism

There are a number of problems with Mill's version of utilitarianism. I will discuss two of them here because they were not included in the earlier section on act utilitarian problems. The first problem involves the procedure for determining good and evil in relation to the quality of pleasures. Mill thinks we can use human preferences to determine quality and, hence, good and evil. He thinks these preferences are consistent and reliable, but in some areas that view is mistaken. Human preferences are notoriously changeable. Sometimes a person prefers watching game shows on television, at other times reading a good book. People sometimes prefer the feeling of satisfaction and the knowledge that they have helped people that comes from giving to charity, and at other times they prefer the satisfaction and pleasure derived from buying luxuries for themselves or their families. Mill thinks people who have had the experience of both higher and lower pleasures will prefer the higher ones, but a more accurate appraisal is that they will sometimes prefer higher ones and at other times lower ones. People are not always constant in their preferences.

The second aspect of the first problem connected to preferences is also related to the idea that people who have been exposed to both higher and lower pleasures will prefer the higher ones. Again, this is simply not true. As evidenced by how they spend their evenings, most Americans seem to prefer television game shows or situation comedies to reading Shakespeare or listening to Mozart. Mill tries to explain this by saying that we all have a capacity to enjoy higher things but that this capacity is easily destroyed by hostile influences or by lack of time and opportunity. This is an inadequate explanation. There is no great hostility directed toward Shakespeare or Mozart, and if people have the time for television game shows or situation comedies, they have the time for higher entertainment. When the movie *Amadeus* became a hit, there was increased interest in Mozart, but this interest waned as people returned to other entertainment. A number of years ago, another popular movie, *Shakespeare in Love,* generated a lot of good publicity for the famous playwright, but the sympathetic atmosphere does not seem to have produced a greater interest in reading his plays instead of watching television. Many people who have been exposed to both simply prefer the "lower pleasures."

The third aspect of the first problem related to preferences is that it is difficult to weigh competing preferences, especially when they are very different kinds of things. This makes it difficult to know what actions are most ethical. Presumably, Mill expects us to choose between actions that satisfy competing preferences by picking the one that informed people would most prefer. How does this work in a real moral dilemma? How do you make decisions about issues like euthanasia, abortion, and gun control, or about less dramatic ones such as lying, breaking promises, and giving to charity? These things involve a wide variety of competing preferences that are sometimes very different. With regard to gun control, how do we weigh the preferences of gun owners to own guns for protection and recreation against the preferences of other people who would feel safer in a society with fewer guns? Mill gives no practical advice about how to weigh them. The general problem is that it is not clear that preferences can be used to create an effective ethical theory along the lines that Mill suggests.

The second problem is that Mill (and Bentham) cannot provide a convincing justification for why rational, self-interested persons will be motivated to substitute the greatest happiness of the majority for their own greatest happiness as their primary motivation. In other words, why will they choose to be utilitarians instead of ethical egoists? People are not merely factors in utilitarian calculations; they are autonomous, rational, self-interested beings. They usually act in their own self-interest. They may at times make sacrifices for those with whom they have close relationships, such as family members and friends. Why, however, would they sacrifice for the general well-being? We might argue that increasing the general well-being will ultimately increase personal well-being, but this is not Mill's program. Moral agents are to be motivated by the general welfare, not their personal welfare. As a practical matter, it is also probable that the best way for me to increase my personal well-being is to act so as to benefit myself directly, not to act to increase the general well-being and hope that some benefit will eventually trickle down to me. Therefore, Mill has a serious problem related to whether or not people will be motivated to act as utilitarians would have them act.

## Rule Utilitarianism

When moral philosophers understand the problems associated with act utilitarianism, some of them turn to a different form of utilitarianism, called rule utilitarianism. Rule utilitarianism does not solve all the problems with act utilitarianism, but it does seem to solve the problems of results contrary to moral intuitions and moral luck. Rule utilitarianism is also a consequentialist ethical theory, but it examines the consequences of generally following moral rules rather than focusing on the consequences of specific actions. The ethical standard for rule utilitarianism might be phrased: *It is good for persons to act from those moral rules, the general following of which would promote the greatest net benefit for the morally significant beings affected; it is bad for persons to act from rules, the general following of which would promote the greatest net harm for the morally significant beings affected.* Based on this standard, an action will be good if it follows from a legitimate moral rule that meets this standard.

Like Kantians, rule utilitarians claim that we can identify a rule to guide any morally significant action. Suppose I send some money to a charity because I believe everyone ought to help those who are less fortunate. The complete description of the action ought to include identification of the rule that guided it. For example, I performed the action—giving this money to this charity—because I thought I should act in accord with my rule: Everyone ought to help those who are less fortunate. The action will be ethical if it follows from the right kind of rule, one whose general following would maximize net benefit for those affected by the persons following it. If the general following of the rule "Everyone ought to help those who are less fortunate" would produce more net benefit than harm for those affected by persons following it, then it is a legitimate moral rule, and we should follow it if we want to be ethical. Thus, rule utilitarianism has two aspects: (1) we should determine the legitimate moral rules that maximize net benefit for those affected by the general following of them and follow these moral rules without exceptions, and (2) if contemplating whether or not to perform an action, we should do so only if it would follow from a legitimate moral rule.

Rule utilitarians must follow legitimate moral rules without exceptions or they would become act utilitarians. An exception would be a particular case where breaking the rule would maximize net benefit in that specific case. Rule utilitarians would not do this because they do not examine the consequences in particular cases. If they examined particular cases and broke their rules in every case where violating the rule would maximize net benefit, they would be no different from act utilitarians and would not be able to avoid the problems specific to act utilitarianism. Rule utilitarians do acknowledge that situations may change. When they do, new rules may be needed because following them will produce more net human benefit than following the old rules. For example, perhaps at one time the general following of the rule "It is unethical to get a divorce" maximized human benefit. If conditions become easier for divorced people (especially single parents), then a new moral rule may be necessary. The inability to make exceptions to moral rules is an essential difference between rule and act utilitarianism. As was mentioned earlier, act utilitarians can use moral rules as timesaving devices, but they must always consider the possibility that an exception will maximize net benefit.

Rule utilitarianism solves the problem with results contrary to moral intuitions because it makes cheating, stealing, and possibly even killing civilians unethical. For example, the general following of the rule "It is unethical to cheat on tests" would produce more net benefit than harm for those affected. If everyone cheats on tests, there will be an enormous amount of harm. Tests will become meaningless, and educators will lose this valuable tool for assessing students. Therefore, the rule is a legitimate moral rule, and we should follow it without exceptions. Cheating is always unethical to a rule utilitarian. Rule utilitarians do not seem to get results contrary to people's moral intuitions.

Rule utilitarianism also greatly diminishes the problem with moral luck. Luck is less of a factor in the consequences of the general following of moral rules than in specific cases. Even though my check to a charity may not get there, and hence sending the check does not produce any beneficial consequences, in general checks usually get to charities. Even with occasional bad luck, the moral rule that "It is ethical for affluent people to help those in need" would maximize net benefit and should always be followed.

Rule utilitarianism will not alleviate the first two aspects of the problem connected to difficulties with doing the calculations. In general, it will be just as difficult to identify and weigh all the consequences connected to the general following of a moral rule as it is to distinguish those resulting from a specific action. Sometimes, determining the consequences for rules may be easier than doing so for specific actions and sometimes harder. For example, it is impossible to know all the consequences of the general following of the rule "It is unethical to ever kill civilians in wartime"; we could only guess whether or not this would produce a net benefit. If it is impossible to calculate all of the consequences of some potential moral rules, then rule utilitarianism can have only limited success in helping us solve moral problems. We would not be able to determine the complete set of legitimate moral rules, but we would be able to sufficiently identify the consequences of some moral rules and evaluate them. Thus, there will be some moral rules for rule utilitarianism to use. Rule utilitarianism also does not alleviate the problem of weighing very different kinds of consequences, such as large sums of money against lives. On this issue, both versions of utilitarianism are equally problematic.

Neither will rule utilitarianism solve the two problems discussed in connection with Mill's ideas. It will not make the attempt to evaluate the quality of pleasures using human preferences any easier. It will also not make it more likely that people will be motivated by the happiness of the greatest number of persons instead of their own personal happiness. Act and rule utilitarianism face these problems equally.

Rule utilitarianism is an improvement over act utilitarianism in a couple of areas, but it is no more successful than act utilitarianism in regard to the other problems. Before we conclude that rule utilitarianism is the best version of utilitarianism, however, we must address a serious criticism act utilitarians bring against rule utilitarianism. If we are really interested in maximizing net happiness or benefit, act utilitarians claim that we would be foolish not to make an exception to a rule when that exception would maximize benefit in a specific case and have no wider implications. They consider rule utilitarians unwise for blindly following moral rules and for never being willing to consider even the most beneficial exceptions. To balance out the problems with injustice and moral luck, act utilitarians contend that their version of utilitarianism will actually produce more net benefit and less net harm.

## Conclusion

In regard to the criteria for evaluating ethical theories, act and rule utilitarianism are only partially successful ethical theories. Both theories do produce a basic ethical guideline and secondary moral guidelines. Both argue that these ethical guidelines are better than others, and both produce ethical guidelines that would prohibit the unlimited pursuit of self-interest. However, both theories encounter problems related to criterion four—that the theory must assist us in solving moral problems successfully. Act utilitarianism is faced with the problems related to results contrary to moral intuitions and moral luck. Rule utilitarianism will be charged with not really maximizing overall benefit. Both theories have problems actually doing the calculations necessary to determine good and bad. Therefore, both ethical theories will only have limited success in helping us solve ethical problems effectively. Both will probably only help us solve ethical problems in relatively simple cases.

Is either act or rule utilitarianism an improvement over Kantian ethics and the four earlier approaches to ethics? These theories do seem better than the first four approaches, but it is not clear that they are superior to Kantian ethics. Both utilitarianism and Kantian ethics satisfied the first three criteria but were unable to completely satisfy the fourth one. Therefore, we should lay them aside for the time being and turn elsewhere to see what other approaches to ethics are available.

In this chapter I briefly discussed the idea of moral rights. Some philosophers believe we can create an ethical theory based on moral rights that would do what rule utilitarianism failed to do—successfully combine the best features of Kantian ethics and act utilitarianism. In Chapter 7 I discuss moral rights theory, which some philosophers think is an improvement over both Kantian ethical theory and utilitarianism.

QUESTIONS FOR REVIEW

*Here are some questions to help you review the main concepts in this chapter.*

1. What is the ethical insight related to utilitarianism?
2. What is a crucial difference between act utilitarianism and ethical egoism?
3. What is Bentham's version of the essential principle or standard of act utilitarianism?
4. According to Bentham, what criterion should we use to determine morally significant beings?
5. What were the six most significant benefits and harms in the automobile safety case? If these were the only consequences, what ethical conclusion would you reach about the decision not to upgrade the safety of the fuel tank?
6. Discuss one justification for the utilitarian ethical standard and the related strength of the act utilitarian theory.
7. How do act utilitarians divide morally significant actions from ones that are not morally significant?
8. What position does act utilitarianism take on each of the three traditional ethical assumptions?
9. What views does act utilitarianism endorse on each of the four ethical themes?
10. Identify one similarity and two differences between act utilitarianism and Kantian ethical theory.
11. What do you think is the most significant problem with act utilitarianism? Why is act utilitarianism only a partially successful ethical theory?
12. Identify two differences between Mill's and Bentham's versions of utilitarianism. Which do you prefer? Explain why.
13. Discuss one of the additional problems with utilitarianism identified in relation to Mill's version of utilitarianism.
14. What is the ethical standard for rule utilitarianism?

15. What problems do act and rule utilitarianism share? Why does rule utilitarianism not suffer from the problems of results contrary to moral intuitions and moral luck?

16. In your opinion, which form of utilitarianism is more effective at helping us solve moral problems? Support your answer.

## NOTES

1. The most common source for Bentham's ideas about ethics is *An Introduction to the Principles of Morals and Legislation* (New York: Hafner Publishing Company, 1948). For Mill, the usual source is John Stuart Mill, *Utilitarianism* (Indianapolis, IN: Hackett Publishing Company, 1979).

2. Jeremy Bentham, *An Introduction to the Principles of Morals and Legislation*, p. 2.

3. I favor formulation of the utilitarian rule in terms of "benefit" rather than "pleasure" or "happiness" because these latter terms can lead people astray. In the ordinary sense of "pleasure" and "happiness," some things may not be pleasant or make us happy, but they may still be good. For example, learning is not always pleasant, nor does it always produce happiness, especially when we have to work very hard to acquire the knowledge. Learning, however, is often beneficial or good even if it is not pleasant. Another consideration is that some people reject the idea that pleasure is good. People sometimes pursue pleasure early in life, but then tire of it. They may then seek success, fame, or power. They may choose to serve others or to serve God in a life of self-sacrifice. They may seek knowledge or enlightenment. Ultimately, they follow the path that seems most beneficial. A key idea for act utilitarianism is that it is good to do things that make morally significant beings better off and bad to do things that make them worse off. In my opinion, "benefit" and "harm" articulate this utilitarian idea better than "pleasure" and "happiness." My version of the utilitarian principle is: What is good is what produces more benefit than harm for the morally significant beings affected; what is bad is what produces more harm than benefit for the morally significant beings affected.

4. Peter Singer, *Practical Ethics* (Cambridge, MA: Cambridge University Press, 1993), p. 57.

5. Ibid., p. 131.

6. See Bernard Williams, "Moral Luck," in *Moral Luck: Philosophical Papers, 1973–1980* (Cambridge, MA: Cambridge University Press, 1981).

7. Mill, *Utilitarianism*, p. 7.

8. Ibid., p. 8.

9. This idea of preferences has been used by some contemporary philosophers as a substitute for pleasure, happiness, or benefit. They claim that good actions provide the greatest net satisfaction of the rational preferences of persons. Sometimes the term "interests" is substituted for "preferences." Most philosophers believe this substitution is not an overall improvement. It improves some aspects while making others worse.

10. Mill, *Utilitarianism,* p. 9.
11. Ibid., p. 11.
12. Ibid., p. 16.
13. Ibid., p. 24.
14. Ibid., p. 25.
15. Ibid.
16. Ibid.
17. Ibid., p. 58.
18. Ibid., p. 52.

# Chapter 7

# *Moral Rights Theory*

Citizens of the United States are familiar with rights. The Declaration of Independence contains the idea that "all men" are endowed by God with certain "unalienable" rights and "that among these are the rights to life, liberty, and the pursuit of happiness." The United States Constitution also talks about rights in a number of areas, such as Article IX of the Bill of Rights, which says, "The enumeration in the Constitution, of certain rights, shall not be construed to deny or disparage others retained by the people." Americans are exposed to the language of rights almost constantly by media coverage of issues involving the civil rights of women, minorities, workers, and so on. International politics frequently focuses on human rights violations, with arbitrary arrests of political dissidents and mass murders of ethnic minorities being common topics. We also encounter the language of rights in discussions of ethical problems such as abortion, affirmative action, euthanasia, and gun control. Because the language of rights is so prevalent, it is important to understand it better. This chapter investigates an ethical theory centered on the idea of rights, the moral rights theory.

An important strength of Kantian ethical theory is that it considers persons as moral equals and requires that they be treated impartially. Kant also asserts that we should always treat persons as ends and never as means only. Part of the reason for this relates to reason and consistency. Another reason is that Kant believes persons have an intrinsic worth or value. For many philosophers, these ideas of the moral equality and the intrinsic value of persons are significant advantages for an ethical theory. Utilitarianism, however, has an important strength that Kantian theory lacks. Utilitarianism provides a clear content for moral good and bad. Moral rights theory is valuable because it has both of these important strengths. First, it asserts the moral equality and value of persons and requires that they be treated with respect. Second, the theory also provides a clear content for moral good and bad. The more important of these strengths is probably the assertion that persons are valuable and we should treat them with respect. Most people would intuitively agree with this idea. Therefore, the ethical insight at the heart of the moral rights theory is that *individual persons are valuable and we should act in ways that respect their value.*

## What Are Moral Rights?

If persons are valuable and if we want to be rational, we ought to act in ways that respect their value because to treat something valuable as valueless would be irrational. One way to respect the value of persons is to assert that they have *moral rights,* rights that are held by all morally significant beings.

The idea of rights was popularized during the seventeenth and eighteenth centuries by such thinkers as Thomas Hobbes and John Locke in Europe, and Thomas Paine and Thomas Jefferson in America. These thinkers referred to rights as *natural rights;* that is, rights that had been granted by God to all human beings—or at least to all adult, white, male human beings. These rights were "natural" because they were part of the nature of human beings, just as being rational was part of human nature. A *right* was considered to be the liberty to do or not do something. The right to self-preservation, for example, was the liberty to do what was necessary to defend oneself. Hobbes claimed that a right "consisteth in liberty to do or to forbear."[1] He thought of liberty as the lack of external impediments, including the lack of laws that would limit people's legitimate range of action. This notion of *liberty rights* is illustrated in Article I of the Bill of Rights of the U.S. Constitution. That article states, "Congress shall make no law respecting an establishment of religion, or prohibiting the free exercise thereof; or abridging the freedom of speech, or of the press; or the right of the people peaceably to assemble, and to petition the government for a redress of grievances." Thus, one view of rights is that they are liberties to believe or act or not to believe or act in certain ways, such as the freedom to speak about a government policy or to not believe in God. This view of rights respects the value of persons by respecting the value of their freedom.

This chapter discusses moral rights, but not moral rights conceived as natural rights. Neither does it discuss civil rights. *Civil rights* are rights that are created and protected by a government. Because the writers of the U.S. Constitution believed in natural rights, they created civil rights such as those set forth in Article I. Article I creates civil rights to freedom of religion, speech, the press, assembly, and petitioning the government. All full-status morally significant beings have moral rights, but only U.S. citizens have the civil rights granted by the Constitution.

Neither are moral rights necessarily the same as the more familiar term *human rights:* rights held by all human beings without regard to race, gender, religion, national origin, intelligence, and so on. If the class of all full-status morally significant beings contains only human beings, then moral and human rights are the same. However, if the class of all full-status morally significant beings extends beyond human beings, then moral rights and human rights are different. This chapter discusses an ethical theory involved with moral rights held by all persons or all morally significant beings. As we shall see in a later section, the correct criteria for morally significant beings remains unresolved.

Another characterization of rights emphasizes their nature as claims.[2] As contemporary philosopher Joel Feinberg phrases it, "To have a right is to have a claim against someone whose recognition as valid is called for by some governing rules or moral principles."[3] He identifies four elements connected to rights as claims. First, the right has a *content,* some good or interest that is the object of the claim. The right is a claim to something. The content is always specified when the right is identified, such as the right to liberty. Second, there is a *holder,* or person, who has the right and can make the claim. Third, there are *addressees,* persons against whom one's claim to something is directed or addressed. The addressees of civil rights are other citizens and the government, whereas the addressees of moral rights are other individual moral agents who are members of the moral community as well as the moral community as a whole (presumably represented by government). As will be discussed shortly, claims are made against addressees, and those addressees have duties related to those claims. Finally, there is a *source of validation,* or system of governing rules or moral principles. The rights holders appeal to the source of validation to justify their assertions that they have these rights. For example, the U.S. Constitution is the source of validation for the civil rights asserted by U.S. citizens.

How do claim rights work? This is a complicated and controversial subject, but it can be made clearer by considering the right to life. Rose has a claim against John, against other individual moral agents who are members of the moral community, and against the moral community as a whole for a right to life. In this instance, the ideas of rights as liberties and as claims can be combined. Rose's right to life gives her a certain liberty, specifically the liberty to defend or not defend her life when under attack. Rose's right to life also allows her to make at least two kinds of claims: one for noninterference and another for protection. Against the specific individual John (and other specific individuals), she can claim that he not interfere with her life or that he not kill her. Against the moral community as a whole, she can claim both noninterference with and protection for her life. Government represents the moral community as a whole, and the government should not wrongfully kill its citizens and should pass and enforce laws against wrongful killing. Thus, the right asserts a certain liberty as well as claims to noninterference and protection. In general, the aspect of moral rights as claims provides persons with legitimate claims to noninterference with and protection for some vital interest, such as life, liberty, or property.

Rose's rights give her claims that are correlated with duties on the part of John, other individuals, and the moral community as a whole. First, moral rights impose duties on specific individuals. If I have a right to life, then other persons have a duty to respect my right to life and not to kill me. This duty is an obligation not to do something; John has a duty not to kill Rose. John would act unethically if he failed to fulfill his duty and violated her right. Claim rights that impose duties on individuals not to do certain things are sometimes called *negative rights.* Duties are also imposed on the moral community as a whole or on its representative, government. The government has an obligation not to wrongfully kill Rose and to protect Rose's life from the actions of others. It can fulfill this second duty by passing and enforcing laws against wrongful killing. The government would act unethically if it wrongfully killed Rose or if it neglected its duty and failed to create and enforce the necessary laws. Thus, claim rights also take the form of *protection rights.* They obligate the moral community as a whole or its representative, government, to provide protection for certain basic interests. Claim rights are often viewed as both negative and protection rights.

As was stated earlier, claim rights have four elements. In this example about the right to life, the *content* of the right is life, the basic good or interest under consideration. The *holder* of the right is Rose. The *addressees* of the right are John, other moral agents who are members of the moral community, and the moral community as a whole. Finally, the *source of validation* is the set or system of legitimate moral rights. The basic rights in this set or system will be enumerated in a later section.

The ethical insight of the moral rights theory is that *persons are valuable and that we should act in ways that respect their value.* The moral rights theory respects individuals' value by protecting their vital interests, such as life and liberty, using rights. A rights-based theory promotes the impartial protection of vital interests. Any full-status morally significant being or person has these rights and is protected regardless of intelligence, sex, race, or religion, and perhaps without regard to species. (This matter is discussed further in a later section.) The ethical standard identified by the moral rights theory is this: *A person acts ethically if his or her action follows from one or more relevant rights and unethically if he or she violates another person's right or rights.* For example, if I steal your legitimately acquired television, I have violated your right to property and have acted unethically. Therefore, the initial claim is that your basic interests should be protected by rights. If someone violates your moral rights by interfering with one or more of these basic interests, that person is acting unethically.

The purpose of moral rights is to respect the value of persons by protecting their basic interests to life, liberty, and property. If individuals require all of these interests to live successfully, then all of them are important and must be protected. There may, however, be cases where it seems that we must violate one right to act in accord with another. Do some rights outweigh other ones? These cases of conflict between rights will be discussed in more detail in the section on problems with moral rights theory. At this point, it can be stated that philosophers have taken two approaches to rights. First, some thinkers assert that basic rights, or some basic rights, are absolute. By "absolute," they mean that it is always unethical to violate them. The right to life is often a candidate for an absolute right. All of a person's basic interests seem to be crucial however, and singling out only one right to be absolute is probably unjustified. Second, some philosophers claim that all or most rights are *prima facie* rights. (*Prima facie* means, roughly, "at first glance.") The idea here is that at first glance or if only one right is relevant, it cannot be violated. All *prima facie* rights are legitimate, but there may be considerations that would outweigh one or more of them. For example, at first glance you have the right to liberty, but there may be other moral considerations that outweigh this right. In light of these considerations, it would not be unethical for someone to infringe upon your freedom of action. This would seem to imply some kind of ranking of rights. If all rights are *prima facie,* then moral agents need to know how to rank them so that they would know which moral considerations outweigh which other ones. Of course, a proponent of the moral rights theory could employ both notions, arguing that one or more rights were absolute and the others were merely *prima facie.* For the moment, this matter can be left open and revisited in the subsequent section on the problem of conflicting rights.

## Another View of Moral Rights: Entitlement Rights

Moral rights are usually seen as assertions of certain liberties and legitimate claims to noninterference with and protection for a basic interest. They can, however, also be viewed as ethical entitlements. *Entitlement* or *positive rights* give a person a legitimate guarantee, or an entitlement, to the satisfaction of some interest. For example, the right to life would not merely protect you against others' taking your life but also would entitle you to the minimum requirements necessary to sustain life. The contrast may be easier to understand if we discuss it in the context of the right to education. If there is a right to education and it is conceived as a negative and protection claim right, the right protects us from other persons' interfering with our getting an education or denying us an education, assuming we have the financial resources and abilities to acquire one. If you have the money, the capabilities, and whatever else you need to attend school, your right to go to school is protected from the actions of other persons or the government. You cannot be prevented from going to school because you are a woman, a minority group member, or for any other arbitrary reason. In the United States, however, the right to education is not merely a negative and protection right. Here, children are entitled to an education up to twelfth grade. If their parents cannot afford private school, children may attend public schools without paying tuition. Entitlement rights do not merely protect things we already have; they impose duties on other persons or the government to provide persons with those things. Social programs in the United States such as the Food Stamp program could be justified with entitlement rights. Persons are entitled to remain alive and in reasonable health. If they cannot secure enough property to sustain their lives and health on their own, the government must assist them.

Entitlement, or positive, rights are also correlated with duties. These rights impose duties on other persons or the government to provide persons with certain things. If the right to life is a positive right, then government has a duty to provide the basic necessities of life to persons who cannot obtain them for themselves. Individuals would have to be provided, at minimum, with food, clothing, shelter, and medical care. Do individual moral agents have this duty also? This is a controversial matter, but for the purpose of this chapter, it is sufficient simply to point out that individual moral agents who are obligated by a positive right to life have a duty to give to charities that help persons who do not possess the basic necessities of life.

Although we can perhaps conceive of the right to life as a positive right, it is hard to interpret the rights to liberty and privacy as entitlement rights. It is difficult to see how persons could be provided with freedom or privacy; instead, it seems adequate to protect persons from other persons' violating their freedom and privacy. Perhaps the most plausible option for those who want to see some rights as entitlement rights is to assert the existence of a mixture of rights, some being positive entitlement rights and others negative and protection rights.

## Who Has Moral Rights?

When we read the works of seventeenth- and eighteenth-century proponents of rights such as John Locke, we might infer that they thought these rights had been given only to adult, white, male human beings. Locke, for example, did not oppose slavery and the subordination of women and children. The idea of who are the holders of moral rights has changed through the years, and rights are no longer seen as being limited to adult, white, male human beings. Women, persons of color, and children are now included as persons having moral rights. There is also considerable discussion of rights for some nonhuman animals.

I use the term "persons" to stand for "full-status morally significant beings" who are entitled to the entire range of moral rights. There might also be partial-status morally significant beings who are entitled to one or more moral rights, but not all of them. Proponents of animal rights sometimes argue that nonhuman animals are partial-status morally significant beings possessing at least the right to life. This is argued especially for gorillas, chimpanzees, dogs, cats, cows, and dolphins, among others. To determine what beings count as persons, we must employ a criterion or set of criteria. We will need another criterion or set of criteria to identify partial-status morally significant beings—if we believe such a category exists. In Chapter 6, we encountered Bentham's idea that any being who could feel pain and pleasure should receive ethical consideration. If we use this criterion for persons, then these other mammals would definitely qualify.

In contrast, moral philosophers working on the problem of abortion have often argued for more demanding criteria for personhood. Mary Anne Warren argues that five traits are central to the concept of personhood: consciousness, reasoning, self-motivated activity, the capacity to communicate, and the presence of a self-concept and self-awareness.[4] Based on these criteria, most, if not all, nonhuman animals would fail to qualify. In fact, some human beings, such as those in a coma or newborn infants, would probably fail to qualify also.

Determining the criteria for full- and partial-status morally significant beings is an important matter. One possibility would be to use Warren's criteria as the standard for full personhood and Bentham's criteria as the measure of partial-status morally significant beings. Many philosophers think Warren's standard is too demanding to be used at all, however, and this issue cannot be resolved here. Moral rights theory will work with any clear set of criteria, so it is possible to understand the theory without resolving this controversy.

## Basic Rights

John Locke claimed that there were three basic natural rights: the rights to life, liberty, and property. As was stated earlier, this chapter discusses moral rights, which are not considered to be part of the nature of human beings. To Locke's list of three basic rights, some proponents of moral rights would add, at a minimum, rights to basic well-being and privacy. Other philosophers argue that the right to well-being is packed into the right to life and that the right to privacy is included in the rights to life and liberty. In 1948, the United Nations adopted the Universal Declaration of Human Rights (Appendix 2), which went far beyond Locke's three and this chapter's five basic rights. Some of the rights included in this document are rights to work, education, and marriage. The next sections discuss the five basic rights that many philosophers consider to be essential to moral rights theory.

### Life

If the right to life is conceived as a liberty right and a negative and protection claim right, it operates in several ways. First, it asserts that persons have the liberty to defend or not defend their lives when under attack. Second, it allows a person to claim against other moral agents that these agents do not interfere with the person's life, that is, that they do not kill him or her. Third, it allows a person to claim noninterference with and protection for his or her life from the moral community as a whole. If the right to life is a negative and protection claim right, it protects a person's existence, but it does not guarantee any particular quality of life. If someone has the right to life, moral agents have a duty not to kill that person except in special cases. For example, if the only way you can defend yourself from someone killing you is to kill that person, you have not violated your ethical duty.

If the right to life is a positive or welfare right, it entitles the person to the basic necessities of life, including at least, food, clothing, shelter, and medical care. The person would presumably be able to claim these benefits from the government, or whomever was the guarantor of these rights. Persons would be entitled to whatever was necessary to keep them alive.

Although the right to life may seem clear and simple, it is not. Ethical issues such as abortion, suicide, euthanasia, and capital punishment raise questions about the right to life. We said that all persons have moral rights, but does the human embryo or fetus meet our criteria for a person? Do any nonhuman animals have the right to life? Is suicide unethical because it violates your own right to life? If a terminally ill person wants to die, does helping that person to die violate his or her right to life? Does the state act unethically when it legally executes someone because execution violates the criminal's right to life? These are only a few of the difficult questions connected to the right to life.

## Well-Being

If we limit the right to life to protecting life itself and do not extend it to protecting some degree of quality of life, then it is important to have a right to basic well-being. I would include both physical and psychological aspects of basic well-being in this analysis, although it will probably be much more difficult to identify cases where someone violates the psychological aspect of the right to basic well-being. Locke does not mention this right (perhaps because he thinks it is packed into the other basic rights), but I think including it clarifies matters. First, this right asserts basically the same liberty as the right to life: the liberty to defend or not defend one's life when under attack. It is an important addition to that right because it makes it clear that persons have the liberty to defend themselves, not only when their lives are in danger but also when they are merely in danger of being harmed. Second, it allows persons to claim against other moral agents that these agents do not interfere with their well-being, that is, that they do not harm them. Third, it allows persons to claim noninterference with and protection for their well-being from the moral community as a whole. If the right to well-being is a negative and protection claim right, it protects basic well-being but does not guarantee any particular level of higher well-being. If Rose has the right to basic well-being, other persons have a duty not to treat her in ways that would seriously harm her. The right to well-being is necessary because John may seriously injure Rose without killing her and violating her right to life. Persons should be protected from serious harm as well as from loss of life. If a moral agent violates a person's right to basic well-being, that individual has acted unethically.

If the right to life is a positive or entitlement right, then the right to basic well-being seems unnecessary because the right to basic well-being, as an entitlement right, would duplicate the right to life. It would entitle the person to the basic necessities of life that produce well-being, including at least, food, clothing, shelter, and medical care. As we have already seen, the entitlement right to life does this also. It might be argued, however, that a positive right to basic well-being entitles us to more than a positive right to life. Besides the necessities of life, it might entitle persons to some level of quality of life. If this were correct, the level of quality of life would be extremely controversial, but there would be a role to play for the positive right to basic well-being.

There are controversies connected to the right to basic well-being beyond the dispute over whether or not such a right exists. Some philosophers question whether a definitive line can be drawn between serious injury, which represents a violation of the right to well-being, and minor injury, which does not. Although I doubt that a definitive line can be drawn, we can surely identify some cases where there is serious injury and the right has indeed been violated. Another objection is that psychological injury should not be included. This objection is probably more practical than theoretical because we know that psychological injury can be as debilitating as physical injury. The concern is presumably not so much whether psychological injury can be serious but whether we can identify it. A related concern is whether we will be overwhelmed with violations of this right if it is included. Once again, although there may be cases where we cannot make a determination, there will be some cases where we can clearly see serious psychological injury. We need to consider such injury a violation of the right.

*Liberty*

The right to liberty asserts that persons have the liberty to make choices and decisions, to speak, to believe, to act to achieve their goals, and so on. The range of choices, beliefs, and actions protected is limited, however. The right to liberty asserts the liberty to act and believe in ways that are ethical and legal—not in all ways. As a claim right, it allows a person to claim against other moral agents that these agents do not interfere with the person's legitimate range of action and belief. It also allows a person to claim noninterference with and protection for his or her legitimate range of action and belief from the moral community as a whole. If the right to liberty is a negative and protection claim right, it protects a person's legitimate range of action and belief, not all actions and beliefs. For example, the right to liberty does not protect your ability to choose to go into a busy street and begin firing your gun at passing cars for target practice. This would be both unethical and illegal. We have a duty to respect the liberty of other persons as long as they exercise it in an ethical and legal manner. If a person prevents you from doing something you legally and morally ought to be able to do, your right to liberty has been violated.

The right to liberty probably generates more controversy than any other right. Although we can all agree that the right to liberty does not protect all actions, disagreements arise over exactly what should and should not be protected. We hear debates over the range of legitimate liberty in connection to issues such as freedom of speech, gun control, and illegal drug use. One guideline employed by moral rights proponents is that actions should be protected as long as they do not violate other basic rights. Other rights advocates worry about this strategy because it implies that other rights are more valuable than the right to liberty. When liberty comes in conflict with another basic right, liberty is the loser. More will be said about conflicting rights in a later section of this chapter.

*Privacy*

When we think of the right to privacy as a liberty right, it asserts our liberty to control information about and access to ourselves, although this control is limited by relationships.[5] As a claim right, it allows a person to claim against other moral agents that these agents do not interfere with the person's legitimate range of control over information about and access to that person. It also allows a person to claim noninterference with and protection for his or her legitimate range of control over personal information and access from the moral community as a whole. If the right to privacy is a negative and protection claim right, it protects a person's legitimate range of control over personal information and access but does not protect all control. For example, when I enter into an employment relationship, I must give the employer certain personal information because it is necessary for the relationship. I must provide data about my family if I want them to be covered by the company health plan. I lose control over this information, relative to my employer, but the employer has not violated my right to privacy because this information was necessary for some aspect of the relationship. A person's legitimate control over information about and access to himself or herself is limited by relationships.

In some cases, acquiring knowledge about a person may not violate the person's privacy even if he or she does not wish you to have the information. Finding out from a third party that one's sexual partner has AIDS does not violate the partner's right to privacy. The nature of the relationship makes it necessary for the person to have this information. Disputes over the right to privacy arise when disagreement exists about whether information is necessary for a relationship. Some companies argue that they should know whether their employees use illegal drugs because this information is necessary for the employment relationship. Companies may institute drug-testing programs to gain this information even though the employees want to keep it secret. Drug testing does not distinguish between drug use on the job and on the employee's own time, and an employee who uses drugs only at home may test positive. Some employees claim that information about drug use away from work is not essential for the employment relationship and that obtaining such information through drug testing is a violation of privacy. Employers counter that view with the response that information about any use of illegal drugs is relevant to the employment relationship; hence, there is no violation of privacy. This controversy illustrates the complicated nature of the right to privacy.

## Property

The right to property, as a liberty right, asserts that persons have the liberty to acquire property, to make any ethical and legal use of it they desire, and to gain any legitimate benefits from that property. Property, in one sense, means the tangible possessions we can legitimately own such as houses, land, cars, and televisions. In another sense, property refers to intangible things such as original expressions of ideas and processes. My television is my property, but so is the song I compose. John Locke wrote more about the right to property than about any other right. He thought that the basis for acquiring property was labor and claimed:

> Though the earth, and all inferior creatures, be common to all men, yet every man has a *property* in his own *person:* this no body has any right to but himself. The *labour* of his body, and the *work* of his hands, we may say, are properly his. Whatsoever then he removes out of the state that nature hath provided, and left it in, he hath mixed his *labour* with, and joined to it something that is his own, and thereby makes it his *property.*[6]

Thus, through labor, people may acquire property and use it to sustain their lives. Without some property, Locke thinks people would be unable to live, therefore property is necessary.

The right to property is also a claim right. It allows a person to claim against other moral agents that these agents do not interfere with the person's legitimate property, either by stealing it or gaining benefits from it that have not been granted them by the owner. It also allows persons to claim noninterference with and protection for their property from the moral community as a whole, or its representative, government. Thus, the right to property protects our property and our ability to gain the benefits of that property. The claim against the government for noninterference with property is limited by the power of a government to tax its citizens and legally take away some of their property. John Locke thought government should tax citizens only to gain funds for things that would benefit them directly. For example, government could tax citizens to build roads that they would use. Today, most philosophers interpret the power of government more broadly. Government can legitimately tax citizens for programs that only indirectly benefit them, such as foreign aid.

Similar to the other rights, there are controversies connected to the right to property. With a piece of property such as a television, we can use sales records to establish ownership. If the television is taken from the legitimate owner, the right to property has been violated. Computer software and videotapes of movies have made the concept of property more difficult for philosophers. A computer program can be copied from a friend's disk, but the original remains with the friend. The software, in contrast to a television, can be used simultaneously by two people in different locations. Companies have tried to resolve this problem with respect to software by licensing consumers to use the software. The license is accompanied by one copy of the software and specifies the terms of the agreement. For example, the user may be permitted to use the software only on a single machine, or to make only one copy for a backup. Most software companies argue that copying this kind of software is unethical as well as illegal. Issues like this one demonstrate that today the right to property is complicated and controversial.

## Justification for the Ethical Standard and Strengths of the Theory

Moral rights theory asserts that persons are valuable and that we ought to respect that value. It encourages this respect by identifying persons' vital interests and protecting those interests from the interference of others. The theory also provides a clear content for moral good and bad related to life, well-being, liberty, privacy, and property. Therefore, moral rights theory provides the emphasis on moral equality and the value of persons that is a strength of Kantian ethics. It also provides the clear ethical content that is a strength of utilitarianism.

Not all philosophers believe in moral rights and the ethical standard connected to these rights. The utilitarian, Jeremy Bentham, thought that the idea of moral rights sounded important but that no such things existed. Philosophers and thinkers who believe in moral rights have offered many justifications for them and the related standard concerning good and bad. This chapter avoids the complicated and difficult justifications that have been offered by some philosophers and focuses on three relatively simple justifications for using the ethical standard. The first relates to the value of persons and consistency. The other two are pragmatic justifications connected to moral equality and a clear content for ethics.

## Rationality and the Value of Persons

One justification for using the moral rights ethical standard and a related strength of the theory is that it is consistent with rationality and the idea that persons are valuable, two important considerations for many people. The moral rights theory asserts that persons are valuable. If persons are valuable and we want to be rational, we ought to act in ways that respect their value. To treat something valuable as valueless would be irrational. For example, if you think your collection of gold coins is extremely valuable, it would be irrational to throw them in the trash. The rational thing to do is to respect their value and protect them in some way. In regard to persons, one way to respect their value is to identify the important aspects of being a person and protect those aspects. This will presumably be more effective than a general and vague injunction to protect persons. Moral rights theory identifies the vital aspects of being a person—life, well-being, liberty, property, and privacy—and uses moral rights to protect them. If these moral rights are effective in providing this protection, then we are justified in endorsing them. Thus, the ethical justification for moral rights is that they are a way to respect the value of persons and that it would be irrational not to respect that value. Moral rights are not necessarily the only way to do this, but the claim is that they are as successful as any other alternative. Moral rights are not a part of innate human nature. They are ethical guidelines endorsed in the name of the value of persons and rationality. This idea, that persons are valuable and that we should treat them with respect, is a strength of the theory for many people.

## Persons as Moral Equals

Another justification for using the ethical standard and a related strength of the theory is that it strongly asserts that persons are moral equals. This is a valuable aspect for many people because it prevents prejudiced attitudes such as racism and sexism. Sexism, for example, goes beyond claiming that women are physically and intellectually inferior and adds that they are morally inferior. If women are morally inferior, then they are not worth as much as men. They would not have the same rights as men, or their rights would lose out when they came in conflict with those of men. Moral rights theory argues that all persons are moral equals, possess the same rights, and have the same strength rights. No man can legitimately claim that women do not have rights or that their rights do not count as much as those of men. No one can violate a woman's rights without acting unethically. Thus, moral rights theory provides the reasoning to refute sexism, racism, and other prejudiced attitudes. This is a justification for using the ethical standard and a strength of the theory for many people.

### A Clear Content for Ethics

A final justification for using the moral rights ethical standard and a related strength of the theory is that the theory provides a clear content for ethics. Ethics is concerned, at least, with the lives, well-being, liberty, property, and privacy of full-status morally significant beings. Of course, if other legitimate rights are identified, then this list would have to be expanded. Moral agents should have a reasonably clear idea about how to interact with other persons. Although there may be some gray areas connected to these basic interests, the content identified by the moral rights theory is clearer than that of Kantian ethics, which offers no specific content. It also is probably clearer than utilitarianism, which contains a significant amount of unclarity in identifying happiness and unhappiness or harm and benefit.

## Determining Morally Significant Actions

Moral rights theory claims that morally significant actions are those that violate a moral right or that follow from a moral right. Things that have nothing to do with moral rights are not morally significant. Killing an innocent person is morally significant because it violates his or her right to life. If horses are not persons or bearers of rights, then killing them is not morally significant unless doing so violates some right of persons (e.g., the right to property of the individual who owns the horses). Thus, the criteria for full-status and partial-status morally significant beings are crucial to what is and is not a morally significant action.

## Moral Rights Theory and the Traditional Ethical Assumptions

Moral rights theory accepts the traditional ethical assumptions. It claims that ethics is rational because we can use reason to reach theoretical and practical conclusions about ethical matters. We can provide reasons, related to the value of persons and moral rights, to support our ethical guidelines and solutions to ethical problems; these reasons and solutions can be evaluated; and some can be evaluated as being better than others. For example, a compelling reason for a moral rights proponent to judge an action to be unethical would be that the action violated some person's right or rights. Persons can use the moral guidelines of the theory to guide their actions. Finally, proponents of moral rights would also agree that well-intentioned persons who share an ethical framework, such as a similar system of moral rights, could discuss moral problems and arrive at mutually acceptable solutions. There is even some ground where advocates of moral rights can agree with proponents of competing ethical theories, especially Kantians.

Philosophers who accept moral rights endorse the view that all persons are moral equals and ought to be treated impartially. All persons have moral rights regardless of race, sex, religion, national origin, or intelligence (or possibly even species) and ought to receive the same ethical protection. According to moral rights theory, there are situations in which to be ethical you must be impartial and act contrary to your own self-interest. I might want to own a certain book that I cannot afford to buy. Perhaps you have this book, and I am certain I could steal it from you without being caught. Although it might be in my self-interest to steal the book, it would be unethical for me to do so because it would violate your right to property. I need to find some legitimate way to acquire the book, otherwise I must do without it so I do not violate your moral rights.

Moral rights theory also accepts the idea of universalizing ethical evaluations. If a particular case is an example of violating a right and is unethical, then any sufficiently similar case is also unethical. It is unethical for me to steal your book, just as it is unethical for anyone else to do so. Regardless of what society or group the person belongs to, all persons have moral rights, and stealing violates the right to property in any society. Thus, persons can universalize some ethical evaluations.

## Moral Rights Theory and the Basic Ethical Themes

Moral rights theory has a position regarding each of the four basic ethical themes discussed in Chapter 1. The first theme was represented by this question: *What kind of moral guidelines makes something good or bad: subjective, relative, or objective ones?* Proponents of moral rights claim that some actions may be said to be objectively good or bad because they are based on objective considerations of reason and fact that do not relate to the attitudes or emotions of specific persons or to social principles. For example, actions such as murder, which violate one or more moral rights, are objectively evil. We must use reason to arrive at the proper description of the act as murder and to know that murder violates the right to life. It must then be a fact that the action is unethical. Actions, such as saving someone's life, which follow from the right to life or another right, are objectively good. Thus, individual actions as well as certain classes of actions are objectively good or bad.

The second theme in ethics was indicated by this question: *What makes something good or evil; is it the consequences that are produced or the reasoning that leads up to it?* Advocates of moral rights focus on the reasoning that precedes an action. If I decide to steal your book because I want a copy of it but cannot afford to buy one, my action is unethical because I have not respected your right to property. I acted on self-interest with no consideration of your moral rights. Instead of thinking that the book was your property and that it would be wrong for me to steal it, I simply did what was in my own best interest. I did not respect your moral rights; therefore, the action is unethical regardless of the consequences it might produce. It is possible that the consequences of the theft may produce a net benefit. For example, perhaps you did not really like the book and were not planning to reread it. I steal it, read it, and get a great deal of pleasure from it. The consequences would seem to be that you were not harmed and that I was benefited; therefore, the good consequence outweighed the bad. To a proponent of moral rights, the action is unethical no matter what the consequences may be. It is the lack of respect for your moral rights that matters, not the results of the action.

The third important theme related to this question: *Are good and bad related to following general rules without exceptions or connected to separately evaluating each action, belief, and so on?* People who believe in moral rights claim that we can construct general rules, justified by statements about moral rights, that can function as ethical guidelines. "Killing innocent persons is evil" is a legitimate moral guideline because killing innocent persons violates their right to life, and "stealing another person's legitimate property is always unethical" is also legitimate because stealing violates the right to property. If a class of action, like theft, always violates a moral right, then one can construct an ethical rule or guideline related to it. These moral rules or guidelines ought to be followed without exceptions.

The fourth theme is connected to the proper focus of ethical attention: *Are good and bad primarily related to the group, community, or majority of persons or should the focus be on the individual?* Advocates of moral rights assert that the focus of ethics should be the individual. Moral rights protect each individual person, and it is always unethical to violate that person's rights, even if doing so would benefit the group or the majority.

## Contrasting Moral Rights Theory with Act Utilitarianism

Moral rights theory and act utilitarianism have some interesting similarities and differences (see Appendix 1). Moral rights theory identifies acting from and violating moral rights as its main ethical guideline, whereas act utilitarianism relates moral good and bad to producing a net benefit or harm for the persons affected. Both moral rights theory and act utilitarianism accept all the traditional ethical assumptions: that people are rational, that they are moral equals and should be treated impartially, and that they can universalize some ethical evaluations. With respect to the four ethical themes, the theories agree on the first ethical theme, that the source of good and bad is objective considerations. The theories disagree, however, on the remaining three ethical themes. They differ regarding how to evaluate good and evil. Act utilitarianism looks at consequences, whereas moral rights theory examines the reasoning that precedes an action. Another difference is that act utilitarianism evaluates acts separately, whereas moral rights theory endorses following general rules without exceptions. Finally, utilitarianism concentrates on the greatest good for the greatest number of persons, whereas moral rights theory protects the individual person.

## Problems with the Theory

Moral rights theory identifies ethical guidelines and argues that these guidelines are superior to those of other theories. The guidelines identified by the theory would also clearly prevent the unlimited pursuit of self-interest. The problems with moral rights theory relate to the fourth criterion: that the theory must produce effective solutions to ethical problems. This section considers a few of the problems with the theory.

### Descriptions of Actions

One problem related to moral rights theory is that it, like Kantian ethics, seems to assume that there is only one accurate description of an action. For example, an action either constitutes theft and violates the right to property or is not theft and does not violate this right. Sometimes, however, there may be more than one competing description of an action. Suppose you want to avoid hurting Rose's feelings, and you tell her you admire her artwork when the truth is that you do not like it. Is the correct description of this action telling Rose a lie, complimenting Rose on her artwork, or trying not to hurt her feelings? If people do not agree on the description of the action, moral rights theory cannot assess whether a particular right was relevant to the case. This problem relates to the fourth criterion for evaluating ethical theories. If we cannot fix the description of an action, we will not be able to identify the appropriate ethical guideline, in this case the relevant moral right. If we cannot identify the appropriate ethical guideline, we will not obtain help in solving the moral problem. Although this is a serious criticism, the theory would still work when there is agreement on the correct description of the action. This criticism demonstrates that moral rights theory is only a partially successful ethical theory.

## Conflicting Rights

Another criticism is that in cases where different rights come into conflict the theory can provide no adequate guidance to resolve these conflicts. This criticism is also related to the fourth criterion for evaluating ethical theories: that the theory must be able to help us solve moral problems. The abortion issue presents a prime example of this problem. Suppose a government that endorses moral rights is trying to create an abortion policy. If officials think the embryo or fetus qualifies as a person, then embryos and fetuses have the right to life. (They might also possess the right to life even if they only qualify as partial-status morally significant beings.) Abortion kills the fetus and would violate its right to life. Thus, a policy allowing abortion would be unethical. The problem is that women have the right to liberty, and many people would argue that this right ought to protect a woman's ability to control what happens in and to her body. If women are to be able to control what happens in and to their bodies, they must be able to control their pregnancies. If they are to be able to control their pregnancies, they must be able to obtain abortions. A policy that would force a pregnant woman to give birth would seem to violate her right to liberty and would also be unethical. Therefore, we have conflicting rights, and it seems that any policy we make would be unethical.

This problem is similar to the problem of conflicting ethical rules that affects Kantian ethics. One way to begin to resolve this problem is to create a legitimate ranking of the moral rights. Assuming that the right to life outweighs the right to liberty, if the fetus is a bearer of moral rights, the anti-abortion policy is an ethical policy. However, no component of this theory allows us to make such a ranking. The theory is designed to protect all of the vital aspects of persons. Intuitively, we usually regard life as more important than liberty. You do not have the freedom to shoot at cars passing by on the highway because the passengers' lives are more important than your freedom. In other cases, however, people seem to claim that liberty is more important. Many people assert that it is ethical for a person to commit suicide. Their position would seem to be that the person's right to liberty should protect the freedom to commit suicide and outweighs the right to life. A skeptic might ask, "Why is life more important than liberty?" The skeptic's question may sound strange, but it points to the real problem. How can we argue that life is more important than liberty without appealing to consequences?

If we start appealing to consequences, we will eventually turn into consequentialists and, probably, utilitarians. Think about the case where a man steals food from a wealthy family to feed his starving children. He could defend his action by saying that the children's right to life outweighed the rich persons' right to property, but this argument is just covert utilitarianism. There is more benefit in saving the children's lives, but maximizing benefit is not supposed to be the focal point of this theory.[7] Even if a legitimate ranking of the moral rights could be achieved, it would not completely solve the problem. There might be cases where we would have a conflict between a very serious violation of a less important right and a minor violation of a more important one, and once again we would be unsure about how to resolve these conflicts.[8]

As the previous criticism shows, moral rights theory has problems producing effective solutions to ethical problems in all cases. The theory does work when there are no conflicting rights and also in conflicts where we can reach compromise solutions that avoid violating either right. Proponents of the theory might insist that violating moral rights is always wrong and that we must search for solutions that resolve the conflicts without violating either party's rights. The potential thief must obtain charity or go on welfare to feed his starving children, and the pregnant woman ought to choose to give birth to her child and put it up for adoption. Opponents will probably say that such compromises are not always available in cases of conflict or that they may be unpleasant for those involved. Proponents of moral rights theory would claim that such compromises are preferable to the more blatant violations of one of those rights. On the whole, this criticism implies that the theory will have only limited success.

### The Community

The final criticism of moral rights theory does not relate directly to the criteria for evaluating ethical theories, but it might help someone compare act utilitarianism with moral rights theory. The criticism is that moral rights lead us to see persons as isolated, egoistic individuals who have no real identity with or obligations to a community, only minimal duties to other individuals. Karl Marx (1818–1883) states a variation of this criticism in his essay "On the Jewish Question":

> None of the supposed rights of man, therefore, go beyond the egoistic man . . . that is, an individual separated from the community, withdrawn into himself, wholly preoccupied with his private interest and acting in accordance with his private caprice.[9]

Marx interprets the right to liberty as the right to be separate from the community and the right to property as the right to act out of self-interest with regard to one's money and possessions. The right to property means that we have no obligation to use our property for the benefit of the community. The general criticism is that the moral rights view stresses individualism, self-interest, and egoism, and sacrifices the community. I believe Marx exaggerates the extent of the egoism, self-interest, and isolation associated with moral rights theory, but it is correct that moral rights theory does not include obligations to the community as a whole, only obligations to individuals. Act utilitarianism operates for the benefit of the majority, and so produces obligations to benefit the majority of people in a community. This is an important difference between act utilitarianism and moral rights theory. Whether or not this criticism is serious depends on whether people can live successfully together using a theory that focuses on the individual and not the community. Philosophers have failed to agree on the answer to this question.

## Conclusion

Proponents of moral rights theory claim that it is superior to Kantian ethics and utilitarianism. They believe it is better than Kant's theory because it gives ethics a clear content and is easier to understand and follow. They claim it is superior to utilitarianism because it avoids the extremely difficult task of identifying and weighing all the harms and benefits for all the persons affected, is more consistent with our moral intuitions, and assures that moral conduct is under the control of the individual moral agent.

Moral rights theory and Kantian ethics are similar. Moral rights theory has been included in this text, however, because the language of moral rights is the most common ethical vocabulary in Western countries. Many people find moral rights more familiar and easier to understand than the various formulations of Kant's Categorical Imperative. Many contemporary ethical problems, such as abortion and euthanasia, are actually discussed by philosophers and nonphilosophers using the language of moral rights. Thus, for some philosophers, moral rights theory is superior to Kantian ethics. In relation to the relative merits of utilitarianism and moral rights theory, the issue may ultimately come down to a moral choice. Based on the value of persons and moral equality, many people believe that it is unethical to sacrifice some individuals without their consent for the good of the majority. All individuals are valuable and equal to all other individuals and therefore cannot be sacrificed without their consent for the good of others. If you agree with this, then you should reject utilitarianism in favor of moral rights theory.

Moral rights theory originates from an extremely valuable ethical insight: that people are valuable and that we ought to act in ways that respect their value. Many philosophers believe this is the vital component of any adequate morality. Moral rights theory has difficulty describing actions and evaluating conflicting rights. Because of these problems, the theory will not always be able to produce effective solutions to ethical problems. Thus, moral rights theory is not completely successful as an ethical theory based on the criteria from Chapter 1. Therefore, we are left with three partially successful ethical theories: Kantian ethical theory, utilitarianism, and moral rights theory.

The next chapter continues the search for a completely successful theory, examining Aristotle's approach to good and bad, called "virtue ethics." Virtue ethics has a familiar ethical vocabulary (courage, generosity, justice, and so on), but it also has some ideas that are not so well known.

## QUESTIONS FOR REVIEW

*Here are some questions to help you review the main concepts in this chapter.*

1. What is the ethical insight at the core of moral rights theory?

2. What are moral rights? Explain rights as liberties, and provide an example of this idea of rights.

3. Explain rights as claims to noninterference and protection. What are the four elements of claim rights? Provide examples of both types of claims.

4. Explain the connection between rights and duties. Provide an example.

5. What is the ethical standard in the moral rights theory?

6. Explain the difference between absolute and *prima facie* rights.

7. Explain the difference between rights as claims to noninterference and rights as entitlements. How would a proponent of each view interpret the right to an education?

8. What criteria would you use to determine status as a person? Do you think we need a category of partial-status morally significant beings? If so, what criteria would you use for this class? What are the implications of your position for moral rights?

9. According to John Locke, what are the three basic rights? According to the text, the proponents of moral rights would identify what five basic rights?

10. How does the right to well-being differ from the right to life? Should the right to well-being be included in the basic rights?

11. What is the right to privacy? How is it different from the right to liberty?

12. Summarize one of the justifications for the ethical standard. How does this justification relate to a strength of moral rights theory?

13. How do proponents of moral rights distinguish between morally significant actions and those that are not morally significant?

14. How does moral rights theory incorporate the traditional ethical assumptions?

15. Explain the moral rights position on each of the four ethical themes.

16. Discuss one similarity and two differences between moral rights theory and act utilitarianism.

17. In your opinion, what is the most serious problem with the moral rights ethical theory? Support your answer.

18. In relation to the criteria from Chapter 1, why is moral rights theory only partially successful as an ethical theory?

## NOTES

1. Thomas Hobbes, *Leviathan,* edited by Michael Oakeshott (Oxford: Basil Blackwell, 1957), p. 84.

2. Perhaps the most influential recent discussion of rights is found in Wesley Hohfeld, *Fundamental Legal Conceptions as Applied to Judicial Reasoning,* edited by Walter Wheeler Cook (New Haven: Yale University Press, 1966). Hohfeld discusses four aspects of rights: rights as liberties, claims, powers, and immunities. In this basic chapter, only the first two will be included.

3. Joel Feinberg, *Rights, Justice, and the Bounds of Liberty* (Princeton, NJ: Princeton University Press, 1980), p. 154.

4. Mary Anne Warren, "On the Moral and Legal Status of Abortion," in *Morality in Practice,* edited by James P. Sterba (Belmont, CA: Wadsworth, 1997), p. 139.

5. I first encountered this definition of privacy in George Brenkert's article, "Privacy, Polygraphs, and Work," *Journal of Business and Professional Ethics,* Vol. 1, No. 1 (Fall 1981).

6. John Locke, *Second Treatise of Government,* edited by C. B. Macpherson (Indianapolis, IN: Hackett Publishing Company, 1980), p. 19.

7. A rough intuitive ranking shows that we run into serious problems if we try to do this. Suppose we create the following ranking of some basic rights: (1) life, (2) well-being, (3) property, (4) privacy, and (5) liberty. Perhaps, however, property should come before well-being. We usually think it is wrong for people to steal, even if they benefit by the theft. In freedom of speech cases, we sometimes allow people to say things that will harm others if the expressions are true. Does this mean that liberty is more important than well-being? These

two examples show the difficulty in creating a ranking based on our intuition. Some component of the theory is needed to order these rights, but there is no general agreement on this component.

8. One of the reviewers of the first edition of this book pointed out this criticism about major and minor violations of moral rights.

9. Karl Marx, "On the Jewish Question," in *The Marx-Engels Reader,* edited by Robert C. Tucker (New York: Norton, 1978), p. 43.

# Chapter 8

# *Virtue Ethics*

One way to determine good and bad is in relation to a goal, a purpose, or a function—something good helps accomplish the goal, promotes achieving the purpose, or helps carry out the function. If the primary function of my university is to educate students, then something that clearly promotes their education would be good relative to that function. For example, skill in teaching is good because it promotes the education of students. If the university had a different primary goal, perhaps to maximize profit, different things would be good. For example, skill in persuading students to pay higher tuition would be good. The idea of good and bad being dependent on a goal, a purpose, or a function is often present in corporations, institutions, and organizations. Many corporations develop a statement of purpose and encourage employees to develop skills and techniques that will promote achieving that purpose. A purpose allows us to evaluate other things in relation to the purpose, but it does not allow us to assess the purpose itself.

In Chapter 1, I stated that the most important function of ethical theories is to help us solve moral problems and live together successfully. The criteria for evaluating a successful ethical theory reflect this basic goal. This goal-oriented approach can be applied to persons as well as to ethical theories. What is the goal of all (or almost all) persons? One plausible answer is that the goal is to live the "good life." People want to live well, to flourish, and to be successful, although they may have different ideas of what allows them to do so. This may be a good opportunity to ask yourself, "What is my idea of the good life?" Would you need to have successful relations with family members, with friends, or with colleagues? Would you have to be healthy, wealthy, or famous, or a great success in your career? Would you require pleasure, excitement, happiness, devotion, or tranquility? Many elements could be important parts of the good life, and your list may be very different from someone else's. Whatever elements you selected, the goal is to live the good life, and whatever promotes or produces the good life is good, whereas whatever detracts from or degrades it is bad.

The Greek philosopher Aristotle (384–322 B.C.E.) uses a goal-oriented approach and a view of the good life to develop a "virtue ethics" based on the distinctive function of human beings. He assumes that all human beings have a basic function or purpose and that a good person is one who is successful at accomplishing it. The key to living the good life, according to Aristotle, is developing certain virtues, such as practical wisdom, courage, and generosity. Thus, his approach to moral good and bad is often called "virtue ethics." Many people would intuitively agree that the virtues help people to live well. Thus, the basic ethical insight associated with virtue ethics is that *the virtues help persons to achieve well-being or to live the good life*. The additional ethical idea that makes Aristotle's virtue ethics distinctive is that there is a basic human function and that the virtues help us to accomplish that function.

## Virtue Ethics, Well-Being, and Reasoning

Virtue ethics, as presented in this chapter, is based on the ideas of Aristotle. This ethical theory emphasizes character and being a good person instead of performing good actions and claims that the virtues are essential to being a good person. There are many possible definitions for virtues, but the one used in this chapter must cover both intellectual and moral virtues. Therefore, *virtues* are character traits that promote the well-being of the person who has them.

Aristotle begins the *Nicomachean Ethics* with a discussion about the goals of human action.[1] He observes that the end, goal, or purpose for an action is always something that is good or that appears to be good. Some goals are means to achieve other ends, and some are ends in themselves. Aristotle is interested in whether there is some ultimate end shared by all human beings. Is there some goal or end that is not a means to anything else but is the ultimate end of all other goals? An answer to this question would reveal the ultimate end for all human beings, not just the ultimate end for some particular person. He believes there is general agreement about the highest of all the goods achievable by action and states:

> Verbally there is very general agreement; for both the general run of men and people of superior refinement say that it is happiness, and identify living well and faring well with being happy; but with regard to what happiness is they differ, and the many do not give the same account as the wise.[2]

The word being translated as "happiness" is the word *eudaimonia*. This word might also be translated as "well-being," or "flourishing." "Happiness" is the usual translation, but I believe this is misleading because for many people happiness implies pleasure. Aristotle rejects the life of pleasure and asserts that the ultimate end is a well-lived life. The well-lived life includes not only pleasure and happiness but also health, longevity, achievement, moral excellence, knowledge, wisdom, and other qualities. Therefore, the ultimate human purpose should be designated as "well-being," which is the concept I will use here.

Aristotle is interested in what constitutes the well-being of humans as opposed to what makes up the well-being of other living things. He observes that some people equate human well-being with pleasure, or wealth, or honor. They also often change their ideas based on their situation; for example, they think well-being is health when they are sick, but wealth when they are poor. Aristotle rejects lives based on pleasure, wealth, and honor as lives that necessarily produce well-being. After rejecting these, he says, "Presumably, however, to say that happiness [well-being] is the chief good seems a platitude, and a clearer account of what it is is still desired. That might perhaps be given, if we could first ascertain the function of man."[3] Aristotle believes human well-being is related to the basic or characteristic function of human beings. Just as a good flute player or sculptor is one who successfully fulfills the distinctive function of a flute player or sculptor, a good human being is one who successfully fulfills the characteristic function of a human being.

Aristotle's idea is that there is a distinctive or proper function for human beings and that that function is related to human well-being. He concludes that the human function is connected to the capacity of humans that he thinks no other living thing possesses—the ability to reason. The essence of reasoning, for Aristotle, is acting in accordance with a rational principle. Therefore, the ultimate good of human beings is well-being, which is realized through excellence in the function that is characteristic to human beings. That function is reasoning or acting in accordance with a rational principle. Human well-being or a well-lived life will be achieved through excellence in reasoning or successfully acting in accordance with rational principles. It is not really necessary to limit this characteristic function to human beings, although Aristotle does so. If there are other beings who also possess reason as their basic function, then this form of well-being would be appropriate for them as well.

Aristotle was primarily interested in good lives or good characters rather than specific good actions. To determine if a person had achieved well-being, the person's complete character or life would have to be examined. In this context, *character* can be considered to be the combination of mental and moral qualities or traits that distinguish an individual. Aristotle would look for excellence in reasoning displayed in all the aspects of character and life. This excellence is not possible unless an individual possesses the virtues. Therefore, it is essential to understand the virtues that a person of good character would possess.

## Intellectual Virtues

How does one achieve excellence in reasoning or the ability to reason well? First, reasoning well means being able to use reason to investigate things and to understand them. Aristotle claims that the proper end of this kind of reasoning is truth:

> Let it be assumed that the states by virtue of which the soul possesses truth by way of affirmation or denial are five in number, i.e. art, knowledge, practical wisdom, philosophic wisdom, comprehension; for belief and opinion may be mistaken.[4]

These five virtues by which people achieve excellence in reasoning and truth may be called the *intellectual virtues*. By "art," Aristotle means knowledge and skill in the arts, which allows a person to produce excellent material things, such as statues or pottery. By "knowledge," he means acquiring knowledge that deals with things that are universal, necessary, and eternal. This knowledge is arrived at by logic and observation. "Practical wisdom" involves excellence in deliberation about the means of achieving a good end, that is, the ability to make sound judgments about the conduct of life. It relates to discovering the appropriate actions to promote well-being as well as controlling the passions that might interfere with these appropriate actions (more will be said about controlling the passions later). "Philosophic wisdom" involves knowledge of the ultimate things, such as the first cause of the universe. Finally, by "comprehension," he means understanding. He claims that understanding and practical reasoning are about the same objects, but there is an important difference between them. "For practical wisdom issues commands, since its end is what ought to be done or not to be done; but understanding only judges."[5] These intellectual virtues are essential to excellence in reasoning, and excellence in reasoning is crucial to well-being.

## Moral Virtues and Vices

Aristotle believes virtue is connected to reasoning well. Therefore, to be virtuous we must not allow our emotions or passions to interfere with our reasoning. We sometimes see a situation where someone is too upset to think clearly; to reason well, we must avoid this. Aristotle claims that a person's emotional response is partly the result of teaching or training in accord with reason. People are taught to feel certain ways in certain situations. This produces habitual responses that are in accord with reason. Thus, a person's emotional response to a situation can be developed in accord with reason through teaching and can also be controlled by using reason.

Intellectual virtue is connected to knowledge and wisdom, but Aristotle claims that "moral virtue" is related to actions and the emotions or passions that accompany them. He states that an excess, a deficit, or an intermediate amount of emotion accompanies actions. An excess or a deficit amount of passion may interfere with acting rationally and choosing the ethical action. Aristotle believes the virtuous person feels a moderate amount of emotion in many situations and chooses the mean in regard to certain actions. He observes:

> Excellence, then, is a state concerned with choice, lying in a mean relative to us, this being determined by reason and in the way in which the man of practical wisdom would determine it. Now it is a mean between two vices, that which depends on excess and that which depends on defect; and again it is a mean because the vices respectively fall short or exceed what is right in both passions and actions, while excellence both finds and chooses that which is intermediate.[6]

The moral virtues are related to feeling a moderate amount of emotion and acting based on the mean. Each virtue is a mean between two vices that involve feeling excess and deficit amounts of emotion and acting inappropriately. An example of a virtue that involves moderation is courage. Courage involves feeling the right amount of fear and confidence when acting in dangerous or difficult situations. In battle, for example, the coward feels too much fear and not enough confidence, whereas the rash person feels too little fear and too much confidence. The coward runs away, and the rash person attacks the enemy foolishly. Neither of these is the ethical or rational action. Courage involves feeling a moderate amount of fear and confidence; this allows the person to act in a rational way. Aristotle calls the virtues connected to moderate emotional responses "moral virtues." The moral virtues also fit the definition of virtues as traits of character that promote the well-being of the person who has them. For example, courage is the disposition to feel the proper amount of fear and confidence in a dangerous or difficult situation, and this disposition promotes the person's well-being.

Moral virtues usually involve emotions and actions wherein excess and deficiency of emotion are wrong. This might lead us to conclude that the vices are always excesses or deficits of an emotion, but this is not true. He observes:

But not every action nor every passion admits of a mean; for some have names that already imply badness, e.g. spite, shamelessness, envy, and in the case of actions adultery, theft, murder; for all of these and suchlike things imply by their names that they are themselves bad, and not excesses or deficiencies of them. It is not possible, then, ever to be right with regard to them; one must always be wrong.[7]

These unethical emotions, such as spite, involve feelings that are evil in any amount, and the unethical actions, such as adultery, are evil, regardless of the feeling that accompanies them. Thus, Aristotle's ethics has a significant objective aspect to it. The intellectual virtues also provide a large objective element because they are always good. There is a subjective element to Aristotle's ethics as well, however, because the mean or proper amount of emotion depends upon a particular individual. The right amount of emotion for a person to feel in a particular situation may vary from person to person depending on the person's nature. Each person must determine the mean in connection with a rational principle that a person of practical wisdom would use for that particular person in that particular situation. The person of practical wisdom is someone who is able to reason correctly about ethical problems and can determine the correct course of action to take.

Aristotle discusses a variety of virtues that involve feeling the right amount of emotion and choosing the mean in regard to action, although for modern readers some of these "emotions" may seem more like attitudes or orientations (see Summary of Some of Aristotle's Moral Virtues). Only some of the virtues he discusses will be enumerated here. Courage is one of his virtues, but was discussed earlier. Another is temperance or self-control, which is moderation in regard to the passion involved with actions motivated by pleasure. An excess of this passion is self-indulgence. Aristotle thinks a deficiency of the desire for pleasure is rarely found. A third virtue is generosity, a mean amount of the emotion and the appropriate actions connected to giving and taking money or gifts. The excess of the passion and action is extravagance and the deficiency is stinginess. In connection with actions related to feelings of anger, people who feel the appropriate amount of anger and act properly are considered to be amiable, another virtue. Those who feel too much anger and act inappropriately are wrathful, and those who feel too little are apathetic. Aristotle also thinks that truthfulness is a virtue where the person has found the mean between being boastful and being self-deprecating. A person who observes the mean in amusing others may be called witty. Someone who goes to excess is a buffoon, and someone who is deficient is humorless. In regard to the emotion and actions related to pleasing others, the virtue is friendliness, whereas excess is obsequiousness and a deficiency is quarrelsomeness or grouchiness. The

SUMMARY OF SOME OF ARISTOTLE'S MORAL VIRTUES

| Area | Defect | Excess | Mean or Virtue |
|------|--------|--------|----------------|
| Fear and confidence in dangerous situations | Cowardice | Recklessness | Courage |
| Desire for pleasure | Hardly ever found | Self-indulgence | Self-control (Temperance) |
| Giving and receiving money and things | Stinginess | Extravagance | Generosity |
| Getting angry | Apathy | Wrathfulness | Amiability |
| Telling the truth | Self-deprecation | Boastfulness | Truthfulness |
| Amusing others | Boorishness | Buffoonery | Wittiness |
| Pleasing others | Grouchiness or quarrelsomeness | Obsequiousness | Friendliness |

common element in all the virtues is that in each of them reason or practical wisdom controls the amount of emotion a person feels and the actions he or she takes.

*Moral virtues* are traits of character concerned with choice that involve moderation in action and emotion; this moderation is determined by a rational principle as discovered by a person of practical wisdom. Therefore, the intellectual virtue of practical reason and the moral virtues are closely related. The origin of action is choice, and the source of choice is desire and reasoning connected to achieving some goal or end. Virtuous action depends on practical wisdom guiding our choices and controlling our emotions.

## The Ethical Person

For the most part, Aristotle thinks people acquire the virtues through education and training. There is also the possibility of emulating a virtuous person. We need to look at a virtuous person for anything resembling an Aristotelian ethical standard. In virtue ethics, the ethical standard will not be a rule or principle that designates ethical actions. Instead, the ethical standard will be *a person who possesses the virtues and does not possess the vices.* In another sense, the ethical standard will be a person who is living the good life. This person can be an actual virtuous individual or a nonexisting ideal person. In either case, the virtuous person will act as a model for others to emulate. If you want to obtain well-being or be an ethical person, you should strive to acquire the virtues, eliminate the vices, and be like the model or ideal person.

What would the virtuous person be like? The first aspect of the ideal or ethical person is that he or she would possess the intellectual virtues. He or she would be wise, knowledgeable, and capable of understanding. This claim that an ethical person is wise, knowledgeable, and capable of understanding may seem to be an odd claim to contemporary people. Many ancient Greek philosophers, however, believed a wise, knowledgeable, and understanding person was living a better life than a foolish and ignorant individual. Knowledge helps persons live better lives because knowledge opens up more opportunities and helps persons make better decisions. The virtuous person will be knowledgeable in a range of areas. Practical wisdom, the tendency or disposition to make sound judgments about the conduct of life, allows the virtuous person to make effective and fulfilling decisions and judgments and to act in appropriate ways. That person will also be able to live a better life than will a foolish person. Understanding will enable the virtuous person to judge correctly, which will lead to a better life than that of someone who judges incorrectly. If we consider knowledge, wisdom, and understanding as character traits, and if these traits can help us live better lives, then these traits fit the definition of virtues. They are character traits that promote the well-being of the person who has them.

As well as having the intellectual virtues, an ethical person must also have the moral virtues. He or she must be courageous, self-controlled, generous, amiable, truthful, witty, friendly, and so on. The common element in all these virtues is that the person does not allow excesses and deficiencies of emotion to interfere with reasoning well or to lead to intemperate actions. In addition to having the virtues, the virtuous person must not have the vices, avoiding emotions such as shamelessness and envy and actions such as adultery, theft, and murder.

Aristotle claims that being a good person involves more than action. First, people must know what they are doing. This relates to the intellectual virtue, knowledge. Second, they must choose the action because it is virtuous and choose it as an end in itself. This relates to practical wisdom. Third, the action must be the expression of their character and must be accompanied by the proper feeling or emotion. This relates to moral virtue. Good people know what they are doing and choose to feel or do something because it is virtuous. Their feelings and actions flow from their character, and their emotions do not interfere with being virtuous. The good person has achieved well-being. Aristotle thought that being a good person and obtaining well-being would only be possible in the presence of certain other factors, such as health, longevity, some degree of material prosperity, and living in a flourishing city. Without these things we would not really be able to live good lives. Thus, the good person must possess a good character and be living the good life. This is such a large requirement, however, one might ask whether there really are any good people. Whether there actually are or are not people who fit the description, anyone can strive to become a good person by trying to become more like Aristotle's model person. The closer one approximates the good person, the better one is.

Aristotle's ethics is different from Kantian ethics, utilitarianism, or moral rights theory. All of these theories focus on actions, either by concentrating on the reasoning that preceded them or the consequences that resulted from them. Aristotle is concerned with character and a person's whole life. Good people have a wide variety of virtues and do not have the vices. Aristotle's view of a good or virtuous person is essential to his theory and constitutes the main ethical standard available to him.

## Justification for the Ethical Standard and Strengths of the Theory

There are a number of justifications for using a model of a good person as an ethical standard, and each of them suggests a related strength of Aristotle's ethical theory.

### An Ethical Theory that Is Not Simplistic

The first justification for the ethical standard is that we should use it because it is not simplistic. Ethics is a comprehensive and complex investigation. The legitimate object of that investigation should be being a good person and living the good life rather than just performing good actions. The focus on performing good actions used by most other ethical theories oversimplifies ethics. Thus, one justification is that Aristotle's ethics is the one theory that does not distort ethics by oversimplifying it. The related strength of the theory is that a theory that corresponds better to the comprehensive and complex nature of ethics is superior to a simplistic one.

### A Practical Ethical Theory

A second justification is that Aristotle's ethics is practical. A person simply needs to find a good person and emulate him or her. This is a fairly common practice and one that is presumably practical. Many people try to emulate the lives of others. People try to live like Christ, a saint, the Buddha, Mohatma Gandhi, Mother Teresa, Martin Luther King Jr., or someone else whom they see as the epitome of goodness. It is a relatively practical endeavor because one can study the person's life and then try to emulate it. The related strength of the theory is that a practical theory is better than one that is impractical because the practical theory will do a better job of helping people solve moral problems and live together successfully.

*A Theory Consistent with Human Nature*

The final justification for using this standard connects to Aristotle's assumption that there is a basic human function—reasoning—and that the well-lived life involves reasoning well. Being a virtuous person will help an individual accomplish the basic human function successfully. If this is correct, then Aristotle's ethical standard is the appropriate one to use because it is consistent with our common human nature and will help us achieve excellence in regard to that nature. The related strength of the theory is that a theory that is consistent with human nature and helps people to achieve excellence in respect to that nature is a better theory that one that is not.

There are a few interesting strengths to virtue ethics theory and also some significant problems, which will be discussed later. Although the theory originates in ancient Greece, it has some adherents today. These philosophers primarily value its holistic nature and its presumed practicality.

## Determining Morally Significant Actions

It is difficult to know exactly how virtue ethics would separate the ethically significant from what is not ethically significant. Aristotle does not discuss this matter because he is focused on character, not actions. One possible answer is that everything that promotes or detracts from well-being might be morally significant. The well-lived life involves knowledge, practical wisdom, feeling the right emotions, and also education, good habits, health, reasonable longevity, and so on. Thus, the range of the ethically significant is enormous. This theory will presumably have a larger set of morally significant actions than any other ethical theory.

## Virtue Ethics and the Traditional Ethical Assumptions

Aristotle would definitely agree with the first of the traditional ethical assumptions: that ethics is rational. He would embrace the notion that persons can reach theoretical and practical conclusions about ethical matters. They can also provide reasons to support ethical guidelines and solutions to moral problems. These reasons and solutions can be evaluated, and some will prove to be better than others. He would also acknowledge that well-intentioned people who share a similar view of human well-being and the basic human function could discuss ethical problems and arrive at mutually acceptable solutions.

The question of impartiality and moral equality is a difficult one for virtue ethics. Aristotle does not seem to have considered persons as moral equals. He endorsed slavery and believed slaves could not achieve the same well-being as citizens as long as they were enslaved. Hence, they were not the moral equals of citizens. For Aristotle, reasoning well and being virtuous depend on opportunity and education. People who lack opportunities and who may be poorly educated will not be the moral equals of those who have more opportunities and are well educated unless they can develop virtuous habits through other means, such as acquiring informal education or emulating ethical persons. Aristotle would at least claim that it would be harder for slaves to live well than for citizens to do so. He also believed a person who is born with a physical or mental disability is morally inferior to a person without such a condition. People with serious mental defects will not have the same opportunities for knowledge and practical wisdom and hence will be hindered in achieving well-being. Similarly, people with serious physical disabilities will not be able to achieve the full degree of well-being and therefore are morally inferior. Finally, Aristotle thought that women are intellectually inferior to men and thus could not achieve the degree of well-being open to males. Therefore, women are also not moral equals. Although Aristotle rejects moral equality and impartiality, does every version of virtue ethics have to do so? If an ethical person is one who is successful at fulfilling the basic function of rational beings (reasoning), then any rational being could, in theory, be ethical by being virtuous or reasoning well. People incapable of complete rationality would still be morally inferior however. Thus, we must conclude that Aristotle's virtue ethics and any theory strictly based on his ideas would not regard all persons as moral equals.

In a similar manner, it is difficult to reach a conclusion about universalizing moral judgments. Aristotle supported universal judgments about actions such as adultery, theft, and murder. He probably would also have claimed that we could universalize judgments connected to the intellectual virtues. He would not have universalized judgments about the actions that flow from moral virtues, such as courage and generosity, and certainly not about what constitutes a moderate amount of emotion. He would claim that the mean with respect to emotion is not the same for everyone in a similar situation. With regard to Aristotle's ideas, we can observe that there are a limited number of moral judgments, for example, ones related to theft, adultery, and murder, which could be universalized.

## Virtue Ethics and the Basic Ethical Themes

Relating virtue ethics to the four basic ethical themes is more difficult than doing so with the other theories. These themes work well with ethical theories focused on actions. Because virtue ethics relates to character, the themes will not be entirely appropriate. For the sake of comparison, however, I will discuss these themes in connection with virtue ethics. The first theme was represented by this question: *What kind of guidelines makes something good or bad: subjective, relative, or objective ones?* Aristotle believes some specific actions may be said to be objectively evil: murder, adultery, and theft. He also claims that certain vices are always evil: envy, shamelessness, and spite. Some virtues, such as practical wisdom, are always good. However, the moral virtues are not objective because the actual amount of emotion that constitutes the moderate amount varies from person to person in similar situations. For example, courage, as it relates to feeling the proper amount of fear and confidence, is subjective. The proper amount of emotion depends on the particular individual. Thus, the moral guidelines that create good and bad are, to a large extent, objective, but there are also subjective moral guidelines that produce other aspects of good and bad.

Another significant theme in ethics was indicated by this question: *What makes something good or evil; is it the consequences that are produced or the reasoning that leads up to it?* Ethical action, with respect to the moral virtues, is primarily related to the proper amount of emotion, not to consequences or reasoning. Therefore, in one sense, this question is not appropriate for Aristotle's ethics. The proper amount of emotion, however, is related to using reason to control the emotions and, therefore, we might say that moral action relates to reasoning. In general, Aristotle thinks that the good life is a life of excellence in reasoning. However, we might also say that virtue ethics is concerned with consequences. Ethical action is related to overall well-being, which is the ultimate goal of human virtue. All ethical actions are a means to achieve the ultimate end of well-being; hence, virtue ethics is also concerned with consequences. The best answer, then, is probably that virtue ethics is concerned with both reasoning and consequences.

The third theme is related to this question: *Are good and bad related to following general rules without exceptions or connected to separately evaluating each action, belief, and so on?* This question misses the point by an even wider margin than the previous one. Proponents of virtue ethics claim that people are not virtuous if they merely act virtuously. Virtuous people have good characters. Even if we do look at action, we see that it has several aspects. Virtuous people know what they are doing, they choose to do something because it is virtuous, and their feeling and actions flow from their character. The last part is crucial; ethical action flows from an ethical character, and an ethical character is a matter of good education and good habits. Ethical people do not need to follow general rules or evaluate individual actions because they have developed a good character and good habits. They act ethically in a spontaneous way, which is a product of character. Thus, the proper answer to this question would seem to be, neither.

The fourth theme is connected to the proper focus of ethical attention: *Are good and bad primarily related to the group, community, or majority of persons, or should the focus be on the individual?* Once again, it is difficult to answer this question definitively. The well-being that concerns Aristotle is the well-being of the individual. The goal of ethics is to discover the best life for an individual to live. Ethics, however, cannot be a matter of an individual acting in isolation. The virtuous person is necessarily social. He or she must live in a flourishing society and receive a proper education. Well-being cannot be achieved in isolation; it must be achieved together. Thus, virtue ethics includes both elements: individuals and the community. The goal of ethics is well-being for the individual, but well-being is necessarily social. Therefore, for lack of a better answer, we might say that virtue ethics involves both the individual and the community.

## Contrasting Virtue Ethics with Moral Rights Theory

Virtue ethics is radically different from moral rights theory and other theories presented here (see Appendix 1). We find four major differences between virtue ethics and moral rights theory even before we look at the traditional ethical assumptions and the basic ethical themes.

The most important difference is the assumption by Aristotle that there is a distinctive human function. Proponents of moral rights theory do not make this assumption. A second major difference is that virtue ethics is more interested in the person's character than in rights and actions. Aristotle's idea is that good actions will flow from a person with a good character. Next, virtue ethics connects the ethical life to factors such as education, health, living in a flourishing state, and theoretical wisdom, which proponents of moral rights theory would say are not essential parts of ethics. Virtue ethics has a wider view of ethical life because it is involved with social, intellectual, and physical factors as well as with making decisions and acting. Finally, the theories have very different ethical standards. Virtue ethics uses the moral model of a good or virtuous person as its ethical standard, whereas moral rights theory claims that people act unethically if they violate another person's right or rights and ethically if an action is in accord with a right or rights.

Virtue ethics and moral rights theory agree on the traditional ethical assumption that ethics is rational. The theories differ, however, regarding whether people are moral equals. Moral rights theory clearly states that all human beings are moral equals and possess moral rights. Virtue ethics claims that all persons are not moral equals because people with physical and mental disabilities, slaves, and persons who are educationally deprived will not be able to achieve complete well-being. Finally, moral rights theory claims that many moral judgments can be universalized, whereas Aristotle would probably claim that a fewer number could be. Because the theories have such different ethical standards, they take very different approaches to making moral judgments and universalizing them.

In connection with the first ethical theme, virtue ethics relates some moral guidelines to objective considerations and others to subjective ones. Moral rights theory endorses only objective ethical guidelines. Regarding the second theme, moral rights theory focuses on the reasoning that precedes action, but virtue ethics looks at both reasoning and consequences. In relation to the third theme, moral rights theory endorses not violating moral rights, a course that is similar to following rules without exceptions. Virtue ethics does not center on either following general rules or evaluating actions; rather, ethical action flows from a good character. Finally, moral rights theory concentrates on the individual, whereas virtue ethics is concerned with both individuals and with the groups in which those individuals must live to achieve well-being.

## Problems with Virtue Ethics

Virtue ethics has a number of strengths, which were discussed earlier. Unfortunately, the theory also has some serious problems, which are discussed in this section.

### Lack of Effective Ethical Guidelines

Aristotle's ethical theory does identify moral guidelines and does argue that some ethical guidelines are better than others. It also identifies ethical guidelines that would prohibit the unlimited pursuit of self-interest. An important problem with the theory, however, is that the ethical guidelines it presents seem inadequate to really help us solve many moral problems. This point relates to criterion four: a successful ethical theory must help us solve ethical problems. Aristotle provides only minimal guidelines about what actions should not be performed: for example, murder, theft, and adultery. Beyond these limited prohibitions, he offers little effective help. Discussion of the intellectual virtues does not help us solve particular ethical problems. Knowledge is required to work out ethical problems, but knowledge alone is not enough to solve them. Practical wisdom is the tendency or disposition to make sound judgments about the conduct of life, and it would certainly lead to successful solutions to ethical problems. However, practical wisdom remains mysterious for Aristotle. The concept of practical wisdom is never extended to identify the solutions to ethical problems that would follow from practical wisdom. The moral virtues provide no specific guidelines related to actions either. Aristotle presents the idea of a moderate amount of feeling, but the amount of feeling does not help us solve moral problems concerning how we should act. Regardless of what we feel, we need help in knowing what to do. In addition, there is not even objective guidance about the proper amount of feeling since the mean is relative to the individual. Aristotle specifies no objective moderate amount of fear and confidence in dangerous and difficult situations that would produce an objective account of courage. In the case of an ethically significant choice, we might have several choices that could be accompanied by a moderate amount of emotion, and several moderate amounts of emotion that might accompany an ethical choice by diferent individuals.

There can be no effective moral guidelines for virtue ethics unless a moral person can be identified, studied, and used as a moral model. The problem is that we are not sure whom to use as our moral model. There are many candidates for a moral person to emulate, and there are numerous differences between these candidates. Aristotle had one vision of the moral person; perhaps he would have identified Socrates. A modern philosopher might reject Socrates, however, and suggest someone else. There does not seem to be an adequate way to resolve this problem of the appropriate moral model. In general, Aristotle has not provided us with ethical guidelines that are adequate to help us solve many moral problems. Therefore, in light of its inability to completely satisfy criterion four, virtue ethics is not an entirely successful ethical theory.

Aristotle would not have viewed this lack of adequate ethical guidelines as a serious problem because he believed good actions would necessarily flow from good character and that education was necessary for the development of good character. He thought education would enable persons to develop the good habits needed to live well. If persons can live well as a result of possessing good habits, then they have no need for more precise ethical guidelines. This does not solve the problem, however; it only pushes it back one level. Aristotle has not provided educators with adequate ethical guidelines or a person to use as a moral model so that they would know how to educate the citizens to achieve good habits.

## Moral Luck

A second problem concerns Aristotle's view that an ethical life contains a variety of components, some of which are beyond the moral agent's control. Well-being requires health, a reasonably long life, and living in a healthy society. None of these requirements is completely within the control of the agent. This produces a version of the problem of moral luck. If the well-being of the individual depends on these factors, then an element of luck enters the moral realm. It is a matter of luck whether I am born a healthy citizen in a flourishing society or a sickly slave in a society on the verge of collapse. Many philosophers would claim that the ability to be a good person should be completely in the control of the moral agent; virtue ethics is seriously flawed in this regard. This problem relates to the fourth criterion for evaluating ethical theories. If I live in an unsuccessful society, I will be less likely to develop a good character. If I do not develop a good character, I will be unable to solve ethical problems successfully. A successful ethical theory is supposed to help us solve moral problems, but Aristotle's theory cannot help us solve ethical problems if we have bad luck. We solve ethical problems successfully because we have good character, and good character depends on luck because many of the social, physical, and intellectual factors necessary to develop a good character are beyond the control of the individual.

## The Fundamental Human Function

The final problem does not relate directly to any of the criteria for a successful moral theory, but it is probably the major reason people reject Aristotle's ethical theory. Aristotle argues that his ethical guidelines are the appropriate ones because they will help us to successfully accomplish the basic human function. He assumes the existence of a basic human function because of his assumption that everything has a basic function. However, Aristotle offers no compelling reasons to accept the position that everything has a basic function and that there is a distinctive human function. In the absence of such reasons, we are free to reject these ideas. If we reject the concept that there is a basic function for human beings, then we would also reject Aristotle's justification for choosing his ethical guidelines and his ethical guidelines.

Even if a person did accept the notion of a basic human function, he or she might not agree with Aristotle that the function was being rational. Aristotle claims that the basic human function must be related to whatever it is that only humans possess, and he thinks that humans alone are rational. Therefore, the human function is rationality. A couple of problems surface in regard to this. First, rationality might not be the exclusive possession of human beings. Our conclusion depends on how rationality is defined. Perhaps a gorilla that can learn to use sign language to communicate about a wide variety of things is rational. If rationality is not an exclusively human possession, then Aristotle's reason for choosing it is based on a mistake. Another problem is that the basic human function might not be related to something only humans possess; perhaps humans share their basic function with other species. It has been suggested that the fundamental human function, like that of any living organism, is to reproduce and pass on its genetic code. If our basic function is shared with other species, then Aristotle's decision to base ethics on our exclusive, basic function is mistaken because humans have no such exclusive, basic function. Finally, even if the basic function is an exclusive human possession, that function might not be being rational. Some Christians believe the fundamental human purpose is to love God and other human beings. Using Aristotle's reasoning, we might argue that the basic human function is to love God and other human beings because we are the only ones who can do so. There are many reasons to reject the most basic part of Aristotle's ethical theory, and subsequently, his ethical guidelines.

## Conclusion

Although virtue ethics begins with an interesting insight, serious problems are revealed with the theory as it is investigated. The theory's greatest strength is that it expands beyond ethical rules and actions the morally significant aspects of being a person. It is also interesting because it illustrates the functional or goal-oriented approach to ethics. One of its main weaknesses is the absence of a convincing justification for the notion of a basic human function that should ground ethical guidelines. This lack of justification illustrates a crucial problem for all functionalist ethical approaches—justification of the purpose or function is typically the weakest part of the theory. Because the theory evaluates everything in terms of the function, it has trouble evaluating the purpose or function itself. In regard to the criteria for a successful ethical theory, virtue ethics can provide some ethical guidelines. It can also argue that these guidelines are better than others. The guidelines endorsed by the theory would seem to prohibit the unlimited pursuit of self-interest. The main problem with the theory relates to criterion four, that the theory must be effective in helping us solve ethical problems. This theory's ethical guidelines are inadequate to help us solve many ethical problems, and it has a serious problem with moral luck. Based on the criteria in Chapter 1, Aristotle's virtue ethics would not be a completely successful ethical theory.

Many philosophers reject Aristotle's virtue ethics based on the distinctive human function of rationality. While discarding Aristotle's distinctive human function, they accept virtue ethics in general, but base it on some different account of the good life. Certainly there is nothing inherently wrong with a goal-oriented approach to good and bad. There is also nothing mistaken about the ethical insight that if we choose the relevant virtues they will help us to achieve the good life. The problem is not so much the goal-oriented approach as it is the selection of the goal. There is nothing internal to a generic version of virtue ethics that requires us to choose a certain goal or vision of the good life.

At this point, four partially successful ethical theories have been discussed: Kantian ethics, utilitarianism, moral rights theory, and virtue ethics. All four assume that ethics is rational, and all have been, to some degree, unsuccessful. One theory, ethical subjectivism, which did not make this assumption, was also unsuccessful. In the next chapter, we look at another theory that does not assume that ethics is rational, the ethics of care. In fact, the ethics of care also rejects the other traditional ethical assumptions of impartiality and universalizability. It is worth investigation because it represents such a different approach to moral guidelines.

QUESTIONS FOR REVIEW

*Here are some questions to help you review the main concepts in this chapter.*

1. What is the ethical insight associated with virtue ethics? What additional idea helps make Aristotle's version of virtue ethics distinctive?

2. In your opinion, what is the good life? What elements would it necessarily contain?

3. What, in general, are virtues?

4. In Aristotle's opinion, what is the distinctive function of human beings?

5. What are the intellectual virtues? How do they help persons achieve well-being?

6. What are the moral virtues? Provide a detailed explanation of Aristotle's account of courage to illustrate a moral virtue. How would courage help persons to achieve well-being?

7. What is the ethical standard for virtue ethics?

8. In your opinion, what is the best justification for using the Aristotelian ethical standard? Discuss the related strengths of the theory.

9. Would virtue ethics endorse any aspects of the traditional ethical assumptions?

10. What position would virtue ethics take on each of the four ethical themes?

11. Identify three major differences between virtue ethics and moral rights theory.

12. Which problem with virtue ethics do you think is the most serious? Explain why.

13. Would virtue ethics be a successful ethical theory based on the criteria in Chapter 1? Explain why, or why not.

14. Do you believe there is a basic human function shared by all people? If so, what is it?

15. Who is your model of a good or virtuous person? If you had to choose someone to emulate, who would it be? Explain why you chose the person you did.

16. What is character? How would you describe your character? If you wanted to improve your character, how would you go about doing so? How would you know that you were headed in the right direction?

## NOTES

1. Aristotle, *Nicomachean Ethics*, in *The Complete Works of Aristotle*, edited by Jonathan Barnes (Princeton, NJ: Princeton University Press, 1984).

2. Ibid., pp. 1730–1731.

3. Ibid., p. 1735.

4. Ibid., p. 1799.

5. Ibid., p. 1805.

6. Ibid., p. 1748.

7. Ibid.

# Chapter 9

# *The Ethics of Care*

To a large extent, our lives are characterized by relationships. We are sons and daughters, fathers and mothers, aunts and uncles, nieces and nephews, cousins, friends, partners, colleagues, teammates, and so on. Traditional moral philosophy, however, has tended to deemphasize relationships in favor of a certain picture of the moral agent and person. The traditional ethical assumptions of rationality and impartiality are crucial to this picture. Several other aspects of the view are individuality, isolation, and freedom. Moral agents are seen as single, distinct beings, isolated in their ability to choose, decide, and act. These choices, decisions, and actions originate from the agent and can be willed in accord with a rational principle. Traditional moral theories provide individuals with the principles that should form the rational basis of action. These principles enable individual moral agents to live together successfully despite their being motivated primarily by self-interest. The unlimited pursuit of self-interest can lead to individuals harming and disrespecting other persons. Individual agents do not need to know anything about the identity of the other individuals to be ethical, however. What is important is whether or not the being is a full-status morally significant being and a moral agent. If the individual is a full-status morally significant being, he or she is a moral equal and should be treated impartially. Impartial treatment, based on moral principles, requires ignoring "irrelevant factors" such as relationships. If the individual is a moral agent, then the person will be expected to act and will be held responsible for those actions. Therefore, traditional moral philosophy has operated with a view of the person and moral agent that is at odds with the fact that to a large extent our lives are characterized by relationships.

In the twentieth century, however, female moral philosophers pointed out the discrepancy between the fact that human experience is to a large degree characterized by relationships and the traditional picture of the person and moral agent. These philosophers emphasized the relatedness or connectedness of human beings. They point out that persons are always related to and interdependent with other persons. Their ethical insight is that *ethics is primarily concerned with relationships between persons*. This emphasis on relationships has produced discussion about the ideal or optimum relationship from an ethical point of view. Some philosophers have suggested that the ideal human relationship can be identified as a relation of care.

This assertion that the relation of care is the optimum human relationship has produced a number of ethical theories that are grouped under the term "ethics of care." One excellent example of the ethics of care can be found in Nel Noddings's book, *Caring: A Feminine Approach to Ethics and Moral Education.*[1] Noddings presents the ethics of caring as an alternative to traditional ethical theories. She believes ethical behavior is connected to human emotional response and the interdependence of people. Therefore, her ethic focuses not on reason and ethical principles but on sentiment and on using ethical caring as the model of an ethical relation.

This chapter is primarily about Nel Noddings's ethics of caring. Noddings's work is an important inclusion in this book because it illustrates the significant contribution to ethics by female moral philosophers during the twentieth century. Noddings, however, is merely one contributor to this female presence. If there is a crucial figure at the beginning of this movement, it is probably Carol Gilligan. Thus, some of Gilligan's ideas are included to "set the stage" for Noddings. Noddings originally referred to her ethics of care as a "feminine ethics," which is often differentiated from "feminist ethics." Thus, the chapter attempts to explain the difference between them and contains a brief section on feminist ethics. Finally, as well as being a theory proposed by a woman, Noddings's ideas are important because they can be used to represent the contemporary ethical thinking that has rejected rationality, impartiality, and universalizability. It is Noddings's focus on feelings or sentiment that enables her to avoid the concentration on rationality. Her position is not, however, without links to the intellectual past.

## The Background to Noddings's Theory

Noddings's ideas about caring fit into a philosophical and psychological background. Her focus on sentiment and not reason is reminiscent of the philosophical ideas of the Scottish philosopher David Hume (1711–1776). Hume's moral ideas are interconnected with the rest of his

philosophy and are difficult, but his position on the relation of sentiment to ethics can be sketched out. Because morals have an effect on
actions, Hume believes they could not be derived from reason. He
observes that reason alone cannot move us to action. He says, "Morals
excite passions, and produce or prevent actions. Reason of itself is
utterly impotent in this particular. The rules of morality, therefore, are
not conclusions of our reason."[2] If morals are not derived from reason,
Hume believes they must be derived from passion. He thinks that moral
judgments are related to a moral sentiment, which provide us with feelings of approbation and disapprobation, or approval and disapproval.
These feelings are aroused by human characters and actions performed
by humans. The feelings and judgments are not voluntary, nor are they
the result of deliberation concerning rational principles or moral laws.
Hume illustrates his view with the following famous example, which I
quote at length because it presents Hume's ethics in summary form.

> Take any action allow'd to be vicious: Wilful murder, for instance. Exam-
> ine it in all lights, and see if you can find that matter of fact, or real exis-
> tence, which you call vice. In whichever way you take it, you find only
> certain passions, motives, volitions and thoughts. There is no other matter
> of fact in the case. The vice entirely escapes you, as long as you consider
> the object. You can never find it, till you turn your reflexion into your
> own breast, and find a sentiment of disapprobation, which arises in you,
> towards this action. Here is a matter of fact; but 'tis the object of feeling,
> not of reason. It lies in your self, not in the object. So that when you pro-
> nounce any action or character to be vicious, you mean nothing, but that
> from the constitution of your nature you have a feeling or sentiment of
> blame from the contemplation of it.[3]

Thus, for Hume moral judgments are the product of a moral sentiment. This is similar to ethical subjectivism, which was discussed in
Chapter 4. Many philosophers consider Hume to be a subjectivist.
Other scholars point out, however, that Hume thought that the moral
sentiment was the same in every "normal" person. If everyone came
equipped with the same moral sentiment that operated in the same
way, all persons would agree on most of their moral judgments. For
example, we all have a sentiment of disapprobation when we witness a
vicious murder. Thus, there is a realist or objectivist element in
Hume's ethics.[4] In any case, Noddings's emphasis on sentiment in relation to moral guidelines fits into a tradition that goes back at least to
David Hume.

Noddings's ethical ideas also can also be located in the context of
the work of two psychologists, Lawrence Kohlberg and Carol Gilligan.
Kohlberg concluded from his research that all human moral develop-

ment follows a necessary path through three levels, although many people do not progress all the way.[5] At the first level, good and bad are understood in relation to power, reward, and punishment. At the second level, good and bad are related to the moral guidelines of groups and society. Finally, at the highest level, people view ethics in terms of objective moral principles. The highest stage for Kohlberg is centered on justice, and among the theories in this book, Kantian ethics would best represent this highest stage.

Carol Gilligan agrees with Kohlberg that there are levels of moral development. She believes, however, that Kohlberg's levels represent a view of moral development centered around justice, which does not explain the moral development of all human beings. She claims (or originally claimed) that this is a masculine way of talking about ethics and suggests that this masculine character may have reflected the fact that Kohlberg used only males in his original studies. Kohlberg's males see the primary moral obligation as "treating people fairly and impartially." They see themselves as acting based on principles, and Kohlberg evaluates their moral levels in connection with the kind of principles they use. Gilligan points out that women often failed to achieve the highest moral stage in Kohlberg's hierarchy.

Gilligan's research suggests a different way of talking about ethics, one more involved with relationships, care, and nonviolence than with justice. The title of her influential book, *In a Different Voice,* highlights the idea that there is an alternative way to talk about ethics.[6] She points out that it is mostly women who employ this different way of discussing ethical problems. Gilligan's women articulate a different moral objective: to care for others and to minimize the harm done to others. They see themselves as acting after a consideration of the effects, especially the harmful effects, of their actions on those real people who would be affected by them. Like Kohlberg, Gilligan asserts that there are three levels to moral development. At the first level, the person is oriented toward individual survival. At the second level, goodness is understood in terms of self-sacrifice. At the third level, nonviolence or the injunction against hurting others is elevated to a principle governing everyone, the moral agent as well as others affected by her actions. It is on this level that care becomes a universal obligation.

For many moral philosophers, and even some psychologists, the Kohlberg/Gilligan theory of progressive moral levels is problematic. As psychologist Norma Hahn points out, these researchers claim to be merely describing the moral development of human beings, but by ranking the various moral orientations, they are inserting their own ethical judgments about what is better and what is worse. She states that researchers cannot rank moral thinking without taking a normative moral position, whether they know it or not.[7] Kohlberg places the justice orientation at the top of his ranking of moral levels because he assumes (perhaps unknowingly) that it is the closest to a legitimate moral theory. He does not reveal the objective criterion or set of criteria he used to rank these approaches to good and evil, nor why this criterion or set of criteria is the best one. Gilligan's approach reveals the same problem. She ranks the nonviolent orientation at the highest level because it fits her normative position. Like Kohlberg, she is not clear about the criterion or set of criteria grounding the ranking, nor why that set is better than any alternatives. Psychologists can certainly identify different ways of talking about good and bad that people actually employ, but they should be careful about ranking these different moral languages. Clear evaluative criteria are needed to produce legitimate rankings, and the psychologists need to explain what their criteria are and why their criteria are the best ones to use.

There has also been a good deal of criticism directed at the idea that men and women have characteristically different "moral languages" or ways of thinking about ethics. Do Kohlberg's men simply represent some men and Gilligan's women some women, or do they represent all the members of their gender? Certainly both of these psychologists used extremely small and socially narrow samples to be drawing such broad conclusions. In addition to this methodological problem, there is a philosophical concern related to gender-based moral languages. Most twentieth-century thinkers endorse the idea that women are the moral equals of men. They are concerned that gender-based differences in moral thinking might undercut moral equality. They would not even be satisfied with the idea that these "moral voices" are different, but equal. This "different but equal" position would still establish gender-based norms for the members of each gender. There would be some moral view that women ought to endorse because they were women and that men ought to endorse because they were men. Thus, men and women would not really be effective moral equals because they would not be held to the same moral standards. This idea of gender-based ethical positions is objectionable to many contemporary thinkers.

We can reject moral hierarchies and gender-based ethical positions and still be interested in the ethics of care. Noddings does not endorse the moral hierarchy view, and this is one advantage of her ideas over Gilligan's. Another reason to use Noddings's ideas instead of Gilligan's is that Noddings provides a more detailed theory. Noddings does, however, retain the idea that the ethics of care is a feminine way of discussing ethics. In this chapter, however, the idea of the ethics of care as a feminine ethical theory will be deemphasized. For the purpose of this text, it is an ethic created by a woman but open to adoption by anyone. The ethics of care is a valuable inclusion in this book because it represents the work of female moral philosophers and because it is representative of contemporary moral theories that reject rationality, impartiality, and universalizability.

## Natural and Ethical Caring

Most of us have been cared for by a person or persons, if only our parents. We value the memories of being cared for and the relationship of caring. The ethical insight of Noddings ethics is that *ethics is primarily concerned with relationships between persons.* The additional idea essential to developing this ethic is that the ultimate relationship, in an ethical sense, is caring.

Nel Noddings claims that human encounter and emotional response are basic aspects of human existence. People are necessarily interdependent and are the products of the various relationships in which they are involved. Ethical action arises out of these relationships, not out of isolated individuals following moral rules. She identifies natural caring—the relation in which we care for another out of love or natural inclination—as the human condition that is consciously or unconsciously perceived to be good. Ethical caring—the relation in which a person meets another morally—arises out of natural caring and can be used as a moral model of the ideal ethical relationship.

Noddings's account of ethical caring identifies three important elements: apprehending the other's reality, engrossment, and motivational displacement. First, ethical caring requires that the one who cares for the other (the one-caring) must try to apprehend the other's (the cared-for) reality. The one-caring must consider the other's nature, way of life, needs, and desires. He or she should try to feel, as nearly as possible, what the other feels. The objective is as complete an understanding as is practical. Second, ethical caring involves engrossment. The one-caring is concerned with the other and must be present in his or her acts of caring and involved with the other. The third aspect of the caring relation is motivational displacement. The one-caring is motivated by the good of the other. There is a displacement of interest from his or her reality to the reality of the other, and the one-caring is motivated more by the good of the other than by his or her own self-interest. Self-interest cannot be ignored completely, but in the midst of the caring relation, most of the motivation is directed toward the welfare, protection, and enhancement of the cared-for. An ongoing caring relationship requires a commitment on the part of the one-caring to act for the benefit of the other. On the other side of the relation, Noddings seems to require very little from the cared-for. That individual must recognize that the one-caring cares for him or her and accept that caring. Overall, Noddings concludes that, "One must meet the other as one-caring. From this requirement there is no escape for one who would be moral."[8]

According to Noddings, ethical caring depends on two sentiments and on memories of caring and being cared for. First is the "sentiment of natural caring."[9] She describes this sentiment as the "natural sympathy that human beings feel for each other."[10] Human beings have a natural emotional response or sympathetic feeling toward other human beings. We feel badly for them when they are in pain and pleased for them when they are happy. At one point, she associates this feeling with the sentiment of natural caring. It is hard to say how close this sentiment is to Hume's "moral sentiment." One similar point is that both thinkers believe sentiment motivates us. For Noddings, the initial "impulse" to care arises as a feeling. For example, we feel badly about another's pain, and this moves us to care. The second sentiment arises when we remember our best experiences of being cared for and caring for others. This sentiment is characterized as a "longing to maintain, recapture, or enhance our most caring and tender moments."[11] The second sentiment reinforces the first. I not only feel badly about the other's pain, but I long to help him or her because of my feelings connected to helping others and being helped.

Based on Noddings's view, the two sentiments are the source of moral obligation. She asks whether we can demand that others care, and answers, "There can be, surely, no demand for the initial impulse that arises as a feeling, an inner voice saying 'I must do something,' in response to the need of the cared-for."[12] She adds, although we cannot demand the initial impulse, we would be repelled by a person who never felt it. Even if someone feels the initial "I must," however, he or she may reject it. It is the second ethical sentiment that reinforces the "I must" or moral obligation in response to the plight of the other. It arises from our evaluation of the caring relation as being superior to other forms of relatedness. We long to be in caring relationships, and that longing provides a major motivation for us to care for others and to be moral. Caring requires a person to respond to the initial impulse with an act of commitment: either overt action or deliberation about how best to promote the welfare of the other. Noddings summarizes her view in this way:

> I am suggesting that our inclination towards and interest in morality derives from caring. In caring, we accept the natural impulse to act on behalf of the present other. We are engrossed in the other. We have received him and feel his pain or happiness, but we are not compelled by

this impulse. We have a choice; we may accept what we feel or reject it. If we have a strong desire to be moral, we will not reject it, and this strong desire to be moral is derived, reflectively, from the more fundamental and natural desire to be and to remain related.[13]

## The Ethical Ideal and the Ethical Standard

Noddings claims that we have memories of those times when we were cared for and in which we cared for others, and that we can choose to use these memories to guide our conduct. When I reflect on the way I am in genuine caring relationships, I form a picture of myself. This picture of myself as cared-for and one-caring is accompanied by an awareness of the goodness of natural caring. In connection with this picture and awareness, I form an ideal picture of myself as one-caring and cared-for. When I am confronted with the plight of an other, I feel compelled to respond because I realize that caring or not caring will enhance or diminish the ethical ideal. I feel that I must do something. The motivational power of this "I must" is related to the value I place on moving toward my ideal picture of myself and on the importance of the relationship of caring. If I want to be ethical, I am obligated to meet the other as one-caring, to increase my virtue as one-caring, and to enhance my ethical ideal. This ethical obligation depends on the existence of or potential for a close relationship with the person and "the dynamic potential for growth in relation, including the potential for increased reciprocity and, perhaps, mutuality."[14] The potential for an effective caring relationship helps to determine whether there is an obligation, and the chance of reciprocity helps us to prioritize our obligations. The greater the potential for a reciprocal relationship of caring, the higher a priority I should give to developing the relationship.

Noddings claims that we form an ideal picture of ourselves as one-caring and cared-for. We realize that how we act toward the other will enhance or diminish this ideal picture. This picture of an ideal caring self can act as a moral model, ethical ideal, or ethical standard. Thus, the ethical standard of the ethics of care is *the ideal picture of myself as one-caring and cared-for.* This ethical standard is similar to the ethical standard of virtue ethics. In virtue ethics, the standard is a good person: one who has the virtues and does not have the vices. According to Noddings, the standard is the person's ideal picture of himself or herself as a good person, that is, as a caring person. She concludes that, "Ethical caring, as I have described it, depends not upon rule or principle but upon the development of an ideal self. It does not depend upon just any ideal of self, but the ideal developed in congruence with one's best remembrance of caring and being cared-for."[15]

We ought to be cautious about this ethical standard, however. Noddings states that her primary focus is not on good and bad but on moral perception and sensitivity, although she does acknowledge that good and bad are useful concepts. The one-caring, she asserts, can make judgments of good and bad by basing them on whether the thing being judged promotes or inhibits caring. For example, hurting people is usually wrong because it inhibits caring for people and detracts from the ethical ideal. Unless I act out of self-defense, hurting some people does not help me to better care for others. She seems to think that I need to examine situations and strive to find ways to care for people without hurting others. I determine right and wrong in relation to my ideal picture of myself as one-caring and cared-for. This picture has objective elements based on my experiences with effective caring; that is, some things have promoted effective caring and others have not. These objective elements related to my actual experiences with caring help prevent the ethic of care from becoming a form of ethical subjectivism.

The ethics of care may not be as precise as some of the other ethical theories, but it is not meant to be. The moral weight is on the person to act for the benefit of the other in a specific caring situation and not on rules or principles. The ethics of care is centered around the ideal picture of the individual as a caring person. Good and bad relate to our moving closer to the ideal or further away from it. A person determines what to do by examining particular cases in light of the caring relation and the ethical ideal. We must still ask, however, to what extent does Noddings expect us to care? Are we expected to care for everyone we encounter, and what about people who we never meet in person?

## The Limit of Ethical Caring and Morally Significant Actions

Nel Noddings denies that we are obligated to care for everyone. Relationships determine the nature of ethical obligation. We should care for those with whom we already have a caring relation or with whom there is potential for an effective caring relation. The relation or the potential for an effective caring relation helps establish the limits of obligation. The greater the potential for an effective and reciprocal caring relation, the higher priority I should give to developing it. We do not have to feel obligated to care for those who are distant and with whom we have no real potential for an effective caring relation unless we abandon already existing caring relations. One metaphor she uses is that of concentric circles: We care most for those in the inner circles, and less as the circles become more distant. She illustrates the point with this example: "I am not obliged to care for starving children in Africa, because there is no way for this caring to be completed in the other unless I abandon the caring to which I am obligated."[16] We may still choose to do something for these children, but we are not obligated to do so. The limit of our obligation is based more on the potential for effective caring and existing caring relationships than on geography. My grown child may move to Africa, but I am still obligated to care for him or her to the best of my ability. Of course, geography makes it much harder to develop caring relationships; it is much easier for me to develop a relationship with the children living in poverty next door than with the impoverished children living in Africa.

Another limitation to the obligation to care is connected to the idea that the one-caring must also protect himself or herself from abusive or harmful relationships that would interfere with the ability to care for others. We are not obligated to care for people who threaten our ability to care for others or ourselves. Those who care must care for themselves as well as others, and they must limit their caring so that they can maintain themselves and their ability to care in the future.

The limits of effective caring would seem to differentiate between what is and is not morally significant, at least in the strongest sense of the morally significant wherein we are obligated to respond to that significance. Things that relate to those we care for are the most morally significant for us, and our moral obligations relate to these relationships of care.

## Justification for the Ethical Standard and Strengths of the Theory

The ethics of care strives to promote the attitude of caring. It is centered on each person's ethical ideal, the ideal picture of oneself as cared-for and one-caring. This ethical ideal motivates us to enter into caring relationships because we know that caring or not caring will move us closer to or further away from our ethical ideal, and our desire is to move closer to it.

### Consistent with the Value of Natural Caring

One justification for the ethical standard is that it is consistent with natural caring, and, according to Noddings, natural caring is good. Thus, we know that ethical caring is good because it is modeled on natural caring, and we intuitively know that natural caring is good. Knowing intuitively that natural caring is good, we ought to engage in natural caring and also in the ethical caring that is modeled on it. This makes the first justification ultimately rather mysterious because it depends on an intuition about natural caring. The intuition does, however, present a nice contrast to Kantian ethics. If you are driven by a respect for rationality, you might become a Kantian; whereas if you are inspired by the intuition that natural caring is good, you might adopt the ethics of care. The related strength of the theory is that it will appeal to people who share the intuition that natural caring is good.

## Harmony with Our Experience of Life

Another justification for the ethical standard and a related strength of the ethics of care is that the theory is in harmony with the observation that specific people and relationships are a vital part of life. Instead of neglecting the importance of relationships, as much Western ethical theory does, the theory asserts that relationships and human encounter are basic aspects of human existence that cannot be neglected by ethics. Thus, the theory is closer to the way we actually live than many other ethical theories, and this will be a strength of it for many people.

## The Problem of Impartiality and Special Relationships

A final justification for using the ethical standard and a related strength of the ethical theory is that it solves a difficult problem that plagues ethical theories that emphasize moral equality and impartiality. Consider how an act utilitarianism would evaluate this case. I have one hundred dollars that I do not need for necessities. I can take my children to a toy store and let each of them spend fifty dollars on toys, or I can donate the money to a legitimate charity that will use it to buy medicine for impoverished people who are in danger of dying from a disease. An act utilitarian would argue that I should do whatever would produce the greatest benefit for those affected by my action. Everyone affected by my action is a moral equal, and I should make my decision about what to do impartially. The toys will make my children happy for a while, and hence benefit them. Buying them toys will also make me happy, and benefit me. My children already have many toys, however, and these toys are not a necessity for them. The medicine will save many people's lives, and it is a necessity for those who are ill and cannot afford it themselves. Thus, the medicine will produce a greater benefit than the toys. I should send the money to the legitimate charity if I want to be ethical. In fact, buying toys for my children would be unethical given the alternative. The implication of this example is that it is unethical to act based on special relationships instead of maximizing benefit for those affected. Theories like act utilitarianism, which stress moral equality and impartiality, seem not only to neglect special relationships but actually undermine them. This is a serious problem for these theories because we value our special relationships enormously. I do not want to be told that it is unethical to buy toys for my children. Thus, I am inclined to reject such a theory because of this problem. A strength of Noddings's theory is that it does not have this problem. It rejects moral equality and impartiality and urges me to act based on caring for my children. I have no caring relation with the dying strangers and, hence, have no ethical obligation toward them. The ethics of caring endorses our special relationships rather than neglecting or being detrimental to them.

## The Ethics of Care and the Traditional Ethical Assumptions

Nel Noddings would reject what I have called the traditional ethical assumptions. She believes ethics is based primarily on sentiment, not reason. Moral obligation relates primarily to the two sentiments discussed earlier and to the value we place on our ideal picture of ourselves as caring individuals, not to rational arguments. She does not, however, dismiss reason completely. Noddings would agree that we could provide reasons for our ethical evaluations, for example, that stealing from someone does not enhance a person's ethical ideal as one-caring. Ultimately, however, she would assert that ethics is not based on reason because caring relationships are founded on sentiment, not reason and rational principles.

Noddings also does not endorse moral equality. We are morally obligated to care for those closest to us, but we are not obligated to care for children in foreign countries. People are not moral equals; the degree to which we should care for them relates to our relationships with them and the potential for developing and maintaining effective caring relationships.

Noddings also rejects the idea of universalizing moral judgments, examining each case in the light of caring to preserve the uniqueness of human encounters. Claiming that subjective experience is essential to ethical encounters, Noddings asserts that conditions are seldom sufficiently similar for one moral agent to declare that everyone who wants to be ethical must perform or not perform this action. She does insist, however, that there is universal access to the caring attitude, but this is not the same as declaring that moral judgments can be universalized.

## The Ethics of Care and the Basic Ethical Themes

The first ethical theme is related to this question: *What kind of guidelines makes something good or bad: subjective, relative, or objective ones?* Noddings believes everyone consciously or unconsciously perceives the relation of natural caring as good, which provides an objective component in the ethics of care. Also, actions that are good must be objectively beneficial to the cared-for and not harmful to the one-caring. For example, it is always good for a person to care for a seriously ill family member when this caring does not harm the one-caring. Noddings is hesitant, however, about this matter; she wants to preserve the subjective aspect of human encounter and examine each ethically significant case separately. Thus, there is a subjective element to these ethical guidelines as well. This theme does not apply very well to the ethics of care, but if we had to respond, we might claim that moral guidelines related to the ethics of care have both an objective and a subjective aspect.

The second ethical theme is indicated by this question: *What makes something good or evil; is it the consequences that are produced or the reasoning that leads up to it?* Noddings is more concerned with consequences than with reasoning. The one-caring must act for the benefit of the cared-for, and this means that consequences are essential. If my caring does not benefit the cared-for, then I have not acted ethically. The focus of the ethics of care is on consequences.

The third theme is connected to this question: *Are good and bad related to following general rules without exceptions or connected to separately evaluating each action, belief, and so on?* Noddings rejects general rules and argues that we must examine each case to see what is best for the person to do.

The fourth theme is related to the proper focus of ethical attention: *Are good and bad primarily related to the group, community, or majority of persons, or should the focus be on the individual?* Noddings believes we must focus on the individual cared-for. We must relate to people as unique individuals, and we must preserve the "subjective aspect" of human encounters.

## Contrasting the Ethics of Care and Virtue Ethics

Nel Noddings's ethics of care is an interesting addition to the ethical conversation and reveals some important differences from virtue ethics and the other ethical theories (see Appendix 1). The ethics of care and virtue ethics have similar ethical standards. Noddings says that the ethical ideal is my picture of myself as a caring person, and virtue ethics makes the ethical standard a good person who has the virtues and does not have the vices. The ethics of care and virtue ethics are in agreement on two further points. Both theories reject moral equality. They also maintain that some actions are objectively good or evil.

One of the main differences between the ethics of care and virtue ethics is that Noddings's theory does not endorse the idea of a basic purpose shared by all human beings. The ethics of care is also much less based on reason. It grounds ethics in sentiments, memories, and an ideal relationship, not in reasoning successfully. Virtue ethics does include sentiment as morally significant but is concerned primarily with moderating sentiment, whereas Noddings endorses the two sentiments connected to ethical caring. The two theories also disagree on universalizing some moral judgments. Noddings strongly opposes universalizing moral judgments.

The two ethical theories disagree on three of the four basic ethical themes, agreeing only that good and bad have both objective and subjective elements. In regard to the other themes, virtue ethics is not focused on rules or actions; it is concerned with both the group and the individual and both reasoning and consequences. The ethics of care centers on specific actions, individuals, and consequences. Because of these important differences, the two ethical theories offer contrasting approaches to ethics.

## Problems with the Ethics of Care

The ethics of care does identify some ethical guidelines and argues that they are better than other possible guidelines. It clearly identifies ethical guidelines that prohibit the unlimited pursuit of self-interest. It does, however, develop some problems related to the fourth criterion: The theory must be able to help us solve ethical problems.

The ethics of care is a contemporary theory, and I will look at another contemporary source to identify some of the main problems with the theory. One of the best of the numerous discussions of Noddings's views is found in Claudia Card's article, "Caring and Evil."[17] Her main question is: "Can an ethics of care without justice enable us adequately to resist evil?"[18] Card identifies problem areas that would seem to indicate a negative answer to this question.

### Incomplete Moral Standard

The first problem area involves the evils that strangers inflict upon strangers. Card states that "resting all of ethics on caring threatens to exclude as ethically insignificant our relationships with most people in the world, because we do not know them individually and never will."[19] No one has the responsibility to care for everyone in the sense of "caring" central to the ethics of care: We do not have the moral obligation to care for Africa's starving children. The implication of this argument is that Noddings has given us no guidance about how to avoid acting unethically in regard to most of the people in the world, people whose lives we may affect for the worse even though we have no personal relationship with them. Because we cannot have caring relationships with most of the people in the world, Card claims that we need other grounds for moral obligations toward them, such as justice. Thus, she believes the ethics of care is incomplete. This criticism relates to the fourth criterion for evaluating ethical theories: The theory must help us to solve ethical problems. If the ethics of care is incomplete and does not provide moral guidelines that relate to most of the world's people, it will not help us solve ethical problems connected to these people. Therefore, it will only partially satisfy criterion four.

## Exploitation of the One-Caring

The second problem area involves the evil that intimates do to each other. According to Card, if we use caring as a base for ethics, we are "in danger of valorizing relationships that are sheerly exploitative of our distinctly human capacity to take another's point of view."[20] That is, the ethics of care might endorse relationships where people who are required to take the other's point of view are valued simply for what they contribute to others or the projects of others instead of being valued for themselves as persons with their own ends and projects. Maintaining the extreme value of caring relationships in all cases will lead to the one-caring being exploited or taken advantage of by the cared-for. Because Noddings claims that if we must exclude someone from our caring we act under a diminished ethical ideal there is ethical pressure to maintain exploitative relationships that perhaps ought to be dissolved. Card observes that there are some caring relationships from which the one-caring ought to be able to withdraw without being "ethically diminished." We must be able to withdraw from exploitative or abusive relationships with intimate partners or family members without diminishing the ethical ideal. Card points out that caring has the consequence of supporting people's projects, and that caring, unrestrained by other values, might lead us to support immoral projects. She claims that "it is better to cease caring than to allow one's caring to be exploited in the service of immoral ends."[21] Once again, Card has identified an area where she thinks the ethics of care is incomplete.

Caring needs to be supplemented with other moral values, such as justice, so that the one-caring can evaluate his or her caring relations and withdraw from those that are supporting unethical projects or exploitation. This criticism also relates to criterion four. If the ethical guidelines identified by the ethics of care are incomplete, then the theory will not be adequate to help us solve all moral problems. The one-caring will not be able to solve all the moral problems connected to caring unless there is some additional ethical standard to enable the person to identify unethical projects and instances of exploitation and to determine what will really promote the welfare of those involved.

## Limits on Promoting Welfare

The final problem concerns one of my own questions about the ethics of care? Why is ethical caring, which limits promoting the welfare of others to a relatively small group of people, preferable to maximizing the welfare of the greatest number of people? We might begin to think about this by asking, "Why is ethical caring good?" Ultimately, the goodness of ethical caring seems to be grounded in the claim that all humans consciously or unconsciously perceive natural caring to be good. This thesis is a factual hypothesis and could be supported with research of the type done by Kohlberg or Gilligan. Noddings, however, offers no empirical evidence for this claim. Of course, even if people do perceive natural caring as good, it does not mean that they ought to do it. To strengthen this theory, Noddings needs an argument to support the claim that we ought to perceive natural caring as good. She then needs another argument establishing a tighter connection between natural and ethical caring, or a separate argument to show why ethical caring is good.

Natural caring is illustrated by a parent's caring for a helpless infant. Natural caring is vital to the survival of the species because human beings are born helpless and must be cared for to survive. If we believe the survival of particular human beings and of the species in general is good, then natural caring is a good means to help accomplish these ends. Ethical caring, however, is not always related to survival. It is related to the well-being of the other, which extends beyond survival. Why is it good to promote the well-being or benefit of others? Utilitarians have one kind of answer to this question, but it is a response associated with happiness or benefit being the ultimate end of action and the ultimate good. If benefit is the ultimate good, then we should try to maximize it for as many people as possible. Noddings thinks we should promote the welfare or benefit of those with whom we have developed relationships of care, but why limit it to these people? Perhaps her answer would be that limiting the number of people whose welfare we promote will make us more effective at helping others. She might believe utilitarianism is ineffective because the ethical concern is spread out over all morally significant beings, whereas the ethics of care is more effective because it concentrates the ethical focus. Would the ethics of care be more effective, and is effectiveness a sufficient justification to choose an ethical theory?

## Feminine and Feminist Ethics

Noddings describes her approach to ethics as a feminine approach. Some philosophers have tried to differentiate a feminine approach from a feminist one. Roughly, the feminine approach is centered around relationships, interdependency, and caring. It usually asserts that these are key elements in an ethics related to women. Women think and talk about ethics using these concepts. Thus, one implication is that women ought to conceive of good and bad in terms of relationships, interdependency, and caring. In contrast to feminist ethics, the feminist approach has at least a couple of different common features. First, feminists observe that women are subordinated by men in contemporary Western societies. Women are subordinated because men have much more political, economic, and social power. In the United States, in spite of a population with slightly more women than men, men hold the majority of political offices and most major corporate positions. Men exert the most social influence too. Women are often discriminated against in a wide variety of ways. A second essential feminist theme is that this subordination of women is morally wrong and should be eliminated. Women are the moral equals of men, and their interests should receive equal weight with those of men. Power should be distributed equally among women and men. Such an egalitarian society would require radical changes in the political and economic structures and in the very nature of society. Feminists are united by their opposition to the inequality between men and women and are dedicated to ending the domination of men. Roughly, a feminist ethics is one that is in accord with at least these two themes.

Another common theme in feminism is that the domination of women by men is social or cultural rather than a biological phenomenon. Many philosophers use the term "sex" to refer to the biological difference. Clearly, men and women have biological differences and constitute two sexes. The term "gender" is used to point to the socially or culturally constructed roles assigned to men and women. It is a "gender difference," not a biological difference, if women are expected to stay home and raise children while men are urged to enter the corporate world to make money. Another gender difference is dressing little boys in blue and giving them toy trucks, while dressing little girls in pink and giving them dolls. The construction of gender starts in the home with the way people raise their children. Society constructs gender in all its aspects: home, school, church, workplace, political arena, and so on. Feminists think these rigid gender differences are factually wrong because little girls may like blue or enjoy playing with trucks, and women can certainly be successful in the corporate world. Little boys might like playing with dolls, and men might be successful at raising children if they were allowed to do such things. Feminists also think that rigid gender differences are morally wrong because one gender occupies the superior position and the other is subordinate, even though men and women are moral equals. The corporate job is superior because it brings a high salary and prestige, whereas being a "homemaker" offers no pay and little recognition. The male gender role is the superior position, and the female gender role is inferior. Thus, society forces women to be inferiors, when they are really moral equals. Gender, as it is constructed by societies like the United States, is unethical because these rigid gender differences are accompanied by greater and lesser amounts of political, economic, and social power.

Thus, we can see why many feminists are concerned about the ethics of care. Because rigid gender-based differences undercut moral equality, the ethics of care might be seen to be forcing women to accept the role of caregiver as a matter of gender. Women will be caring for others, and this role may be an inferior one because these others may exploit or take advantage of the women. Feminists would not even be satisfied with separate but equal rigid gender roles because this would limit the freedom of the individual. Why should women be forced to be homemakers even if this role brought with it a large salary and enormous prestige? Why should women be obligated to be caregivers simply because they are women? Free individuals ought to be able to choose the social roles they will occupy and the ethical theory they will endorse. To uphold moral equality and freedom, all social roles must bring relatively equal amounts of power and be open to anyone. In a similar manner, to uphold moral equality and freedom, persons must be able to choose their approach to moral good and bad based on reasons, not gender. Rigid gender-based roles make women inferior and limit their freedom and are opposed by feminists.

Feminists do not have to be only women. To be a feminist, in the sense indicated here, is to think that male domination is wrong and that something must be done about it. Men who oppose inequality, male domination, and rigid genders are feminists in this sense. If someone thinks that male domination is wrong, he or she must have some moral view that justifies this moral judgment. Feminists are found among ethical relativists, Kantians, utilitarians, moral rights advocates, and proponents of many other theories.

## Conclusion

The idea that an ethic could be based on care generated a considerable amount of interest among moral philosophers. Most moral philosophers, however, still seem more comfortable with an ethics based on rules and principles rather than one based on relationships and care. In spite of the problems with this theory, the ethics of care is an interesting addition to the ethical conversation. The greatest strengths of this theory are that it is in harmony with the fact that relationships are vital to our lives and it allows special treatment for those who are closest to us without this special treatment being unethical. Most traditional ethical theories emphasize moral equality, neglect relationships, and cannot respond to the special relationships we have with friends and family members. The theory does seem to be incomplete, however, and therefore it will not always be successful in helping us solve moral problems.

In the preceding chapters, I have briefly examined nine ethical theories and found that there are problems with all of them. In Chapter 10, I discuss the possibility that a pluralistic ethics, which uses more than one ethical theory, can do a better job of solving moral problems and helping us live together successfully than can any single ethical theory.

## QUESTIONS FOR REVIEW

*Here are some questions to help you review the main concepts in this chapter.*

1. What problem arises with the traditional view of the person and moral agent?

2. According to David Hume, what is the source of moral judgments?

3. Identify one similarity and two differences between Kohlberg's and Gilligan's views of morality.

4. According to Noddings, what is natural caring?

5. What are the key elements of ethical caring?

6. What are the two sentiments essential to ethical caring? Why are they essential?

7. What is the ethical ideal, and how do we enhance it or detract from it?

8. How does a person make judgments about right and wrong based on the ethics of care?

9. Does the ethics of care accept the traditional ethical assumptions? Support your answer.

10. How does the ethics of care relate to the four ethical themes?

11. What are two differences between the ethics of care and most of the other ethical theories discussed in the text?

12. Which problem with the ethics of care seems most serious to you? Explain why. Why would the ethics of care not always be successful in helping us solve ethical problems?

13. Do you think there are distinctively masculine and feminine approaches to ethics? Support your answer.

14. What two themes are common to the different versions of feminism?

15. Explain what is meant by the "social construction of gender," and discuss why feminists object to the construction of rigid gender roles.

## NOTES

1. Nel Noddings, *Caring: A Feminine Approach to Ethics and Moral Education* (Berkeley: University of California Press, 1984).

2. David Hume, *A Treatise of Human Nature,* edited by L. A. Selby-Bigge (Oxford: Oxford University Press, 1968), p. 457.

3. Ibid., pp. 468–469.

4. See, for example, David Norton *David Hume* (Princeton, NJ: Princeton University Press, 1982).

5. Lawrence Kohlberg, "Moral Stages and Moralization: The Cognitive-Development Approach," in *Moral Development and Behavior,* edited by T. Lickona (New York: Holt, Rinehart & Winston, 1976). Each of Kohlberg's levels has two stages. To simplify things, I have only summarized the levels.

6. Carol Gilligan, *In a Different Voice: Psychological Theory and Women's Development* (Cambridge: Harvard University Press, 1982).

7. Norma Haan, "Can Research on Morality Be Scientific?" *American Psychologist,* October 1982, 37(10): 1096–1104.

8. Noddings, *Caring: A Feminine Approach to Ethics and Moral Education,* p. 201.

9. Ibid., p. 79.

10. Ibid., p. 104.

11. Ibid.

12. Ibid., p. 81.

13. Ibid., p. 83.

14. Ibid., p. 86.

15. Ibid., p. 94.

16. Ibid., p. 86.

17. Claudia Card, "Caring and Evil," *Hypatia,* 1990, 15(1): 100.

18. Ibid., p. 101.

19. Ibid., p. 102.

20. Ibid.

21. Ibid.

# Chapter 10

# *A Pluralistic View of Ethics*

In Chapter 1, I claimed that the most important function of ethical theories is to identify moral guidelines that can help us solve ethical problems and live successfully with other persons. None of the theories discussed in this book is able to accomplish that function with complete success. Because there are problems with all the theories, you may conclude that learning about ethical theories is a waste of time. I think this conclusion is a mistake. Even though no one ethical theory can be applied in every case, many of the ideas presented do have merit.

The key to understanding the value of ethical theories is to see them as tools to help us solve ethical problems and live successfully with other persons. Like our familiar hand tools, each one is best at helping us accomplish a certain job, and none of them is appropriate for every job. A hammer is useful for driving nails, but if you need to tighten a bolt, you should use a wrench. Living successfully with other people may seem like one "job" that can be accomplished by one theory, but I believe it involves many jobs because it involves many people with whom we have different kinds of relationships. We need more than one theory to provide the guidelines that will help us solve moral problems related to these people and to live successfully with them. The ethical insight and standard associated with each theory and the positions taken by the theory on the ethical assumptions and themes are clues to the kind of ethical job each theory is best suited to address.

In this final chapter, I outline a way of thinking about ethics that is called ethical pluralism. This model employs more than one ethical theory and is characterized by a second feature—the assumption that we should attempt to live successfully with *all* other persons. This assumption is essential to this version of ethical pluralism. The outline provided here is only a sketch of an approach to ethics, and I encourage you to try to fill it out for yourself.

Although more than one theory can be helpful in solving ethical problems and helping us live successfully with all other people, not all theories are useful for this purpose. Some theories have problems with one of the first three criteria for a successful ethical theory. If the theory cannot produce ethical guidelines, demonstrate that some are better than others, or prohibit the unlimited pursuit of self-interest, it cannot help us live together successfully. Other theories meet the first three criteria but have problems with the fourth, and I believe these theories can be useful in obtaining our objective. Based on this position, we can eliminate divine command theory, ethical egoism, ethical subjectivism, and ethical relativism. We will retain utilitarianism, Kantian ethics, moral rights theory, virtue ethics, and the ethics of care.

## Ethics and Relationships

The ethics of care pointed out that, to a large extent, our lives are characterized by relationships.[1] We are sons and daughters, fathers and mothers, aunts and uncles, nieces and nephews, cousins, friends, partners, colleagues, teammates, and so on. We treat people differently based on the kind of relationship we have with them. I do not treat my daughter in the same way that I treat a colleague at work. This observation seems to conflict with the demands of egalitarian ethical theories, which claim that persons are moral equals and that we ought to treat them impartially if we want to act morally. Egalitarian theories have a problem related to the special treatment of family and friends and impartiality. The problem was illustrated in Chapter 9 with this example involving act utilitarianism. Assume that I have one hundred dollars that I do not need for necessities. I can take my children to a toy store and let each of them spend fifty dollars on toys, or I can donate the money to a legitimate charity that will use it to buy medicine for impoverished people who are in danger of dying from a disease. An act utilitarian would argue that I should do whatever would produce the greatest benefit for those affected by my action. Everyone affected by my action is a moral equal, and I should make an impartial decision about what to do. The toys will make my children happy for a while and, hence, benefit them. Buying them toys will also make me happy and benefit me. My children already have many toys, however, and additional toys are not a necessity for them. The medicine will save many people's lives and it is a necessity for the people who are ill and cannot afford it themselves. The medicine will produce a greater benefit than the toys. Therefore, I should send the money to the legitimate charity if I want to be ethical. In fact, buying toys for my children would be unethical given the alternative. The implication of this example is that it is often unethical to act based on special relationships instead of maximizing net benefit. This result conflicts with the normal practice of treating people differently based on the kind of relationship we have with them. It would also seem to create a problem for the pluralist who wants to live successfully with all other persons.

If we treat people with whom we have special relationships impartially, we will not be able to live successfully with these people as daughters, wives, friends, and colleagues. If I treat my friend the same way that I treat a stranger, he or she will not remain my friend for very long. Friends expect us to give them special treatment: to spend time with them, to help them, to look out for their best interests. If I always acted to maximize benefit, I would probably do very little for my friends because most of them are relatively well off. My money and time can certainly produce more net benefit by being spent on the poor and the sick instead of on my friends. If I spend little or no time with my friends, however, sooner or later I will not have any friends. My colleagues at work also expect me to act in ways that do not maximize overall net benefit. They expect me to show up for committee meetings and help solve mundane problems—even though I could produce more benefit elsewhere. If I ignore my minor responsibilities and make them do the trivial work by themselves, they will resent and dislike me. I might be able to keep my job, but I will not get along very well with my coworkers. Therefore, we must give persons special treatment if we want to live successfully with these people as daughters, colleagues, and so on.

Suppose Rose treats everyone impartially, and after a period of time she has no friends or colleagues who like her. Could she live successfully with these people simply as "persons" or morally significant beings? It seems doubtful that she could. People are always already in relationships with persons, and if they deny those relationships, problems will result. The fact is that many people are already more than simply persons to Rose. She cannot reduce the relationship from daughter, friend, or colleague to simply person and expect her life to proceed successfully. The psychologist Abraham Maslow argued that a hierarchy of needs motivates human beings. Satisfying these needs is essential if people are to flourish or thrive.[2] Once the physiological needs (food, water, and so on) and the safety needs (physical security, stability, and so on) are satisfied, Maslow thought that people are motivated by needs related to love and belonging. They are motivated to obtain close relationships with other people and to be part of various groups. People desire to have friends, a spouse, and children and to belong to clubs or organizations.

Failure to satisfy these belonging and love needs can lead to psychological maladjustment. Therefore, if Maslow is correct, people need to have close relationships with other persons to maintain good mental health. They cannot simply treat everyone as persons, and a satisfactory ethical approach needs to take special relationships into account.

If people want to live successfully with other persons, they must have ethical guidelines that enable them to maintain their special relationships with particular persons. At this point, we might ask whether we could simply use the ethics of care to guide our relations with everyone. That theory would justify special treatment to family and friends. As we saw in Chapter 9, however, the ethics of care provides an incomplete ethical standard: No one has the responsibility to care for everyone. For example, we do not have the moral obligation to care for Africa's starving children or even acquaintances at work. The ethics of care provides no guidance about how to avoid acting unethically in regard to most of the people in the world, people whose lives we may affect for the worse even though we have no personal relationship with them. We cannot use the ethics of care to guide our conduct with most of the people in the world. Thus, neither an egalitarian ethical theory nor the ethics of care would seem to be adequate by itself.

If neither of these approaches to ethics is adequate by itself, then perhaps ethical pluralism should be considered. Ethical pluralism provides multiple ethical guidelines, which will allow all of these relationships to be maintained. Using the pluralist strategy, we can consider the various kinds of relationships people have and then ask which ethical theory would best help us solve moral problems related to those people and live successfully with them. In the interest of keeping this chapter relatively short, these relationships will be organized into four groups: (1) family and friends; (2) colleagues, teammates, and members of organizations; (3) members of the same ethnic group, gender, or nation; and (4) other persons. After discussing the best ethical theory to use with each group, I will relate that theory to the ethical problems identified at the beginning of the book.

## Relationships with Family and Friends

The first relationships to consider are the closest ones, family and friends. It is not appropriate to use an egalitarian ethical theory to help us live successfully with our families and friends. If I treat my family and friends the same way I treat strangers, I will alienate my family and lose my friends. To solve moral problems related to family and friends and to live successfully with them, we need an ethical theory that will endorse giving these people special consideration. The insight and the essential ethical ideas of the ethics of care are best able to justify such special consideration. The ethics of care asserts that I should strive to care for certain people, including my family and close friends. I will give them more attention, concern, and assistance than I would give a stranger or colleague. I will try to apprehend their reality and promote their welfare. This endorsement of special treatment for those for whom we care will enable us to maintain our special relationships with family and friends.

Most of the problems mentioned in Chapter 1 dealt with friends or intimates. Because the ethics of care is best equipped to endorse special treatment for such people, it is the appropriate ethical resource to use with these persons. To solve problems using this ethic, we must apprehend the other's reality and promote his or her welfare. We must figure out how best to care for all those involved. Noddings provides suggestions related to a couple of the questions in Chapter 1. She claims that we ought not to steal and would argue that it is unethical to steal a book from a friend.[3] She also claims that a woman should care more for herself and those she already cares for than for an embryo with whom she has not established a caring relationship. An abortion is not unethical if it is necessary for one to continue to be successful as a one-caring (to oneself and to others).[4] Solving the other moral problems from Chapter 1 will be more difficult. We must apprehend the reality of the people involved in these situations and try to determine how best to promote their welfare. In relation to the problem of whether or not to tell your friend about his or her cheating partner, you should not lie to a friend, but neither should you hurt that person. You should probably try to get the person who is cheating to end the relationship or to be honest about what is going on. A relationship that involves deception on the part of one person is not really in the best interest of either person. In relation to the problem about whether or not to leave your lover for another person, the situation is more difficult. How can you best care for both of these people? Will you now think less of the first person and always regret not entering the new relationship? A proponent of the ethics of care would conclude that you cannot stop caring for the first person, but as long as you continue to care, it would probably be ethical to end the romantic aspect of the relationship and become involved with the new person. Based on the ethics of care, the suicide case seems relatively easy. If you really care for your family and your friends, you will not kill yourself. Suicide devastates the family and friends of the person who dies, and this act would be contrary to caring for these people. Finally, consider the case where you are paralyzed from the neck down and ask a friend or family member to kill you. If you really care for this person, you would not put him or her in this position. Doing so does not reflect an appreciation of the other person's reality and a concern for his or her welfare.

### Relationships with Colleagues, Teammates, and Members of Organizations

In addition to our family and friends, we also have relationships with people who belong to the same corporation, business, university, team, club, and so on. If we value our relations with colleagues, teammates, and members of organizations, an ethical resource is needed to help us live successfully with them. What consideration about these relationships will enable us to choose the appropriate ethical theory or resource to use with these communities? The most relevant moral factor, I believe, is that the members of these collectives share a common goal or purpose. Organizations, universities, and corporations often have mission statements or statements of purpose. Teams usually share the goal of winning. Virtue ethics best takes these shared goals, missions, or purposes into account. As the insight and essential ethical ideas show, virtue ethics is centered around a purpose or function, whereas egalitarian theories and the ethics of care do not recognize the moral significance of such organizational, team, or corporate purposes. The goals, missions, or purposes can replace Aristotle's human function as the foundation of a version of virtue ethics. The goal (or mission statement or statement of purpose) can provide one component of a well-lived life and can be used to identify the practices and virtues that will help to accomplish the goal or purpose and achieve this aspect of the good life. A well-lived life, in the corporate or organizational context, is one in which the person thrives as an individual but also is successful at supporting the corporate or organizational mission. Persons who think only of themselves and do not help achieve the corporate, team, or organizational goal or purpose will be unsuccessful in the context of that collective. The significant virtues will vary based on the relevant goal, but hard work and teamwork would be virtues for any of these organizations.

If we value our relationships with colleagues, teammates, and members of organizations, we ought to act ethically toward the members of these collectives. Virtue ethics provides a moral resource to help us do this. We should not expect that virtue ethics will be completely successful at helping us live successfully with the members of these collectives, but it will be more useful than the other ethical theories. Of course, virtue ethics will not provide us with the resources to evaluate the basic goal, mission, or purpose itself. We must assume that the basic purpose is ethical and worthwhile. (A questionable purpose is discussed in a later section on misguided purposes or goals.)

One of the ethical problems from Chapter 1 dealt with an organization or institution, a university. The problem involved whether or not you should cheat on a test. One mission or function (perhaps *the* function) of a university is to educate students and to evaluate students fairly to determine their educational progress. Honesty is a necessary virtue for achieving this mission or function. Teachers must be honest in assessing their students, and students must be honest in completing the assessment instruments, such as tests and papers. Cheating is dishonest and undermines the function of the university. Therefore, cheating on the test would be unethical.

### Relationships with Members of the Same Ethnic Group, Gender, or Nation

People often identify with members of the same ethnic group, gender, or nation. If they value successful relationships with these people, they need some ethical resource to guide their conduct toward them. What binds these people together besides the accidental factual connection of being of the same race, ethnicity, or gender, or of being citizens of the same nation? As with corporations and organizations, I suggest that it is a common purpose or goal that is of the greatest ethical relevance. Many people might resist the idea that a country's citizens could believe their nation has a purpose, but it is hard to dismiss the idea out of hand. For example, many citizens of the United States believe our national purpose is to protect the rights of our citizens and perhaps also to promote the spread of democratic governments. Many women share the common feminist purpose of eliminating the male domination of women. W. E. B. DuBois wrote about African Americans as having a mission to deliver a spiritual message to the world.[5] If members of these communities share a purpose, then that purpose is ethically relevant.

Not all people value or even acknowledge these kinds of relationships, but for those who do value them, virtue ethics is superior to an egalitarian theory or the ethics of care as a moral resource. As the insight and essential ethical ideas show, virtue ethics is centered around a purpose or function, whereas egalitarian theories and the ethics of care do not recognize the moral significance of such a purpose. Aristotle's basic human purpose might be replaced with a national, gender-related, or ethnic purpose. If there is such a purpose or goal, we can develop a view of a well-lived life in connection with achieving that purpose or goal. Virtues can then be identified that will help achieve that well-lived life, although these virtues will probably not be understood in the way Aristotle conceived of them. Patriotism and civic duty are two virtues related to the United States and democracy, justice is a crucial virtue for feminists, and DuBois talked about racial pride and honesty in connection with African Americans.

If we can identify a purpose shared by the members of the same ethnic group, gender, or nation, then virtue ethics will be a valuable moral resource in helping us to solve moral problems related to that purpose and to live successfully with others. We should not expect a version of virtue ethics to be completely effective at helping us live successfully with the members of these groups, but the theory would provide more useful assistance than the other ethical theories. Of course, virtue ethics will not provide us with resources to evaluate the basic purpose itself; we must assume that the basic purpose is ethical and worthwhile. (A questionable goal or purpose is discussed in a later section on misguided purposes.)

None of the ethical problems identified in Chapter 1 deal with persons as members of an ethnic group or gender or as citizens of the same country. Therefore, in my view, virtue ethics is not the best theory to use to solve any of the problems, although Aristotle would have provided clear answers for several of them. Based on his ethical ideas, you ought to tell the truth if someone asks you a question, no matter how upset the person may be with you for telling the truth. You ought to care more for the truth than for what other people think of you. If your friend asks you if he or she is being deceived, you should tell your friend the truth. Aristotle identifies stealing as one of the actions that is always evil no matter what emotion accompanies it. He would argue that it would be unethical of you to steal the textbook. Finally, he would reject committing suicide. To kill yourself to escape from suffering or a broken heart is the act of a coward. You ought to be courageous and face hardship.

## Relationships with People as "Persons"

Most of the world's people are persons with whom we have no special relationship. It is possible to try simply to ignore these people, but many believe we do have a relationship with these people. We have the common bond of all being human beings or persons together, and we have bonds of sympathy and empathy. Finally, many believe all persons are valuable, even when we have no special relationship with them. These considerations connect us to other persons and may produce certain kinds of actions. For example, some people donate to charities that help people they do not know. They may make these donations because they feel some connection to these people and want to help them.

If someone wants to assert a connection or relationship with other persons simply as persons, he or she will need some relevant moral guidelines. What ethical theory best provides us with guidelines to solve moral problems and to help us live successfully with persons we do not know? When we interact with persons only as "persons," or full-status morally significant beings, we should disregard factors that are irrelevant to this moral status, such as age, gender, and color, and treat them as moral equals. Because these persons are moral equals, an egalitarian ethical theory is a reasonable moral resource to use to help us live successfully with people with whom we have no special relationship. We have discussed three egalitarian ethical theories: utilitarianism, Kantian ethics, and moral rights theory. How do we choose a theory or theories that will help us live successfully with all these people?

One assumption of ethical pluralism is the commitment to attempt to live successfully with *all* persons. If we want to maintain a successful relationship with all persons, we must eliminate utilitarianism as our theory of choice.[6] Utilitarians act for the greatest good of the greatest number of people and must be willing to sacrifice a minority for the greater good of the majority. If we want to live successfully with all persons, we cannot sacrifice some of them for the good of others. We need a theory that regards all persons as valuable to increase our chances of living successfully with all of them.

The insights and themes show us that both Kantian ethics and moral rights theory regard persons as moral equals who are all valuable. Kantian ethics is related to the insight that there are moral laws that apply to all persons. For Kantians, persons are moral equals, and our ethical treatment of persons in sufficiently similar situations ought to be consistent. According to proponents of this theory, we must act only from those personal rules that we can at the same time will to be moral laws, and we must also act in regard to all persons in ways that treat them as ends in themselves and never simply as means to accomplish the ends of others. These principles could be used as an ethical guide to help us live more successfully with persons in general. Moral rights theory also produces a useful set of ethical guidelines. This theory claims that individual persons are valuable and that we need to act in ways that respect their value. Moral rights are used to respect their value by giving persons legitimate claims to protection for their vital interests. Avoiding violations of the moral rights of others would also help us live successfully with these persons.

Both moral rights theory and Kantian ethics can help us understand our moral obligations to persons with whom we have no special relationship. It is in regard to this aspect of ethics that moral equality is essential. We need to protect equally all full-status morally significant beings, and we need a moral resource to help us do so. Neither of these theories would be a complete success, but both establish a kind of "moral minimum" with regard to persons in general. For practical reasons, I prefer moral rights theory. Avoiding violations of moral rights seems clearer and more precise to me than acting from those personal rules that a person could will to be moral laws. Choosing between these two theories is not crucial, however, because either one would provide an appropriate moral minimum.

Egalitarian ethical theories such as utilitarianism, Kantian ethics, and moral rights theory relate best to persons simply as equal morally significant beings. Historically, these theories have tended to elevate moral obligations to "persons" above obligations related to special relationships. The proponents of egalitarian ethical theories have emphasized our moral obligations to all full-status morally significant beings and downgraded our moral relationships to persons who occupy more specific roles (e.g., family members, friends, and neighbors). I believe egalitarian ethical theories put too much emphasis on our moral obligations to all full-status morally significant beings to qualify as our only ethical resource. These theories assume that "ethical" is inexorably linked with the moral equality of all full-status morally significant beings and that general moral obligations always outweigh everything else. This viewpoint neglects the reality that moral considerations should be related to special relationships too.

Why should moral obligations to persons in general take precedence over obligations to people with whom we have special relationships? The traditional answer is that general obligations are *moral* obligations and that obligations connected to special relationships are not considered to be moral obligations. The corollary to this is that moral obligations outweighed non-moral ones. The pluralist approach widens the notion of moral obligations. Egalitarian ethical theories and persons in general need not take precedence over other approaches to ethics related to persons with whom we have special relationships. Egalitarian theories attempt to articulate our moral relationship with persons in general, but they are not the whole of ethics. These egalitarian theories have an important role to play, but they are only one element in ethical life. They should not necessarily take precedence over everything else.[7]

It is possible, of course, that an egalitarian theory might be the most important ethical resource for an individual whose loyalty and connection to persons in general is greater than his or her loyalty and connection to the persons with whom he or she has special relationships. This would tell us something about the person's allegiances and loyalties, but not something about ethics in general.

Developing a pluralistic ethical position enables us to use multiple ethical resources to help us live successfully with all persons. When trying to solve an ethical problem, we need to identify the relationship or relationships with the person or persons involved and use the appropriate ethical theory or theories. If persons with whom we have different kinds of relationships and therefore different ethical theories are involved, we will need to see if both theories produce the same answer. When they do not, there will be a conflict. (I will discuss such conflicts in the next section.)

The main purpose of ethical theories is to help us to solve ethical problems and to live more successfully with other persons. I have suggested that the best way to utilize ethical theories to accomplish this purpose is to use different theories for persons with whom we have different relationships. I have sketched out the bare bones of this approach, and I encourage you to try to fill it out. In the next section, I turn to the major problem with this pluralistic approach to ethics—the problem of conflicting moral obligations.

## Conflicting Moral Obligations

If we have valuable but different relationships with persons and are trying to live successfully with all of them, we will encounter cases that involve conflicting moral obligations. Sometimes, the different ethical guidelines will create conflicting obligations. At other times, we possess limited resources and must decide who will receive them. For example, I have only limited time on a Saturday; should I spend it fixing a house for an impoverished family, working at the office, or taking my children to a baseball game? Each individual must decide whether he or she will act in the name of the good related to family, friends, neighbors, co-workers, ethnic groups, other citizens, persons in general, or some combination of these. How should we arbitrate the competing obligations related to different persons?

Two basic kinds of conflicts may arise involving the obligations generated by the ethical theories we employ. In some situations, conflicting moral obligations of two or more persons may allow us to act only in accord with one of them, but in making this choice, we will not violate the ethical guidelines of the other theory. I could spend the day kayaking with a friend or taking my children to a baseball game, but not both. In this situation, either choice seems ethical. In contrast, the second kind of case involves conflicting moral obligations wherein acting in accord with the obligations generated by one theory associated with one person or group would violate the ethical guidelines of another theory connected to another person or group. Taking my family to a baseball game on a Saturday when the other employees at my office are struggling to meet a crucial deadline and need my help may be judged as unethical by these other employees because my disregard for my responsibilities will interfere with achieving the corporate purpose. What should we do in cases of such conflicts?

These conflicts might be described as a problem about which relationship is most important to us. Human beings have different kinds of relationships, and perhaps some are more important than others. Certainly many of us claim that our families are the most important to us, but the way we spend our time would seem to call this into question. Most of us spend much more time on our jobs than we do with our families. I claim that my family is my priority, but I have spent countless hours on weekends doing work related to my job. Is there one group of people that should be our highest priority? In line with this, should the ethical guidelines provided by one ethical theory take precedence over the others?

I believe all our relationships to persons are crucial because these relationships help to define us as individuals. To adapt an idea from Sarah Conly (although I will reach a conclusion different from hers), a person needs a way of life that will enable the person to maintain a general harmony among his or her relationships. Without such harmony, the person will not be an integrated individual.[8] Suppose Rose has many relationships that she thinks are valuable, with family, friends, her teammates on her adult soccer team, her colleagues at work, other members of her ethnic group, other women, and persons in general. Instead of making the ethical obligations to the members of one group more important than the others, she might strive to achieve an overall balance among the moral obligations connected to the various persons. Her identity depends on successfully maintaining her ties to all of these persons; therefore, she will not want to sacrifice any of them completely. She is a daughter, sister, and friend but also a teammate and a colleague. In an effort to maintain all these relationships, it is useful for her to act, as much as possible, in accord with all the various ethical guidelines connected to each person. In cases of conflict, she should seek some kind of overall balance. This is not to suggest some absolute equality among the competing obligations; each one must receive what is necessary to maintain the connection.

Obligations to family members often outweigh obligations connected to the other members of an organization, but the demands of the organization must be satisfied to a degree sufficient to maintain the relationships with colleagues. In a particular instance, Rose might weigh the competing claims and decide in favor of the one that would lead to the greatest overall balance in maintaining all her valuable relationships. In one case, she might act in accord with the moral rights of persons with whom she has no close relationship, in another because she "cares for" a friend, in a third in accord with the virtue of concern for her customers' satisfaction, and so on. This would enable her to maintain her connection to all the persons that are important to her. The key is to act in ways that minimize conflict among the various ethical obligations connected to the different persons and, when conflicts are inevitable, to try to obtain an overall balance regarding the fulfillment of the obligations generated in connection with all of them.

This solution to the problem of conflicting obligations does not eliminate conflicts. Instead, it makes a person aware that maintaining the connection to all the important persons in his or her life will require an overall balance. It may require moral sensitivity and creativity to identify and achieve this balance, but I believe doing so is worthwhile. An individual needs a variety of relationships to live an interesting and fulfilling life, but the individual also needs to create some coherence and harmony among the obligations connected to the persons so that he or she can maintain a consistent self-identity. An important part of what a person is results from all the relationships in which he or she is involved.

## Misguided Purposes or Goals

I argued that virtue ethics was the best theory to use with members of corporations, organizations, clubs, teams, ethnic groups, genders, nations, and so on. Virtue ethics is centered around a purpose, and this raises the question of a misguided goal or purpose. For example, suppose someone belongs to a racist organization whose members regard persons of color as inferior and whose mission is to drive them out of predominantly white neighborhoods. Based on this mission or purpose, the members of the organization might guide their conduct by a dubious set of "virtues" connected to their mission. They might use intimidation and violence against their victims; they might regard members who are particularly strong and violent as individuals for others to emulate. Based on the ethical guidelines connected to their mission, their conduct would be ethical to them, but most of us would believe they are acting unethically. Are proponents of a pluralistic ethics justified in condemning and trying to stop such conduct?

I first noted this problem in the discussion of virtue ethics. Although a purpose allows us to ethically evaluate other things, it does not allow us to evaluate the purpose itself. The key to understanding why pluralists see some purposes or goals as misguided and unethical is that they have adopted an overriding goal or purpose: to try to live successfully with *all* persons. Specific purposes—such as driving away people of color—that would conflict with this overriding purpose are unethical. Pluralists cannot tolerate conduct that would harm or humiliate persons because it would prevent their living successfully with these persons.[9] Of course, we will not be able to ethically evaluate the overriding pluralistic purpose. The commitment to living successfully with all other persons is ultimately what makes people pluralists. It is simply the ground on which they stand.

## Conclusion

I have sketched out a way to use multiple ethical theories to try to help us live successfully with others and to solve moral problems. This pluralistic approach views egalitarian moral theories as important resources but not as the only appropriate ethical resources. We are closely tied to our family and friends and need few reminders of their importance to us, but our identification with and relation to persons we do not know is often weak. The task of the proponents of egalitarian ethical theories is not merely to express our universal moral obligations but also to illustrate and strengthen our bonds with persons in general. Developing the moral sensitivity to see beyond our families, friends, and colleagues and to realize our connection with other persons simply because they are persons is a valuable ethical achievement.

This pluralistic approach to ethics takes for granted the overriding value of attempting to live successfully with all persons. It endorses striving to balance the moral obligations to all the persons who are important to us. Our identities depend on successfully maintaining all our important relationships.[10] Therefore, we must try to minimize conflicts among the various ethical obligations connected to different persons and, in cases where conflict is unavoidable, to seek some kind of overall balance.

I began this chapter by acknowledging that no single ethical theory is completely effective at helping us live successfully with others and solving ethical problems. Nor is ethical pluralism a complete success, but, for several reasons, it is an improvement over a single theory. First, if we use the theory that fits best with each group of persons rather than only one theory, our chances of solving moral problems and living successfully with all other people should be improved. A pluralistic approach ought to do a better job of helping us maintain our relationships. Second, ethical pluralism eliminates some of the problems that plague single theories. Using a pluralistic approach eliminates the Kantian problem with exceptions to moral laws, the moral rights problem with community, the virtue ethics problem with the fundamental human purpose, and the ethics of care problems with an incomplete moral standard and limits on promoting welfare. By eliminating even some of the problems with these theories, ethical pluralism should make it easier for us to solve moral problems. Finally, a pluralistic ethics also has the advantage of pointing out the incredible diversity, richness, and complexity of ethical life. It shows us how being ethical involves many different people with whom we have many different relationships, including our families, friends, neighbors, teammates, colleagues, members of the same ethnic group, gender, and nation, and others with whom we simply share the bond of moral personhood.

## QUESTIONS FOR REVIEW

*Here are some questions to help you review the main concepts in this chapter.*

1. What is the most important function of ethical theories?

2. Explain the problem related to impartiality and special treatment for family and friends.

3. Why does the author claim that we cannot treat all people simply as "persons," ignoring all special relationships.

4. What ethical theory is the best moral resource to use with friends and family? Explain why. With colleagues, teammates, and members of the same organization? Explain why. With members of the same ethnic group, gender, or nation? Explain why. With persons with whom we have no special relationship? Explain why.

5. Is utilitarianism the best theory to use with people simply as "persons"? Why, or why not?

6. What is the ethical pluralist position regarding egalitarian theories? How is this view different from the one endorsed by most of the proponents of egalitarian theories?

7. How does the author suggest that we resolve moral conflicts among the contending moral obligations connected to persons with whom we have different relationships?

8. Discuss the difference between a dispute involving the moral obligations related to two persons with whom you have different relationships and a conflict involving the moral obligations connected to another person and self-interest. To be ethical, must we sometimes sacrifice our self-interest? Why, or why not?

9. What is the overall purpose underlying ethical pluralism? How does this purpose help us identify misguided goals or purposes?

10. Choose one of the moral problems identified in Chapter 1 and explain how a pluralistic ethics would solve that problem. Why would a pluralistic ethics solve it in this way?

11. Is ethical pluralism an improvement over using a single ethical theory? Support your answer with examples from your own experience.

## NOTES

1. In the first edition of this book, the ethical pluralist position was developed in terms of loyalty to moral communities. In this edition, I decided to develop the position based on relationships. I still believe there are such things as moral communities, but our primary ethical obligations and connections are to persons. For example, I am more concerned with my colleagues and students than I am with the university as a community of people. Designating the university as a moral community and directing my ethical consideration toward it has come to seem like a less valuable move than simply directing my ethical consideration toward specific persons. The result is that the "groups" associated with an ethical theory are labeled by relationships instead of by moral community. It is not really much of a difference. If the reader wishes to compare the two approaches, read Chapter 8 from the first edition or read the inspiration for that chapter, a paper entitled "Loyalties," by Andrew Oldenquist (although my position differed from his). See Andrew Oldenquist, "Loyalties," *The Journal of Philosophy*, 1982, 79: 173–193.

2. See Abraham Maslow, *Motivation and Personality*, 3rd ed. (New York: Harper & Row, 1987).

3. Nel Noddings, *Caring: A Feminine Approach to Ethics and Moral Education* (Berkeley: University of California Press, 1984), p. 93.

4. Ibid., pp. 87–89.

5. W. E. B. DuBois, "The Conservation of Races," in *The Oxford W. E. B. DuBois Reader*, edited by Eric J. Sundquist (New York: Oxford University Press, 1996).

6. Some readers will believe I have too quickly dismissed utilitarianism. For me, the willingness to sacrifice a minority for the good of the majority is the most significant difference between utilitarian and deontological theories. Because pluralists believe in trying to live successfully with all persons, they cannot endorse sacrificing some of them. I also have serious practical concerns about utilitarianism. Act and rule utilitarianism are not successful at solving problems whose consequences are impossible or very difficult to predict. The abortion case mentioned in the first chapter, for example, could not be solved using a utilitarian theory. It is impossible to predict the consequences because we would have to know what harm and benefit would result if the fetus were allowed to live. Would the resulting person grow up to invent a cure for cancer or become a mass murderer? These determinations are impossible to make; therefore, utilitarianism cannot be used to solve such moral problems. Even in a case where utilitarian theory would seem to work much better, I still have

concerns. Regarding the problems connected to cheating on a test or stealing a book, a person should be able to predict with reasonable accuracy the harms and benefits for everyone produced by each outcome. The problem, of course, is to predict the probability of being caught. I am not sure we can ever accurately make these predictions. In the case where a person has been paralyzed, this person thinks that he or she can predict the future with great accuracy—a life filled with pain and humiliation—but is this really correct? I appreciate the insight connected to utilitarianism, but I do not feel comfortable using the theory to solve ethical problems.

7. I first encountered this idea that ethical theories were only one aspect of moral life in Lawrence Blum, *Friendship, Altruism and Morality* (Boston: Routledge & Kegan Paul, 1980).

8. Sarah Conly, "The Objectivity of Morals and the Subjectivity of Agents," *American Philosophical Quarterly,* 1985, 22: 281.

9. An ethical pluralist can, of course, harm others in self-defense. We should try to live successfully with everyone, but if others threaten our lives, we must defend ourselves and may be forced to harm them.

10. It should be pointed out that someone can have more than one relationship with a single person. I have colleagues who are also my friends. In such cases, my interaction with these people is guided by more than one ethical theory.

## Ethical Insights

| | |
|---|---|
| Divine Command Theory | Legitimate guidelines for how to live are necessarily related to God. |
| Ethical Relativism | Legitimate moral guidelines are necessarily related to an actual society. |
| Ethical Egoism | Legitimate moral guidelines necessarily have something to do with particular individuals. |
| Ethical Subjectivism | Legitimate moral guidelines necessarily have something to do with particular individuals. |
| Kantian Ethics | There are moral laws and these laws apply to all persons. |
| Utilitarianism | An action is morally bad if it harms someone, whereas it is morally good if it helps or benefits someone. |
| Moral Rights Theory | Individual persons are valuable, and we should act in ways that respect their value. |
| Virtue Ethics | The virtues help persons to achieve well-being or live the good life. |
| Ethics of Care | Ethics is primarily concerned with relationships between persons. |

## Ethical Standards

| | |
|---|---|
| Divine Command Theory | What God commands people to do is good, and what God forbids people to do is bad. |
| Ethical Relativism | A society's actual moral guidelines determine good and bad. |

| | |
|---|---|
| Ethical Egoism | What is good is what produces a net benefit for a particular individual, and what is bad is what produces a net harm for the individual. |
| Ethical Subjectivism | What is good is what produces a positive attitude or emotional response in a specific individual, and what is bad is what produces a negative attitude or emotional response in a specific individual. |
| Kantian Ethics | (1) Act only from those personal rules that you can at the same time will to be moral laws. (2) Act in regard to all persons in ways that treat them as ends in themselves and never simply as means to accomplish the ends of others. |
| Utilitarianism | (Bentham) Actions are good and bad according to the tendency they have to augment or diminish the pleasure or happiness of the parties whose interests are in question. |
| | (Mill) Actions are good in proportion to which they tend to promote happiness and bad as they tend to produce unhappiness. |
| Rule Utilitarianism | It is good for persons to act from those moral rules the general following of which would promote the greatest net benefit for the morally significant beings affected; it is bad for persons to act from rules the general following of which would promote the greatest net harm for the morally significant beings affected. |
| Moral Rights Theory | A person acts ethically if his or her action follows from one or more relevant rights and unethically if he or she violates another person's right or rights. |
| Virtue Ethics | An individual should strive to be a person who possesses the virtues and does not possess the vices. |
| Ethics of Care | I should strive to maintain and enhance my ideal picture of myself as one-caring and cared-for. |

## Traditional Assumptions

ASPECTS OF THE TRADITIONAL ETHICAL ASSUMPTIONS

| Ethical Theories | Is ethics rational? | Are people moral equals? | Can we universalize some ethical evaluations? |
|---|---|---|---|
| Divine Command Theory | No | Yes | Yes |
| Ethical Relativism | No | No | Yes (No) |
| Ethical Egoism | Yes | No | No |
| Ethical Subjectivism | No | No | No |
| Kantian Ethics | Yes | Yes | Yes |
| Utilitarianism | Yes | Yes | Yes |
| Moral Rights Theory | Yes | Yes | Yes |
| Virtue Ethics | Yes | No | Yes |
| Ethics of Care | No | No | No |

## Ethical Themes

| Moral Theories | What kind of guidelines makes something good or bad? | Should we focus on consequences or reasoning? | Should we focus on rules or actions? | Should we focus on the group or the individual? |
|---|---|---|---|---|
| Divine Command Theory | Objective | Reasoning | Rules | Individual |
| Ethical Relativism | Relative | Reasoning | Rules | Group |
| Ethical Egoism | Objective | Consequences | Either | Individual |
| Ethical Subjectivism | Subjective | Neither | Actions | Individual |
| Kantian Ethics | Objective | Reasoning | Rules | Individual |
| Utilitarianism | Objective | Consequences | Either | Group |
| Moral Rights Theory | Objective | Reasoning | Rules | Individual |

## Ethical Themes (*continued*)

| Moral Theories | *What kind of guidelines makes something good or bad?* | *Should we focus on consequences or reasoning?* | *Should we focus on rules or actions?* | *Should we focus on the group or the individual?* |
|---|---|---|---|---|
| Virtue Ethics | Objective/ Subjective | Both | Neither | Both |
| Ethics of Care | Objective/ Subjective | Consequences | Actions | Individual |

# Appendix 2

## The United Nations Universal Declaration of Human Rights, 1948

*Preamble*

Whereas recognition of the inherent dignity and of the equal and inalienable rights of all members of the human family is the foundation of freedom, justice and peace in the world,

Whereas disregard and contempt for human rights have resulted in barbarous acts which have outraged the conscience of mankind, and the advent of a world in which human beings shall enjoy freedom of speech and belief and freedom from fear and want has been proclaimed as the highest aspiration of the common people,

Whereas it is essential, if man is not to be compelled to have recourse, as a last resort, to rebellion against tyranny and oppression, that human rights should be protected by the rule of law,

Whereas it is essential to promote the development of friendly relations between nations,

Whereas the people of the United Nations have in the Charter reaffirmed their faith in fundamental human rights, in the dignity and worth of the human person and in the equal rights of men and women and have determined to promote social progress and better standards of life in larger freedom,

Whereas Member States have pledged themselves to achieve, in cooperation with the United Nations, the promotion of universal respect for and observance of human rights and fundamental freedoms,

Whereas a common understanding of these rights and freedoms is of the greatest importance for the full realization of this pledge,

Now, therefore,

*The General Assembly Proclaims*

This Universal Declaration of Human Rights as a common standard of achievement for all peoples and all nations, to the end that every individual and every organ of society, keeping this Declaration constantly in mind, shall strive by teaching and education to promote respect for these rights and freedoms and by progressive measures, national and international, to secure their universal and effective recognition and observance, both among the peoples of Member States themselves and among the peoples of territories under their jurisdiction.

*Article 1*  All human beings are born free and equal in dignity and rights. They are endowed with reason and conscience and should act towards one another in a spirit of brotherhood.

*Article 2*  Everyone is entitled to all the rights and freedoms set forth in this Declaration, without distinction of any kind, such as race, colour, sex, language, religion, political or other opinion, national or social origin, property, birth or other status.

Furthermore, no distinction shall be made on the basis of the political, jurisdictional or international status of the country or territory to which a person belongs, whether it be independent, trust, non-self-governing or under any other limitation of sovereignty.

*Article 3*  Everyone has the right to life, liberty and security of person.

*Article 4*  No one shall be held in slavery or servitude; slavery and the slave trade shall be prohibited in all their forms.

*Article 5*  No one shall be subjected to torture or to cruel, inhuman or degrading treatment or punishment.

*Article 6*  Everyone has the right to recognition everywhere as a person before the law.

*Article 7*  All are equal before the law and are entitled without any discrimination to equal protection of the law. All are entitled to equal protection against any discrimination in violation of this Declaration and against any incitement to such discrimination.

*Article 8*  Everyone has the right to an effective remedy by the competent national tribunals for acts violating the fundamental rights granted him by the constitution or by law.

*Article 9*  No one shall be subjected to arbitrary arrest, detention or exile.

*Article 10*  Everyone is entitled in full equality to a fair and public hearing by an independent and impartial tribunal, in the determination of his rights and obligations and of any criminal charge against him.

*Article 11*  1. Everyone charged with a penal offence has the right to be presumed innocent until proved guilty according to law in a public trial at which he has had all the guarantees necessary for his defence.
2. No one shall be held guilty of any penal offence on account of any act or omission which did not constitute a penal offence, under national or international law, at the time when it was committed. Nor shall a heavier penalty be imposed than the one that was applicable at the time the penal offence was committed.

*Article 12*  No one shall be subjected to arbitrary interference with his privacy, family, home or correspondence, nor to attacks upon his honour and reputation. Everyone has the right to the protection of the law against such interference or attacks.

*Article 13*  1. Everyone has the right to freedom of movement and residence within the borders of each state.
2. Everyone has the right to leave any country, including his own, and to return to his country.

*Article 14*  1. Everyone has the right to seek and to enjoy in other countries asylum from persecution.
2. This right may not be invoked in the case of prosecutions genuinely arising from non-political crimes or from acts contrary to the purposes and principles of the United Nations.

*Article 15*  1. Everyone has the right to a nationality.
2. No one shall be arbitrarily deprived of his nationality nor denied the right to change his nationality.

*Article 16*  1. Men and women of full age, without any limitation due to race, nationality or religion, have the right to marry and to found a family. They are entitled to equal rights as to marriage, during marriage and at its dissolution.
2. Marriage shall be entered into only with the free and full consent of the intending spouses.
3. The family is the natural and fundamental group unit of society and is entitled to protection by society and the State.

*Article 17*  1. Everyone has the right to own property alone as well as in association with others.

2. No one shall be arbitrarily deprived of his property.

*Article 18* Everyone has the right to freedom of thought, conscience and religion; this right includes freedom to change his religion or belief, and freedom, either alone or in community with others and in public or private, to manifest his religion or belief in teaching, practice, worship and observance.

*Article 19* Everyone has the right to freedom of opinion and expression; this right includes freedom to hold opinions without interference and to seek, receive and impart information and ideas through any media and regardless of frontiers.

*Article 20* 1. Everyone has the right to freedom of peaceful assembly and association.
2. No one may be compelled to belong to an association.

*Article 21* 1. Everyone has the right to take part in the government of his country, directly or through freely chosen representatives.
2. Everyone has the right of equal access to public service in his country.
3. The will of the people shall be the basis of the authority of government; this will shall be expressed in periodic and genuine elections which shall be by universal and equal suffrage and shall be held by secret vote or by equivalent free voting procedures.

*Article 22* Everyone, as a member of society, has the right to social security and is entitled to realization, through national effort and international co-operation and in accordance with the organization and resources of each State, of the economic, social and cultural rights indispensable for his dignity and the free development of his personality.

*Article 23* 1. Everyone has the right to work, to free choice of employment, to just and favourable conditions of work and to protection against unemployment.
2. Everyone, without any discrimination, has the right to equal pay for equal work.
3. Everyone who works has the right to just and favourable remuneration ensuring for himself and his family an existence worthy of human dignity, and supplemented, if necessary, by other means of social protection.
4. Everyone has the right to form and to join trade unions for the protection of his interests.

*Article 24* Everyone has the right to rest and leisure, including reasonable limitation of working hours and periodic holidays with pay.

*Article 25* 1. Everyone has the right to a standard of living adequate for the health and well-being of himself and of his family, including food, clothing, housing and medical care and necessary social services, and the right to security in the event of unemployment, sickness, disability, widowhood, old age or other lack of livelihood in circumstances beyond his control.

2. Motherhood and childhood are entitled to special care and assistance. All children, whether born in or out of wedlock, shall enjoy the same social protection.

*Article 26* 1. Everyone has the right to education. Education shall be free, at least in the elementary and fundamental stages. Elementary education shall be compulsory. Technical and professional education shall be made generally available and higher education shall be equally accessible to all on the basis of merit.

2. Education shall be directed to the full development of the human personality and to the strengthening of respect for human rights and fundamental freedoms. It shall promote understanding, tolerance and friendship among all nations, racial, or religious groups, and shall further the activities of the United Nations for the maintenance of peace.

3. Parents have a prior right to choose the kind of education that shall be given to their children.

*Article 27* 1. Everyone has the right freely to participate in the cultural life of the community, to enjoy the arts and to share in scientific advancement and its benefits.

2. Everyone has the right to the protection of the moral and material interests resulting from any scientific, literary or artistic production of which he is the author.

*Article 28* Everyone is entitled to a social and international order in which the rights and freedoms set forth in this Declaration can be fully realized.

*Article 29* 1. Everyone has duties to the community in which alone the free and full development of his personality is possible.

2. In the exercise of his rights and freedoms, everyone shall be subject only to such limitations as are determined by law solely for the purpose of securing due recognition and respect for the rights and freedoms of others and of meeting the just requirements of morality, public order and the general welfare in a democratic society.

3. These rights and freedoms may in no case be exercised contrary to the purposes and principles of the United Nations.

*Article 30*   Nothing in this Declaration may be interpreted as implying for any State, group or person any right to engage in any activity or to perform any act aimed at the destruction of any of the rights and freedoms set forth herein.

# Index

act utilitarianism, 9, 85–98
  calculations, 88–90
  contrasted with moral rights theory, 127–128
  and the ethical standard, 86
  and the ethical themes, 93–94
  justification and strengths, 91–92
  and morally significant actions, 92
  problems with, 95–98
  related ethical insight, 84, 85
  and the traditional ethical assumptions, 92–93
applied ethics, 3
Aristotle, 136–152, 181
attitudes, 4, 23, 52, 57–59, 64–66

Bentham, Jeremy, 85–90, 98–101, 123

Categorical Imperative, 71–72
character, 136–139, 143, 147
civil rights, 112
Conly, Sarah, 185
consequentialist ethical theories, 50, 53, 68, 84, 85
cultural relativism, 33, 36, 37

deontological ethical theories, 69
deontologists, 13
divine command theory, 17–31
  contrasted with ethical relativism, 40–41
  and the ethical standard, 18
  and the ethical themes, 23–24
  justification and strengths, 19–21
  and morally significant actions, 21
  problems with, 24–28
  related ethical insight, 18, 30
  and the traditional ethical assumptions, 21–23
DuBois, W. E. B., 180, 181

emotions, 23, 156
emotivism, 57–59
ethical assumptions, 7–11, 15, 21, 38
  and act utilitarianism, 92–93
  and divine command theory, 21–23
  and ethical egoism, 52
  and ethical relativism, 38–39
  and ethical subjectivism, 12
  and the ethics of care, 165
  and Kantian ethics, 77

and moral rights theory, 125–126
  and virtue ethics, 144–146
ethical consequentialists, 13
ethical egoism, 10, 13, 48–56, 63, 68, 85
  contrasted with Kantian ethical theory, 78–79
  and the ethical standard, 49, 50
  and the ethical themes, 52–53
  justification and strengths, 50–51
  and morally significant actions, 51–52
  problems with, 54–56
  related ethical insight, 48
  and the traditional ethical assumptions, 52
ethical insights, 18
  related to divine command theory, 18
  related to ethical egoism, 48
  related to ethical relativism, 32
  related to ethical subjectivism, 48
  related to the ethics of care, 155–159
  related to Kantian ethics, 68, 69
  related to moral rights theory, 112, 114
  related to utilitarianism, 84, 85
  related to virtue ethics, 136
ethical pluralism, 174–175, 177, 182, 187, 188
ethical problems, 2–3
ethical relativism, 32–47
  contrasted with ethical egoism, 53–54
  and the ethical standard, 33
  and the ethical themes, 39–40
  justification and strengths, 35–38
  and morally significant actions, 38
  problems with, 41–46
  related ethical insight, 32
  and tolerance, 34–35
  and the traditional ethical assumptions, 38–39
ethical subjectivism, 12, 56–66
  and the ethical standard, 59
  and the ethical themes, 62–63
  justification and strengths, 60–61
  morally significant actions, 61
  problems with, 64–65
  related ethical insight, 48
  and the traditional ethical assumptions, 61–62

# ROBIN HOOD

A GRAPHIC NOVEL

BY AARON SHEPARD,
ANNE L. WATSON, &
JENNIFER TANNER

STONE ARCH BOOKS
A CAPSTONE IMPRINT

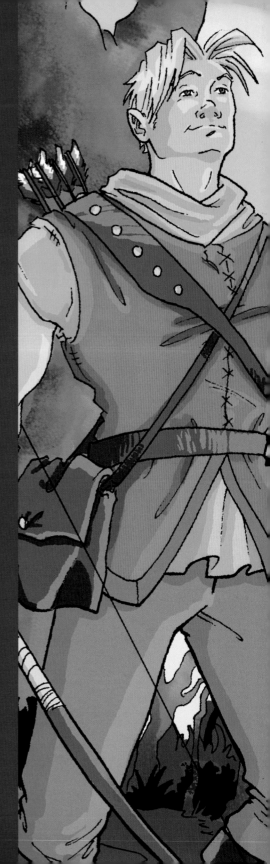

Graphic Revolve is published by Stone Arch Books
A Capstone Imprint
1710 Roe Crest Drive, North Mankato, Minnesota 56003
www.capstonepub.com

Cataloging-in-Publication Data is available at the Library
of Congress website.
Hardcover ISBN: 978-1-4965-0007-6
Paperback ISBN: 978-1-4965-0026-7

Summary: Robin Hood and his band of outlaws are
the heroes of Sherwood Forest. Taking from the rich
and giving to the poor, Robin Hood and his loyal
followers fight for the oppressed and against the evil
Sheriff of Nottingham.

Common Core back matter written by Dr. Katie Monnin.

Designer: Bob Lentz
Assistant Designer: Peggie Carley
Editor: Donald Lemke
Assistant Editor: Sean Tulien
Creative Director: Heather Kindseth
Editorial Director: Michael Dahl
Publisher: Ashley C. Andersen Zantop

Printed and bound in China. PO4399

# TABLE OF CONTENTS

# ABOUT ROBIN HOOD

The stories of Robin Hood's adventures were first told hundreds of years ago in England. The earliest known written story, *The Gest of Robin Hood*, was written around 1500. The word "gest" means deed. This early version includes Maid Marian, Little John, and the Sheriff of Nottingham.

In the 1800s, Howard Pyle, an American illustrator and writer, loved reading about Robin Hood. He retold these popular stories in 1883 in his book *The Merry Adventures of Robin Hood*.

Sherwood Forest, the setting for the tale of Robin Hood, still exists in England. However, the forest today is a much different place than it was in the late 1100s. Back then, the forest belonged to the King of England. Only he and other noblemen were allowed to hunt there. Also, the sheriffs, friars, and bishops collected taxes and **tithes** from the people who lived in the communities near Sherwood Forest. Most of these people were poor farmers who worked hard to feed their families. These people relied on the goods of the forest — from the wood for heat and shelter to the plants and wildlife for food. Many people poached, or hunted illegally, in order to provide their families with food even though they could be hanged for breaking the law. Those who were in trouble with the law, like Robin Hood, often hid deep in the forest.

The story of Robin Hood, whether it is true or not, gave people hope that such an unfair way of living would eventually come to an end.

Marian

# Robin Hood

Will Scarlet

Little John

Edward

King Richard

Sir Stephen

David of
Doncaster

Will
Stutely

Sheriff of
Nottingham

Bishop of Hereford

Alan-a-Dale

Eleanor

Friar Tuck

7

The band grows.

And Robin takes a new name. A name heard through all England. A name that draws blessings from the poor and curses from the rich . . .

. . . Robin Hood.

The next day . . .
Would Eleanor marry you against her father's wishes?
Yes!
I know a **friar** with no love of the rich and mighty.
Just through those trees is where you'll find **Friar** Tuck.

31

Robin sells the horse, the cart, and its meat to another butcher. Then they start off with the Sheriff.

This is Sherwood Forest! Heaven save us from Robin Hood!

I know this Robin Hood well.

You're as safe from him as you are from me.

You know him?

Look, there's our herd now!

Naughty beasts! Right where we left them.

How do they look to you, Sheriff?

43

Most of the archers do well.

But only four qualify for the second round.

56

## ABOUT THE RETELLING AUTHOR AND ILLUSTRATOR

**Aaron Shepard** and **Anne L. Watson** are a husband and wife writing team. Aaron is the award-winning author of many retellings of folktales and world classics for young readers. His books include *The Legend of Lightning Larry* and *The Sea King's Daughter.* Anne is a novelist as well as a photographer.

When she was young, **Jennifer Tanner** loved to draw humorous comics about dogs who went on spectacular adventures through time and space, meeting alien creatures along the way. She's never lost that love for telling stories with pictures. She attended the Savannah College of Art and Design where she received her degree in Sequential Art. Today she spends her time illustrating many comic books.